Viewpoints

Exploring the
Reformed Vision

Viewpoints

Exploring the
Reformed Vision

Edited by James D. Bratt

A joint publication of the
Education Department, CRC Publications
Christian Reformed Church in North America
and the
Office for Christian Education and Youth Ministries
Reformed Church in America

Acknowledgments
The publishers are grateful to Dr. James D. Bratt for compiling and introducing the readings in this book. Dr. Bratt, who also took part in the introductory video session of *Viewpoints*, is a specialist in Dutch-American history who teaches history at Calvin College, Grand Rapids, Michigan.

Library of Congress Cataloging-in-Publication data
Viewpoints : exploring the Reformed vision: selected readings /
    edited by James D. Bratt.
        p. cm.
    Includes bibliographical references and index.
    1. Reformed Church—United States—Theology. 2. Reformed
(Reformed Church)—United States—Religious life. I. Bratt, James D.,
1949-
BX9424.5.U6V53 1992   92-18723
285.7—dc20   CIP
ISBN: 1-56212-024-7

Contents

Preface   9

Introduction

Our identity as Christians in the Reformed/Presbyterian tradition
Heidelberg Catechism Q & A 1, 54   15
From *On Being Reformed: Distinctive Characteristics
and Common Misunderstandings,* by I. John
Hesselink   16
From *From Generation to Generation: The Renewal
of the Church According to Its Own Theology and
Practice,* by John H. Leith   19
From *An Introduction to the Reformed Tradition:
A Way of Being the Christian Community,* by
John H. Leith   19
From "Reformed and American," by George M.
Marsden   22

Viewpoints on Being a Christian

1. What does it mean that we are sinners?
Belgic Confession, Art. 15   29
Canons of Dort, III/IV: Art. 3   29
From *Our Song of Hope: A Provisional Confession of
Faith of the Reformed Church in America,* by
Eugene P. Heideman   30
From *Creation Regained: Biblical Basics for a
Reformed Worldview,* by Albert M. Wolters   32
From *The Christian Looks at Himself,* by Anthony A.
Hoekema   35
"Incarnation," by Rod Jellema   38

2. What do we believe about salvation?
Canons of Dort, III/IV: Art. 10, 16   41
From "God Glorified in Man's Dependence," by
Jonathan Edwards   42
From *The Reformed Imperative: What the Church
Has to Say That No One Else Can Say,* by John H.
Leith   42
From *Union with Christ: A Biblical View of the New
Life in Jesus Christ,* by Lewis B. Smedes   45
From *Called to Holy Worldliness,* by Richard J.
Mouw   48

3. How do we respond to the gift of salvation?
Heidelberg Catechism Q & A 32   51

From *On Being Reformed: Distinctive Characteristics
and Common Misunderstandings*, by I. John
Hesselink 52
From *Christian and Reformed Today*, by John Bolt 53
From *Until Justice and Peace Embrace*, by Nicholas
Wolterstorff 57
From *An Introduction to the Reformed Tradition:
A Way of Being the Christian Community*, by
John H. Leith 59
"The Sea of Forgetfulness: Lake Michigan," by
Sietze Buning 59

Viewpoints on Being a Member of Christ's Church

4. How shall we worship?
Heidelberg Catechism Q & A 103 63
Our Song of Hope, st. 15 63
From *Into His Presence*, by James A. De Jong 64
From "The Need and Promise of Reformed
Preaching," by Howard G. Hageman 68
From *Pulpit and Table: Some Chapters in the History
of Worship in the Reformed Churches*, by Howard
G. Hageman 70
"A Thirst for Expressive Worship," by David Beelen 72
"Lord, Have Mercy: Lakeside Church Wrestles with
Raised Hands," by James Calvin Schaap 75
"Holy Water," by Sietze Buning 79

5. How do we view the Bible and the creeds?
Belgic Confession; Art. 3, 5 81
From *Acts of Synod 1975* of the Christian Reformed
Church 82
From *Creeds of the Churches: A Reader in Christian
Doctrine from the Bible to the Present*, rev.; ed.
John H. Leith 83
From "The Inspiration and Authority of the Holy
Scripture," by Herman N. Ridderbos 85
From *Reformed and Feminist: A Challenge to the
Church*, by Johanna W. H. van Wijk-Bos 88

6. How do we organize the life of the church?
Belgic Confession, Art. 31 93
From *The Spirit of the Reformed Tradition*, by
M. Eugene Osterhaven 94
From "Foreword," by Cynthia M. Campbell in
Presbyterian Policy for Church Officers 95
From "Equipping the Saints: A Church Political
Study of the Controversies Surrounding
Ecclesiastical Office in the Christian Reformed
Church in North America, 1857-1982," by
Henry De Moor 99
From *A Teachable Spirit: Recovering the Teaching
Office in the Church*, by Richard Robert Osmer 102

Viewpoints on Our Public Life as Christians

7. **What is our responsibility as stewards of creation?**
   Heidelberg Catechism Q & A 110-111   109
   "Calvinist Farming," by Sietze Buning   110
   "Obedience," by Sietze Buning   112
   From *Thine Is the Kingdom: A Biblical Perspective on
   the Nature of Government and Politics Today*, by
   Paul A. Marshall   114
   From *Earthkeeping: Christian Stewardship of Natural
   Resources*, ed. Loren Wilkinson   118
   From *Leadership Is an Art*, by Max De Pree   121

8. **What responsibilities do we have for justice in our
   society?**
   Belgic Confession, Art. 36   125
   From *Thine Is the Kingdom: A Biblical Perspective on
   the Nature of Government and Politics Today*, by
   Paul A. Marshall   128
   From "Christian Action and the Coming of God's
   Kingdom," by James W. Skillen   132
   "The Americanization of Reformed Confessions,"
   by Eugene P. Heideman   136

9. **How do we carry out the task of evangelism?**
   Heidelberg Catechism Q & A 86   141
   From "General Overview of the Relationship of
   Covenant and Mission in the Reformed
   Tradition," by John H. Kromminga   142
   From "The Changing Face of Ministry: Christian
   Leadership in the 21st Century," by George R.
   Hunsberger   145
   From *Mission in Christ's Way: Bible Studies*, by
   Lesslie Newbigin   149

Viewpoints on Our Private Life as Christians

10. **How should we use the gifts and abilities
    God has given us?**
    Heidelberg Catechism Q & A 55   155
    Our Song of Hope, st. 14   155
    From *Leadership Is an Art*, by Max De Pree   156
    From *Testament of Vision*, by Henry Zylstra   158
    From *Christian and Reformed Today*, by John Bolt   160

11. **Why are families important to our lives as
    Christians?**
    Heidelberg Catechism Q & A 104   165
    Our World Belongs to God, st. 47   165
    From *I Pledge You My Troth: A Christian View of
    Marriage, Family, Friendship*, by James H. Olthuis   166
    From *Mere Morality: What God Expects from
    Ordinary People*, by Lewis B. Smedes   168
    From *Gender & Grace: Love, Work & Parenting in a
    Changing World*, by Mary Stewart Van Leeuwen   172
    "Heading In," by Rod Jellema   175
    "The Work of Our Hands," by Rod Jellema   176

12. How should we spend our work and leisure time?

Our World Belongs to God, st. 51   177

From "Calling, Work, and Rest," by Paul A.
    Marshall   178

From *The Fabric of This World: Inquiries into Calling,*
    Career Choice, and the Design of Human Work,
    by Lee Hardy   181

From "Theology and the Playful Life," by Lewis B.
    Smedes   184

Contributors   189

Bibliography   193

Contributors   189

Bibliography   193

Preface

Jesus assured his disciples in one of his last talks with them that his Father's house has many rooms (John 14:2). Over the centuries Jesus' followers have made good on this saying in their earthly pilgrimage, although not necessarily in the way Jesus intended; they have taken the house called Christianity and divided it into many rooms. Or, to change the metaphor, through the centuries Christianity has diverged into several large streams, each of which has developed multiple currents along the way.

Character

One of these streams is Reformed Christianity, sometimes known as Calvinism. It emerged in Switzerland in the 1520s as part of the broader Protestant Reformation. From there it moved quickly down the Rhine Valley and into France, Hungary, and the British Isles. Later it spread across the oceans to every continent on earth. While numerically one of Christianity's smaller families, the Reformed have held a vision and character distinctly their own, and they continue to be a vital force in the Christian faith today.

This selection of readings collects contemporary voices from a couple of neighboring currents in the stream of Reformed Christianity. Most of the statements come from people connected in one way or another with the Reformed Church in America (RCA) or the Christian Reformed Church (CRC), two North American denominations originally founded by immigrants from the Netherlands. Other selections come from American Presbyterians, whose church roots go back to Scotland and Ireland, and still others represent the Reformed Churches in the Netherlands, the United Reformed Church in the United Kingdom, and American Congregationalism in the days of the Puritans.

Purpose

This book has been commissioned by the education departments of the CRC and RCA to update, to honor, and to encourage their members in one of the strongest features of the Reformed tradition: the informed, critical application of Christian teachings to the different domains of life. These readings aim at acquainting people with what Reformed Christianity teaches and why, and with the tensions it struggles with. Ultimately this book challenges believers to test the Reformed legacy in the light of the gospel message. Only in this way can a Reformed tradition be truly owned by those who find themselves in it. Only in this way can their tradition be corrected, preserved, and revitalized so that it moves closer to realizing the aim it set for itself from the start: to be a full and faithful witness to Jesus Christ.

Why study tradition?

North Americans may enjoy talking about various traditions, but denominational identity increasingly gets ignored. Many have suggested that the day of strong denominational loyalty in North America has passed. The emphasis today often falls on a more ecumenical empha-sis—Christians from diverse backgrounds meeting and cooperating in their shared faith. So the question naturally arises as to why we should study a distinct stream of Christianity. Besides, didn't Jesus call his disciples to become not Catholics, Calvinists, or charismatics but simply followers of his way? So why study "human" conclusions and conflicts that come with a specific tradition? Why not return to the pure and simple gospel? Why not urge people to be "just Christians"?

Charles Hodge, a great American Presbyterian theologian of the nineteenth century, gave a good answer. "No one is a Christian in the general [sense]," Hodge observed; in other words, no one is "just a Christian" but always a particular kind of Christian. Even those who want to identify themselves as "just Christians" will find this true. Labeling oneself as "just a Christian" turns out to be as much of a tradition, with its own distinct history and theology, as labeling oneself as Reformed or Presbyterian. There always have been and always will be, until Christ's return, different strands, different understandings, different constructions of the faith.

When traditions become ends in themselves, when people uncriti-cally accept all that a tradition gives them, then traditions become idolatries, false gods. But when people live consciously and discerningly within a tradition, then a tradition can provide rich resources for understanding the faith and conversing with other believers.

No one comes to the faith in a "pure" form. The mighty river of Christianity began with the outpouring of the Holy Spirit at Pentecost. Since then that river has flowed, branched, and branched again. But the stream of living water flows from the death and resurrection of Jesus Christ. We all come into the stream at some particular point, on some particular branch. Exploring and understanding the currents and forces in their own branch of the stream can help believers appreciate better the currents that have carried others and the special gifts each current offers within the larger stream of the faith.

Old models, new twists

One of Reformed Christianity's strengths lies in its persisting effort to fathom what the faith implies for the various dimensions of life. This effort became an especially self-conscious enterprise in the Neo-Calvinist movement that emerged in the Netherlands more than a century ago. This enterprise found a home in North America in the CRC. Under the leadership of Abraham Kuyper, Neo-Calvinism sought to establish fixed principles of Reformed conviction and then to apply these in the "spheres" of church, home, school, society, politics, and art. But Kuyper's rivals in the Dutch national-church tradition (reflected in the RCA) were not other-worldly pietists; they, too, pursued a program of instituting Reformed Christianity in society, although by a different model.

This book therefore picks up an old practice but gives it a couple of twists. First, because of changes over the decades, the Neo-Calvinist and national-church currents have merged in several ways. You will find evidence of this in the following readings and also in the dual church sponsorship of *Viewpoints*. Second, those changes over the decades have struck at some fundamental assumptions and approaches. The

10

national-church line has seen secularization erode the old hope of being a dominant, inclusive faith for an entire society (see, for example, the readings from Eugene P. Heideman and George R. Hunsberger in sections 8 and 9). On the other hand, the Neo-Calvinist method of first determining principles of Reformed conviction and then applying them to life no longer describes—if it ever did—how people operate. Instead, convictions and consequences, theories and experience emerge together, continually circling back on each other. So on either side today people are not as sure of their model as they used to be, and they incur greater risk as they go. That can lead to mush and muddle, but it can also lead to a humbler, more venturous, and more faith-filled life as pilgrimage. Christians everywhere, especially Reformed people in North America, are newly conscious of being on such a pilgrimage. This book—with apologies to *The Wizard of Oz*—hopes to give Reformed believers a little more heart, head, and courage on their journey.

Usage and content

Some headnotes and selections use the terms *Calvinist* or *Calvinism* synonymously with *Reformed*. While many figures besides John Calvin have shaped the Reformed movement, his name is closely associated in history and commentary with that movement, especially with respect to its social, political, and cultural outgrowth. The terms should be understood in that light.

Reformed, to reiterate a point made above, refers not to a "faith" but to a branch of the Christian faith, and that faith does not believe in itself but in the God who called it into being.

Church sometimes denotes the institutional operations associated with staff, buildings, and Sunday services; other times it means the sum total of Christian believers in their daily activities. Readers will need to determine which sense applies in each instance.

Most of the following selections are excerpts from much larger works. This volume is best read as an invitation to explore those works in greater detail. Each section begins with excerpts from official confessions or testimonies, most of them centuries old. We include these to recall the roots of the Reformed tradition, to show contemporary statements as commentary on its classic themes, and to challenge us all to make our lives a fitting testimony to the ancient hope by which we are called.

—James D. Bratt

Introduction

Our identity as Christians in the Reformed/Presbyterian tradition

Q. What is your only comfort
   in life and in death?

A. That I am not my own,
   but belong—
       body and soul,
       in life and in death—
   to my faithful Savior Jesus Christ.

   He has fully paid for all my sins with his precious blood,
   and has set me free from the tyranny of the devil.
   He also watches over me in such a way
   that not a hair can fall from my head
   without the will of my Father in heaven:
   in fact, all things must work together for my salvation.

   Because I belong to him,
   Christ, by his Holy Spirit
   assures me of eternal life
   and makes me wholeheartedly willing and ready
   from now on to live for him.

   —Heidelberg Catechism Q & A 1.

Q. What do you believe
   concerning "the holy catholic church"?

A. I believe that the Son of God
       through his Spirit and Word,
       out of the entire human race,
       from the beginning of the world to its end,
   gathers, protects, and preserves for himself
       a community chosen for eternal life
           and united in true faith.
   And of this community I am and always will be
       a living member.

   —Heidelberg Catechism Q & A 54.

Scholars have long searched for the core doctrine, the distinctive spirit, of the Reformed tradition. Some have found it in "the sovereignty of God," in the sense of "living in the presence of God," or in a particular understanding of law and grace. But many, including most laypeople, have seen it in the moving declaration of the Heidelberg Catechism's opening words: "I am not my own, but belong—body and soul, in life and in death—to my faithful Savior Jesus Christ."

This belonging cannot remain only a private, warm relationship with the Savior. Belonging to Christ comes inseparably with belonging to Christ's people, the church—and not just to the church in general but to some piece of it in particular. Even so, particulars can be cold comforts compared to an ideal Jesus. Finding the body of Christ in them may require delving below parochial customs to their enduring substance.

I. John Hesselink recounts his own voyage of discovery in a context that will strike a chord among many people who have been raised on midwestern American Calvinism. The following selection prefaces Hesselink's own book *On Being Reformed* and speaks for this volume of selected readings as well.

From *On Being Reformed*, by I. John Hesselink:

I AM BULLISH ON BEING REFORMED. It was not always so. If I had remained in the areas where my roots are—Grand Rapids, Michigan, and Pella, Iowa—I would not sing quite the same song, or at least not in the same way! When you are too close to something or someone, you tend to see only the warts. Distance and time give a more balanced perspective.

As a small boy, I knew of no other churches than Reformed and Christian Reformed. This was true both in Grand Rapids, where I was born, and in Leighton, Iowa (ten miles from Pella), where we moved when I was eight years old. Pella is a small town—now over 7,000 people—located forty miles southeast of Des Moines. Settled in 1847 by a group of Dutch immigrants led by the Reverend Hendrik Scholte, the town still reflects its Dutch Reformed heritage in distinctive religious and cultural ways. Since my father is a minister, I heard occasionally about other churches but I had no experience of them. I still have vivid recollections of the cultural-ecclesiastical shock of attending a Disciples of Christ church in Memphis, Tennessee, when I was twelve, an evening service in a Nazarene church in Illinois when I was fourteen, and very sophisticated services in Methodist, Congregational, and Episcopal churches in Evanston, Illinois, when, at sixteen, I spent a summer at Northwestern University. These other ecclesiastical worlds seemed extremely strange and alien.

Much more familiar and real were the little skirmishes between the two churches in Leighton (a town of about 125 people)—one Reformed, the other Christian Reformed. We argued about Christian schools, doctrinal purity, and use of the Dutch language. Above all, we argued about what one could properly do on Sundays besides go to church and read religious literature. Petty legalisms, a peculiar Dutch-American piety and church loyalty, and a strait-laced, very orthodox father (who has become more open and genial as he has aged) were the leading influences in my boyhood development as a Christian.

As I look back on those days, I am surprised that I never rebelled against this rather narrow version of the Christian faith—and the whole Reformed tradition! There were, fortunately, family friends and relatives—particularly a very literate, liberal uncle—who broadened my horizons and helped me see life whole. In any case, despite occasional questions and misgivings, I grew up as a loyal and generally appreciative son of the church. But I really did not have a very clear idea as to what was distinctive about the larger Reformed tradition as such. To be Reformed, at that point, meant basically: 1) to be orthodox; 2) to go to catechism; and 3) to go to church faithfully Sunday morning *and evening* and to honor the rest of the Sabbath Day in an appropriately sedate manner. That, needless to say, does not well represent the genius of the Reformed tradition! Even so, I shall always be grateful for this godly heritage and for the Reformed Church in America which brought it to me.

While in college and seminary, I gradually was exposed to what made "us" different from "them" (i.e., all those other Christians of non-Reformed background). I was introduced to our Reformed "father," John Calvin. In my senior year at seminary, we made a cursory review of our standards of unity, but I was not especially impressed even by the Heidelberg Catechism. I had also married a Reformed minister's daughter who had also grown up in the Midwest, in a greater variety of places, but all traditional Reformed centers.

When we sailed to Japan as missionaries in 1953, we were well-grounded theologically but had not had our inherited Reformed convictions tested and tried. Moreover, I had a bit of a minority complex, coming, as I did, from a very small town, a small college, a small seminary, and a small denomination, none of which were known in most parts of the United States.

Our missionary experience in Japan changed all that. We suddenly were exposed to missionaries of all stripes. There were liberals, who believed very little but had great compassion for the Japanese. There were fundamentalists, who seemingly had all the answers but cared little for the Japanese (except to add converts' scalps to their belts), or anyone else for that matter. Between these extremes was a growing circle of friends who both challenged and chastened us. They ranged from Southern Baptist and Pentecostal to Lutheran and Roman Catholic. This was enriched by deepening relationships with Japanese Christians and non-Christians, and a host of international contacts during my three years of doctoral work in Basel, Switzerland. From the time I left Western Seminary as a young graduate in 1953 until the time I returned to become president of the seminary in 1973, I was in the United States only a little more than two years. During that time, and for extended periods, we worshiped with Southern Baptists, English Anglicans, American Lutherans, and Christian Reformed, along with local Japanese and Swiss churches.

This cultural and ecclesiastical diversity led into a period of intensive theological reflection and soul-searching. We were constantly being asked about our denomination and what we believed. There were occasions when I was charged with being liberal by fundamentalists (who regarded anyone with my kind of background and associations as suspect) and other occasions when I was called a fundamentalist by my liberal acquaintances. Thus, I was forced to reexamine everything that I had once assumed and taken for granted.

This process was aided and abetted by my more formal theological studies and professional associations. During my first year in Japan, I had the opportunity of studying with Emil Brunner, one of the most famous theologians of the time. He was a man whom I had read, admired, and attacked as a student. In the mysterious providence of God I soon found myself doing doctoral work in Basel with *the* theologian of our time, Karl Barth, regarded as liberal by some conservatives and as too orthodox by many liberals. I was also exposed to radical theologians such as Rudolph Bultmann and Fritz Buri, as well as more traditional scholars like Oscar Cullmann. More important, I had come to a fresh appreciation of Calvin while teaching an English Bible class in a Tokyo high school. To my surprise, I found Calvin's commentaries more helpful—and more inspiring—than most of my contemporary commentaries. The result was that I ended up writing my doctoral dissertation on Calvin's concept of the law. It was something I would not have dreamed of while in seminary.

All of these experiences—academic, spiritual, ecumenical, and international—over a twenty-year span meant an increasing under-standing and appreciation of what was distinctive and beautiful about the Reformed tradition. Much of what I learned and experienced is spelled out in the chapters of this book. In general, I discovered that we represent a middle way. We are neither liberal nor fundamentalist. At our best we share many liberal concerns (scholarly openness, social justice, etc.) as well as fundamentalist doctrines (a high view of the inspiration of Scripture, the virgin birth, the second coming of Christ, etc.). We are neither high church nor low church, dispensationalists nor latitudinarians. Above all, we take Scripture seriously—all of it, not simply those parts which appeal to evangelistic types, on the one hand, and social activists, on the other.

At the same time I was coming to appreciate our tradition more and more, I also came to see more clearly where we had failed to measure up to that tradition at its best. I learned a lot from my Southern Baptist, Lutheran, Anglican, Catholic, liberal, charismatic, and evangelical friends. I found that each of these traditions had something to offer, often something we were lacking. Every "misunderstanding" of the Reformed tradition is based on a degree of truth: where there is smoke, there is usually fire.

It may seem paradoxical that as I grew more appreciative (and less judgmental) of other traditions I became more enthused about my own. I recognize far better now than twenty years ago the foibles and failures of our particular expression of that tradition in the Reformed Church in America, but I also love and appreciate it now as never before.

Hence with a chastened realism and unashamed pride I gladly and gratefully acknowledge my Reformed heritage and tradition. The purpose of this book is to encourage and elicit a similar appreciation in those for whom being "Reformed" is new as well as others who have grown up in my tradition or in other branches of the broader Reformed tradition.

—pp. vii-ix.

....

I n the next two readings, John H. Leith reflects on the virtues, defects, and necessity of tradition. For him, *tradition* is a verb as well as a noun, a process of nurturing over time that is vital for every believer and for the church as a whole.

From *From Generation to Generation,* by John H. Leith:

The Christian tradition shares many characteristics with other human traditions. Traditions grow out of the experience of community and they take shape in time. They cannot be momentarily and rationally created, nor can they be imposed on a community. The traditioning of the faith does not exhaustively or finally express what is believed, taught, and confessed. Handing on the faith is not static but alive with argument, correction, and fulfillment, trial and error. The apostolicity of the church, the continuity of the faith, is personal and communal and never finally expressed in propositions or structures. Traditions grow slowly, taking at least three generations to become established or for practices to become an ongoing way of life.

The act of traditioning at its best enlarges the human understanding of that which is traditioned. The Christian witness cannot simply go back to the sources, cannot merely read the Bible, cannot just repeat what a previous generation has said. There is inescapably the translation of the tradition into the language and idiom of the time. The task of translation not only enhances the understanding of the tradition but also entails the possibility of the distortion, dilution, or corruption of the tradition. Ideally every Christian recapitulates the church's witness to and reflection upon Jesus Christ as the rite of passage into full membership in the community. Traditioning the faith is an awesome responsibility on the one hand to incorporate each new person and generation into the community of faith and on the other hand to do so in a self-critical manner which maintains the faith without distortion, dilution, or corruption.

—p. 36.

From *An Introduction to the Reformed Tradition,* by John H. Leith:

Tradition is not a "good" word in common speech. For many it means old-fashioned, out of date, rigid and fixed, or past-oriented. Good reasons are in part responsible for the various negative connotations of the word. The negative impressions are rooted in the fact that traditions may die at some fixed point. Having died, they can only be repeated in a legalistic way by their adherents. When traditions die and become fixed, they may be discarded, or they may become oppressive burdens upon those who continue to live by them. The negative impression of tradition also has its source in traditionalists for whom the past is so good that the future has no possibilities of its own.

Tradition in itself is a good word. More than that, it is virtually an indispensable word. Human beings are distinguished from animals by a cultural memory, by a capacity for tradition. Animals have no traditions and no cultures. By tradition people are saved from the tyranny of the moment, and by it they gain some transcendence over time. A traditionless person is tossed about by every wind that blows at a particular moment and is bereft of perspective by which to judge the future. Tradition properly enables one to live out of the resources of the past with an openness to the future. In fact, appeal to tradition has been historically one way of opening up the future to change, even to revolution.

Tradition, as has been indicated, is a human act. In the church, traditions have taken wrong turns, have turned in on themselves, and have become prematurely fixed. Contemporary fundamentalism and some types of liberalism represent the fixation of conservative and liberal traditions in the nineteenth century. There have always been liberal and conservative components of the Christian traditions. The problem arises not in the liberal and conservative components of the traditions themselves but with the fixation of the traditions in a particular time and place so that those who come after can only repeat what has been fixed in another time and place. The tradition, whether liberal or conservative, is no longer alive but dead and fit only for sterile repetition.

Traditions also have a way of isolating themselves and living according to their own internal principles. Sometimes this internalizing of tradition is a means of self-protection in the context of a hostile society . . . . Yet too great an internalization of a tradition, even when necessary, always erodes its vitality. Traditions have been strongest when they have lived not only by their own internal principles but also in dialogue with the total culture.

The discarding of traditions, however, is no adequate answer to the problem of dead and aborted traditions or of traditions that are turned in upon themselves. This is abundantly clear in much contemporary church life. Since 1955, theology and churchmanship have been plagued by lust for novelty and narcissistic delight in being original. The result has been faddism. In a single decade it has been possible for one person to have passed through the civil rights movement, the theology of the secular, the theology of hope, black theology, political theology, the women's liberation movement, and the theology of play. In addition, there has been the Jesus movement. Some have gone from movement to movement with no place to call home. All of these movements have their positive contributions to make to the life of the church and have their rightful claim to the attention of all. Yet these movements and thematic theologies became nonproductive of constructive achievement when they monopolized the attention and energies of their adherents and thus lost perspective and the capacity for critical self-criticism. Two basic criticisms that can be made of most of the theological and social enthusiasms of the 1960s are lack of gratitude for what is given by the past and lack of capacity for critical self-judgment. The same complaints can be made concerning rootless churchmanship that has also been tossed about by every new form of worship, or experimental ministry, or management system.

The great asset of a tradition is its provision of a rich resource of accumulated wisdom that gives perspective to the present moment. Its wisdom has been tested and tried in the crucible of life, not once or twice, but many times over. Out of the wisdom and stability of living tradition, it is possible to carry on dialogue or debate with all that is contemporary and new without being tossed about by every new wind that blows. Tradition provides criteria that enable one to test the spirits. Furthermore, traditions preserve resources from the past that otherwise would be lost when they are most needed. Many elements of the Christian tradition only seem to die, and they have an amazing capacity for "resurrections from the dead." . . . Tradition "saves" many valuable components of the Christian experience that are prematurely dismissed as dead but which are sources of light in new situations. Thus traditions give both perspective and depth to the Christian community.

Inordinate love of the past, the repetition of dead traditions as laws for contemporary life, the refusal to change are clearly destructive ways of life. Yet change in itself is not necessarily good. The future is not automatically an open door to inevitable progress. The wisdom of the past has not been outdated because it is the integrity that has been wrested out of actual human experience. Human nature is still human nature. The temptation of the liberal spirit to reject all traditions uncritically deprives the church of a great resource for facing the future. A more productive procedure is to test the traditions and in particular the ones by which we live; all traditions must continually be critically reviewed and open to self-reformation. They must live and develop not only in terms of their own internal principles but also in dialogue, even debate and confrontation, with other traditions, movements, and events. . . .

The living and open tradition of the church has its liberal and conservative components. It has assimilated in a living way the wisdom of the past, and it is open to the future. The living tradition of the church is the indispensable link between the believing community today and the events, witness, and interpretation that are its origin. A historian of doctrine has put it very well. Tradition is the living faith of dead people. Traditionalism is the dead faith of living people. For this reason tradition is a source of the church's vitality and traditionalism the occasion of its death.

God's salvation of men and women in Jesus Christ has been handed on in many diverse ways. Some ways have been good, some have been bad, and some have been indifferent. Every generation must therefore test the tradition or traditions to see how clearly they represent God's grace and action in Jesus Christ to the life of faith and obedience today. Therefore, all traditions must be received with gratitude and with critical judgment.

The Reformed tradition does not claim to be the only Christian tradition. It does claim to be *one* way the one, holy, catholic, apostolic church has lived, handing on its faith and life to every new generation. It does claim to be an authentic form of the Christian community that has its special strength and also its weaknesses and problems. It intends to be the people of God in all their fullness. On the basis of this claim, it asks for both acceptance and criticism.

—pp. 28-31.

....

George M. Marsden summarizes his own experience among the variety of Reformed people in North America. His conclusion returns us to the opening words of this introductory section, for if assurance comes from belonging to God, so should humility.

From "Reformed and American," by George M. Marsden:

What sense does it make in late twentieth-century America to talk about being "Reformed"? For most Americans the word conveys no clear meaning. Very few would think of it as a religious designation at all, and most of those would think it referred to Judaism. Even if, as in the present work, we limit the audience to those who have some notion of "Reformed theology," we are left with the problem that even among such a select group, "Reformed" has numerous differing connotations. In the United States alone there are about a dozen Reformed denominations and perhaps another half-dozen with a Reformed heritage. Within each of the Reformed denominations varieties of meanings are given to being "Reformed." These may reflect European traditions, such as Scottish or Dutch, or continental neoorthodox, as well as a variety of American developments. Each such type includes differing subtypes. For instance, within the Reformed Church in America alone, ten distinct approaches to the Reformed faith have been identified. Differences across denominational lines may be sharper. A strictly confessional member of the Reformed Presbyterian Church in North America (Covenanters) might be most unhappy with the preaching at Robert Schuller's Crystal Cathedral. A fundamentalist Bible Presbyterian would refuse fellowship with almost any member of the United Church of Christ. And within most of the larger Reformed denominations, conservatives and progressives are locked in intense struggles over the true meaning of the faith.

A major purpose of this essay is to cut through the bewildering confusion of the many meanings of "Reformed" by reducing the categories to the three major Reformed emphases that have flourished in the American cultural setting. Not every Reformed heritage can be subsumed under these categories and the categories are ideal types or models rather than fully nuanced representations of the growth of each type. Nonetheless, these are the major subgroups that have been prominent among the Reformed throughout American history. So if we understand something of these three developments and emphases we can gain a fairly good picture of the main varieties of being "Reformed" in the American cultural setting.

Perhaps an illustration from my own experience can make clear the characters of the differences among these major American Reformed traditions. Most of my life I have lived in one or the other of two communities that placed great merit on being Reformed. The central meaning of "Reformed," however, has differed greatly in these two communions. The Orthodox Presbyterians, among whom I was reared, meant by "Reformed" strict adherence to Christian doctrine as contained in the infallible Scriptures and defined by the standards of the Westminster Assembly. Only Christians whose creeds were fully compatible with Westminster's and who viewed subscription to them as paramount were fully within the pale. Other factors were important to Christian life, especially a proper emphasis on the law of God as the central organizing principle in the Westminster formulations. But the operative test for "Reformed" was, with this important practical proviso, always doctrinal.

In the other community in which I have spent many years, the progressive wing of the conservative Christian Reformed Church, being "Reformed" is also taken seriously, but with very different meaning. There, a "Reformed" Christian is one who has a certain view of the relationship of Christianity to culture. She or he must affirm the lordship of Christ over all reality, see Christian principles as applicable to all areas of life, and view every calling as sacred. Although subscription to the authority of the Bible and classic Reformed creeds is significant in this community, the stronger operative test for admission is support for separate Christian schools at all levels (except, oddly, the graduate university), where the "Reformed" world-and-life view can be exemplified and taught.

I have also spent some time at institutions of mainstream American evangelicalism, such as Trinity Evangelical Divinity School and Fuller Theological Seminary, where one finds still another meaning to being "Reformed." In this context being "Reformed" must be understood in the framework of being "evangelical." "Evangelical" is a word with a more elusive meaning than "Reformed." Basically it refers to anyone who promotes proclamation of the gospel of salvation through the atoning work of Christ and has a traditional high view of Scripture alone as authority. Evangelicalism is thus much larger than just the Reformed tradition. Within American evangelicalism, however, there is an important subgroup that might be called "card-carrying" evangelicals. These are persons who think of themselves primarily as "evangelicals" and who, as such, identify at least as much with evangelicalism as a movement as with their own formal denomination. Billy Graham, *Christianity Today*, *Eternity*, Inter-Varsity Christian Fellowship, Wheaton College and its imitators, and seminaries such as Trinity, Fuller, and Gordon-Conwell have been prototypes of this influential interdenominational evangelicalism.

In this evangelical fellowship the dominant theological tradition is Reformed. It is by no means, however, the only tradition. One trait of this type of being "Reformed," unlike the other two, is that it is tolerant of diversity to the point of keeping close fellowship with persons of other traditions. The operative tests for fellowship among the Reformed in such communities are those of the broader American evangelical-pietist tradition—a certain style of emphasis on evangelism, personal devotions, Methodist mores, and openness in expressing one's evangelical commitment. To be "Reformed" in this setting means to find in Reformed theology the most biblical and healthiest expression of evangelical piety.

The differing emphases of these three communities suggest that in America there are at least three major meanings to being "Reformed." There are, of course, also a number of other Reformed traditions and styles in America. These include the southern, ethnically and racially defined groups, smaller denominations, progressive Reformed in mainline denominations, and some neoorthodox. Nonetheless, the three we have begun with suggest classically distinct types of emphasis that give us some working categories. Many of the developments of America's Reformed groups can be understood as variations on these typical themes.

For convenience' sake, we shall designate these three types as doctrinalist, culturalist, and pietist. In doing so, it is important to remark again that the terminology refers to "ideal types" or descriptive models emphasizing one dominant trait. In reality all three groups typically embody the traits dominant among the other two. Thus a "pietist" is not typically a person who is lax in doctrine or lacking in cultural concern. Similarly, to call people doctrinalists or culturalists does not imply lack of the other two traits. . . .

The American Reformed community today, then, still includes substantial representation of the three classic emphases, doctrinalism, pietism, and culturalism. These three are, of course, not incompatible and the unity of Reformed Christians in America would be much greater were this compatibility recognized and emphasized.

The question of unity, however, is complicated by the twentieth-century divisions of modernists and fundamentalists that have cut across the traditional divisions. Neoorthodox and dispensationalist variations add further complications. Moreover, among those who are primarily culturalists, conflicting political allegiances subvert Reformed unity. Nonetheless, there remain a substantial number of Reformed Christians whose faith reflects a balance, or potential balance, of the three traditional emphases. It is these Christians who need to find each other and who might benefit from reflecting on what it should mean to be Reformed.

They can also learn from considering the characteristic weaknesses, as well as the strengths, of their tradition. Perhaps the greatest fault of American Reformed communities since Puritan times is that they have cultivated an elitism. Ironically, the doctrine of election has been unwittingly construed as meaning that Reformed people have been endowed with superior theological, spiritual, or moral merit by God himself. The great irony of this is that the genius of the Reformed faith has been its uncompromising emphasis on God's grace, with the corollary that our own feeble efforts are accepted, not because of any merit, but solely due to God's grace and Christ's work. The doctrine of grace, then, ought to cultivate humility as a conspicuous trait of Reformed spirituality. A strong sense of our own inadequacies is an important asset for giving us positive appreciation of those who differ from us.

Yet too often Reformed people have been so totally confident of their own spiritual insights that they have been unable to accept or work with fellow Reformed Christians whose emphases may vary slightly. Perhaps some review of the rich varieties of theological views among the Reformed in America today will contribute to bringing tolerance and search for balance. Moreover, the unmistakable minority status of the "Reformed" in America today should help foster the need for mutual understanding and respect. Above all, however, a revival of the central Reformed distinctive—the sense of our own unworthiness and of total dependence on God's grace, as revealed especially through

Christ's sacrificial work—should bring together many who in late twentieth-century America still find it meaningful to say "I am Reformed."

—*Published in* Reformed Theology in America, *ed. David F. Wells; pp. 1-3, 10-11.*

Viewpoints on Being a Christian

1. What does it mean that we are sinners?

The Doctrine of Original Sin

We believe
that by the disobedience of Adam
original sin has been spread
through the whole human race.

It is a corruption of all nature—
an inherited depravity which even infects small infants
    in their mother's womb,
and the root which produces in man
    every sort of sin.
It is therefore so vile and enormous in God's sight
that it is enough to condemn the human race,
and it is not abolished
    or wholly uprooted
    even by baptism,
        seeing that sin constantly boils forth
        as though from a contaminated spring.

Nevertheless,
it is not imputed to God's children
for their condemnation
but is forgiven
by his grace and mercy—
    not to put them to sleep
    but so that the awareness of this corruption
    might often make believers groan
    as they long to be set free
    from the "body of this death."

Therefore we reject the error of the Pelagians
who say that this sin is nothing else than a matter of
imitation.

—*Belgic Confession, Art. 15.*

Total Inability

Therefore, all people are conceived in sin and are born children of
wrath, unfit for any saving good, inclined to evil, dead in their sins,
and slaves to sin; without the grace of the regenerating Holy Spirit
they are neither willing nor able to return to God, to reform their
distorted nature, or even to dispose themselves to such reform.

—*Canons of Dort, III/IV: Art. 3.*

I n this opening section we consider the bedrock themes of Reformed theology. We follow the three-part order of the Heidelberg Catechism: sin-salvation-service, or guilt-grace-gratitude.

Calvinism has often been lampooned for its emphasis on sin and people's inability to escape or change this condition on their own. In truth, the criticism is sometimes deserved because of Reformed people's own misuse or misunderstanding of the doctrine.

As the following excerpt assumes, the Reformed focus on sin is simple realism, an accurate depiction of the natural state of human affairs. Eugene P. Heideman's depiction of "original sin" comes from his commentary on Our Song of Hope, "a contemporary statement of faith adopted by the Reformed Church in America in 1978."

We know Christ to be our only hope.
We have enmeshed our world in a realm of sin,
   rebelled against God,
   accepted inhuman oppression of humanity,
   and even crucified God's son.
God's world has been trapped by our fall,
   governments entangled by human pride,
   and nature polluted by human greed.
               —*Our Song of Hope*, st. 2.

From *Our Song of Hope: A Provisional Confession of Faith of the Reformed Church in America*, by Eugene P. Heideman:

This stanza makes clear who it is that is singing Our Song. We confess that those of us who join our voices together are a crowd of sinners, living in a realm of sin. . . . We are so thoroughly disappointed when we look at ourselves that we can hope only in God.

It is line 2 with its "realm of sin" that sums up our condition. We are not simply talking about a list of individual sins which each one of us has committed. We are faced with an unfathomable, interrelated complexity of sin in which individual sins are inextricably intertwined with each other. No longer can we see where one sin begins and another leaves off. What began with the eating of a piece of fruit ended as murder; what began as a story of a baby born in Bethlehem ended as an event in which all of the rulers and peoples of the world com-bined to crucify the only righteous person around.

We are enmeshed in systems of life which embody the sin of our race. That sin reaches into our political, economic, social, educational, and even into our religious institutions. The way we speak our words, frame our thoughts, and eat our food is part of that realm of sin. It not only touches our souls; it reaches into our bodies, causing blindness in some, malnutrition in others, and kills those who do little harm to others. In the words of the Scriptures, we battle not against flesh and blood but against powers and principalities, against the rulers of this age. We feel ourselves caught in a web of evil even when we cannot locate the sources of that iniquity. This web of sin in which we are trapped is what the theologians in the past called "original sin," or even "inherited sin." By this phrase they did not mean that God had created an evil world. On the contrary, they always insisted that God had created the world good; it was man who had invented sin. Neither did they mean to say that sin was some kind of a biological inheritance, due to the fact that we are caught up in a world of matter. What they indicated by this phrase was the fact that so soon as we accept in any way our place in the human race, we willingly participate in the whole nexus of sin in the world. By accepting language, family life, money, clothing, food, etc., we accept the way in which a fallen race does things and begin to participate in that realm of evil ourselves. Modern psychologists and sociologists have traced out in detail the struggles, clashes, and jealousies which take place in families. They have shown how even sexual union, that beautiful gift of God for human love, has been corrupted into a battle ground.

In Our Song, we frankly admit that we see no way out. We dare not even say that we are not responsible because the system was planned and developed by our forefathers since the time of Adam. We know that we ourselves all too willingly accept the system; we even add our own inventions to the sins of the fathers. Like the sinners of old, we continue to build the tower of sin higher, hoping thereby to displace God from the heavens.

Thus we do not talk about the fall of the race as if it happened long before we were born. We know that it happened way back at the beginning of our race, but it has been happening and becoming greater in each generation. Even when we can no longer make contact with our ancestors, the doctrine of the fall of man remains true. From the time of Cain murdering Abel we know that man has been adding to his oppression of man. We too have entered into that realm of oppression; so satisfied are we with the system that when someone proposes to change it to make for a little justice in human life, we often oppose the change because of what it would cost us.

We like to complain about how others mis-use the creatures of God, while we continue in our own life and society to pollute the world and neglect the environment ourselves. We are not nearly so concerned about our children as we claim to be, and we willingly ignore those older than ourselves. Reading in the Scriptures that we can inherit the earth, we act as if it is already ours to use as we please, without regard for any other creature.

But the depth of it all comes when we see what happened to Jesus. So long as we analyze our lives with the tools of history sociology, and psychology, we still hope that we ourselves may be able to earn salvation. So long as we are in those realms of thought, we can argue about whether mankind is fallen or still in a position where it could lift itself up by its own bootstraps. But when we look at Jesus, crucified on a cross, we know the truth about ourselves. What we did to Jesus is what we will always do to a righteous man. We cannot tolerate his presence; he makes us change too much. We are willing to defend our realm of sin, injustice, and oppression to the death. There is no sense in talking about our fathers; it is our own sin which is caught up in the death of Christ.

We like to avoid the doctrine of original sin, according to which, in the words of our fathers, we are inclined by nature to hate God and our neighbor. We want to talk about the individual sins of ourselves and others. In that way it becomes possible to measure our individual sins against the sins of others and to conclude that we are not as bad as they are. By emphasizing individual sins, we can easily begin to feel that our own wills remain somewhat neutral between good and evil, sometimes choosing to do a good deed and at other times an evil one. When we emphasize individual sins to the neglect of original sin, we can easily think of the human race as a series of isolated individuals, with some going on the way to hell and others on the road to glory. We can accept Jesus in our personal lives without being concerned about how He encounters the sin of the world.

Our Song of Hope knows that we cannot cut ourselves off from the sin of others. We are involved in their sin as they are involved in ours. Our only hope lies in Jesus Christ, for the Scriptures tell us that he died for the sin of the world.

—pp. 20-23.

....

While "natural," sin is not "creational"; it is not part of God's original and enduring intention for this world. Missing that distinction is a mistake Reformed people have made too often, distorting the rest of their thought and action. Albert M. Wolters addresses that error here.

From *Creation Regained,* by Albert M. Wolters:

In the early church there was a heresy called Gnosticism that denied the goodness of creation in a fundamental way. It held that the Creator of Genesis 1 was a subordinate evil deity who had rebelled against the supreme good God, and that the world he made was an evil place, a prison from which people had to be rescued. The Gnostics considered salvation to be a flight away from this evil world in withdrawal and detachment in order to achieve a kind of mystical union with the supreme God. Gnosticism posed a significant threat to the early church and was fiercely attacked by such Church Fathers as Irenaeus. Already in the days of the apostles the danger of such a heresy was apparent. This is what Paul seems to have had in mind when he wrote to Timothy about a special message from the Spirit in regard to a demonic teaching that would appear "in the last days" prohibiting marriage and the eating of certain kinds of foods. Such a message, warns Paul, depreciates God's good gifts, "which God created to be received with thanksgiving by those who believe and know the truth." He then adds the following ringing manifesto: "For everything created by God is good, and nothing is to be rejected if it is received with thanksgiving; for then it is consecrated [or: sanctified] by the word of God and prayer" (1 Tim. 4:4-5, RSV). If Timothy will drive home *this* point to the believers, says Paul, then he will be "a good minister of Christ Jesus" (v. 6). Against the Gnostic maligning of God's creation (or some part of it) he must proclaim the goodness of all creation.

The ramifications of this basic confession are far-reaching, especially if we recognize that creation includes everything wrought by God's wisdom (including such institutions as marriage). It is the biblical antidote to all worldviews, religions, and philosophies that single out some feature or features of the created order as the cause of the human predicament, whether that be the body, temporality, finitude, emotion-ality, authority, rationality, individuality, technology, culture, or what have you. All of these have been scapegoats that have drawn attention away from the real root of the trouble, human religious mutiny against the Creator and his laws for the world—a mutiny that most assuredly is *not* part of God's creation and its goodness. Deeply ingrained in the children of Adam is the tendency to blame some aspect of creation (and by implication the Creator) rather than their own rebellion for the misery of their condition. . . .

It is one of the unique and distinctive features of the Bible's teaching on the human situation that all evil and perversity in the world is ultimately the result of humanity's fall, of its refusal to live according to the good ordinances of God's creation. Human disobedience and guilt lie in the last analysis at the root of all the troubles on earth. That the fall is at the root of evil is most clear for specifically human evil as it is manifested, for example, in personal, cultural, and societal distortions. Since all have fallen in Adam, evil in human life in general originates in enmity toward God.

But the effects of sin range more widely than the arena of specifically human affairs, touching also the nonhuman world. Two biblical passages in particular make this wider scope of sin unmistakable. The first is Genesis 3:17, in which immediately after the fall God says to Adam, "Cursed is the ground because of you." The very soil is affected by Adam's sin, making agriculture more difficult. A more extensive passage is the one in Romans to which we have already alluded. The passage as a whole reads as follows:

> The creation waits in eager expectation for the sons of God to be revealed. For the creation was subjected to frustra-tion, not by its own choice, but by the will of the one who subjected it, in hope that the creation itself will be liberated from its bondage to decay and brought into the glorious freedom of the children of God. We know that the whole creation has been groaning as in the pains of childbirth right up to the present time. (Rom. 8:19-22)

Paul states that the whole creation, not just the human world, was subjected to frustration (i.e., to "vanity" or "futility" or "pointlessness") by the will of "the one who subjected it" (i.e., Adam, through his disobedience). That vanity seems to be the same as the "bondage to decay" from which creation will be liberated. Thus, we learn from Paul that the creation in its entirety is ensnared in the throes of antinormativ-ity and distortion, though it will one day be liberated.

All of creation participates in the drama of man's fall and ultimate liberation in Christ. Though the implications are not easy to under-stand, this principle is a clear scriptural teaching. We will see it empha-sized again when we come to speak of the kingdom of God as the restoration of creation. At bottom, it seems, all kinds of evil—whether sickness or death or immorality or maladjustments—are related in the Scriptures to human guilt.

The Relation of Sin and Creation

If it is true that Adam's sin carries in its train the corruption, at least in principle, of the whole of creation, then it becomes very important to understand how this corruption is related to the originally good creation. This relation is crucial for a Christian worldview. The central point to make is that, biblically speaking, sin neither abolishes nor becomes identified with creation. Creation and sin remain distinct, however closely they may be intertwined in our experience. Prostitution does not eliminate the goodness of human sexuality; political tyranny cannot wipe out the divinely ordained character of the state; the anarchy and subjectivism of much of modern art cannot obliterate the creational legitimacy of art itself. In short, evil does not have the power of bringing to naught God's steadfast faithfulness to the works of his hands.

Sin introduces an entirely new dimension to the created order. There is no sense in which sin "fits" in God's good handiwork. Rather, it establishes an unprecedented axis, as it were, along which it is possible to plot varying degrees of good and evil. Though fundamentally distinct from the good creation, this axis attaches itself to creation like a parasite. Hatred, for example, has no place within God's good creation. It is unimaginable in the context of God's plan for the earth. Nevertheless, hatred cannot exist without the creational substratum of human emotion and healthy assertiveness. Hatred participates simultaneously in the goodness of creation (man's psychic makeup as part of his full humanity) and in the demonic distortion of that good creation into something horrible and evil. In sum, though evil exists only as a distortion of the good, it is never reducible to the good.

Perhaps the point can be made plain by speaking here of two "orders" that are irreducible to one another. In the words of John Calvin, we must distinguish between "the order of creation" and "the order of sin and redemption," which relate to each other as health relates to sickness-and-healing. These two orders are in no sense congruent with each other. At every point, so to speak, they stand at right angles to each other, like the length and width of a plane figure. The perversion of creation must never be understood as a subdistinction within the order of creation, nor must creation ever be explained as a function of perversion and redemption. As fundamental orders of all reality they coexist—one original, the other adventitious; one representing goodness, the other involving deformity.

Or, to clarify the point further, we may say that sin and evil always have the character of a caricature—that is, of a distorted image that nevertheless embodies certain recognizable features. A human being after the fall, though a travesty of humanity, is still a human being, not an animal. A humanistic school is still a school. A broken relationship is still a relationship. Muddled thinking is still thinking. In each case, what something in fallen creation "still is" points to the enduring goodness of creation—that is to say, to the faithfulness of God in upholding the created order despite the ravages of sin. Creation will not be suppressed in any final sense.

In the present context we must stress again that these two orders are in no sense on a par with each other. Sin, an alien invasion of creation, is completely foreign to God's purposes for his creatures. It was not meant to be; it simply does not belong. Any theory that somehow sanctions the existence of evil in God's good creation fails to do justice to sin's fundamentally outrageous and blasphemous character, and in some subtle or sophisticated sense lays the blame for sin on the Creator rather than on ourselves in Adam.

—pp. 42-43, 46-49.

....

Another misconception about sin can keep believers from appreciating the joy and power that come with salvation. Anthony A. Hoekema discusses the status of the old person of sin after salvation has come in Christ.

From *The Christian Looks at Himself,* by Anthony A. Hoekema:

If we who claim to be Christians are honest with ourselves, we shall have to admit that many of us tend to have a self-image that over-accentuates the negative. Many of us commonly see ourselves through the purple-colored glasses of our depravity—sometimes even called "total depravity." I do not deny that according to the Scriptures we are all by nature depraved or sinful in every aspect of our being, but the same Scriptures teach us about redemption and renewal. Sad to say, however, many of us tend to look only at our depravity and not at our renewal. We have been writing our continuing sinfulness in capital letters, and our newness in Christ in small letters. We believe in our depravity so strongly we think we have to practice it, while we hardly dare to believe in our newness. . . .

This is the problem with which we must now deal. In trying to find a solution to it, let us first of all consider what the Scriptures teach about the concepts "old man" and "new man." A better understanding of these concepts than is sometimes held will, I believe, help us to answer the question posed above.

It has been rather commonly held by Christians that in the believer there is a continual struggle between two aspects of his being, the "old man" which he is by nature and the "new man" which he puts on at the time of regeneration and conversion. According to this view, the old man and the new man are distinguishable "parts" of the believer. Before conversion he is only an old man; at the time of conversion he is said to put on the new man—without, however, totally losing the old man. The converted person, or believer, is understood to be partly new man and partly old man. At times the old man is in control, whereas at other times the new man is in the saddle; the struggle of life, therefore, is the struggle between these two aspects or parts of his being (also sometimes called the "new nature" and the "old nature").

This understanding of the old and the new man can easily lead to a negative self-image. One may, of course, think of himself as primarily new man, and only secondarily old man, but even in such a case his self-image will be of a person who is partly new and partly old—partly obedient to God and partly in rebellion against God. One might, however, also think of himself much more pessimistically, as primarily old man and only occasionally and rarely new man—in which case his self-image would be negative indeed.

It is to be seriously questioned, however, whether the view of "old man" and "new man" described above is the right one. In his *Principles of Conduct,* John Murray has rejected the idea that the believer is both old man and new man. It is just as wrong to call the believer both a new man and an old man, he argues, as it is to say that he is both regenerate and unregenerate (p. 218). Murray contends that since according to New Testament teaching the believer has put off the old man and put on the new, we must think of him as a new man—though a new man not yet made perfect, and still the subject of progressive renewal. This renewal, however, is not to be conceived of as the progressive putting off of the old man and putting on of the new (pp. 218-19).

In his study *Paulus,* Herman Ridderbos offers an interpretation similar to Murray's. When Paul speaks about the old man and the new man, writes Ridderbos, he is not concerned primarily with the change which takes place in the life of an individual Christian after conversion, but with what took place once and for all in Christ (pp. 61-62). Christ, as the second Adam, died on the cross and arose from the grave for His people. Since Christ's people are one with Him in corporate unity, what happened to Christ has therefore also happened to His people. By His death on the cross Christ dealt a death-blow to sin as the power which had been enslaving His people; by His resurrection He opened up a new way of living for His people: the way of living associated with God's new creation. . . .

Our self-image as Christians, therefore, must be of ourselves as persons who have decisively rejected the old way of living which is called the old man, and have permanently adopted the new way of living which is called the new man. Paul himself describes what the self-image of the believer ought to be in Romans 6:11, a few verses beyond the passage where he says that our old man was crucified with Christ (v. 6): "So you also must consider yourselves dead to sin and alive to God in Christ Jesus." This is as clear a biblical statement of the Christian's self-image as one can find anywhere. Because of what Christ has done for us, and because we, enabled by His Spirit, have appropriated all His benefits by faith, we are now to look upon ourselves as no longer identified with the way of living called the old man, but as identified with the way of living called the new man. I am to look upon myself, therefore, not as partly old man and partly new man, but as a new man in Christ.

Does this mean that for the believer the struggle against sin is over? No. The New Testament is full of the language of struggle: the Christian life is called a battle, a race, and a wrestling against evil spirits; we are told to be good Christian soldiers, to fight the good fight of the faith, to resist the devil, to take heed lest we fall, and to put on the whole armor of God. Moreover, in this struggle we do not always win, we do not resist every temptation. On the contrary, we hear New Testament saints confessing that they are far from perfection, that they have not yet attained, that in many things they all stumble. We hear John saying in his first epistle, "If we say we have no sin, we deceive ourselves and the truth is not in us" (1:8). The point is, however, that when we do fall into sin, we are momentarily living according to the old man, or the old way of living, which we have actually repudiated. We are then living contrary to what we really are in Christ. Though we are regenerate, we are then living contrary to our regenerate life. Though we have put on the new man, we are then living contrary to the new man, as if we were still the old man.

But the fact that this does happen—and may, indeed, happen frequently—does not mean that we must therefore revise our self-image as having to include both old man and new man. For—and this is a most important point—when we slip into an old-man way of living, we are living contrary to our true selves; we are denying our true self-image. Paul does not say in Romans 6:11, "Consider yourselves to be *mostly* alive to God and *mostly* dead to sin." What he says is, "Consider yourselves dead to sin and alive to God." *This, then, must be our Christian self-image.* We must consider ourselves to be new men in Christ, who have once and for all turned our backs upon the old way of living called the old man, and who therefore refuse to be identified with it any longer. . . .

This is a good point at which to consider a problem many people have with the cultivation of a positive self-image. The problem is this: How can one have a positive self-image and still avoid spiritual pride? Will not such a self-image bring with it a kind of holier-than-thou attitude? Will it not lead a person to think of himself as superior to others?

The Bible warns us sharply against such thinking. Jesus' words are well known: "Whoever exalts himself will be humbled, and whoever humbles himself will be exalted" (Matt. 23:12). Paul warns us not to think of ourselves more highly than we ought to think (Rom. 12:3), and Peter says "God opposes the proud but gives grace to the humble" (I Pet. 5:5).

How, then, can one have a positive self-image and still avoid this kind of pride? The answer is to be found in a proper understanding of the Christian self-image. The Christian is not to think himself *apart from Christ* as someone worthy of high esteem. But the image the Christian should have of himself is of someone who is *in Christ* and is *therefore* a new creature. The proper Christian self-image, in other words, does not imply pride in ourselves but rather glorying in what Christ has done for us and continues to do for us.

It will be recalled that this was precisely the case with the Apostle Paul. Though he calls himself the chief of sinners and the least of all the saints, he yet says, "By the grace of God I am what I am" (I Cor. 15:10). He claims that his sufficiency is not in himself but only in God (II Cor. 3:5). His boasting is in the Lord rather than in himself; as far as his own person is concerned, he boasts of his weaknesses, so that the power of Christ may fully rest upon him (II Cor. 12:9). Paul's positive self-image, therefore, is not an evidence of spiritual pride, but rather a fruit of his faith in Christ.

—*pp. 18, 42-43, 45-47, 56-57.*

....

Still, Reformed realism must say, in line with Article 15 of the Belgic Confession, that sin does haunt the redeemed: in themselves, when they are tempted to pride in their own righteousness; and in the world, where it persists so painfully. As the previous selection linked

sin to salvation, so Rod Jellema's poem "Incarnation" ties salvation back
to sin via images of the Savior.

Incarnation

Coming home through snow, I think the grey face
of my father, little physician, knew cells. Faces.
Loved most his alcoholic patients, tender
toward their long thirst for a home
that denies our only home.

Addiction, he said, is 80-100 proof
that spirit is,
craves to be flesh.
He understood about incarnation.

But my father still had the dazed Galilean
fisherman's habit of looking up.
His eyes pleaded with red cancer to hurry
as though it were a skyriding pillar of fire,

but it was cancer flowering down in the flesh,
and down in grey cells under skull-bone,
in an old synapse, is where God the Father
was speaking Dutch to a child
when my father said *tot ziens* and died.

(*Tot ziens*: "until we see."
Never mind *wiedersehen*, seeing again,
that German illusion. God and the Dutch tongue
know we have never seen much.)

Home. Make the second sandwich while eating the first,
the third while eating the second.
At seven p.m. there is light enough
at the open refrigerator.
Reach into the light for milk, drink it
from the wax lips of the carton. Rinse
the knife. Now tilt the lamp. Spend
the evening reading the morning paper.

But the sky out there will have to be more
than a capsule under a tooth
hissing blue and then black in God's throat.
My furnace burns blue, rattles death
down the hall that goes nowhere but out, out
across snowfield city and faces,
the making of tracks across morning papers.

Christ resurrected as nigger or honky,
broken and waiting for what,
something has to stop this news from becoming home,
these burnings, body counts, thrusts
of needles and rockets into fleshless non-worlds.

How god damned whited and cold
like a sheet of paper I am now,
making tracks, thinking the lines of faces
at the bars, each face as sharply its own
as the labels on bottles that reverse the mirrors,
imprinting the only news for now.

Face by false ascent by phrase
by face by riot I learn, learn that words matter
like bodies, learn not to look up
for some pure-spirit godkin
Christ but down the lost faces
the Word became
before we made it mere word again,
mere tracks in the snow.

—*Rod Jellema. From* The Eighth Day,
pp. 52-53.

2. What do we believe about salvation?

Conversion as the Work of God

The fact that others who are called through the ministry of the gospel do come and are brought to conversion must not be credited to man, as though one distinguishes himself by free choice from others who are furnished with equal or sufficient grace for faith and conversion (as the proud heresy of Pelagius maintains). No, it must be credited to God: just as from eternity he chose his own in Christ, so within time he effectively calls them, grants them faith and repentance, and, having rescued them from the dominion of darkness, brings them into the kingdom of his Son, in order that they may declare the wonderful deeds of him who called them out of darkness into this marvelous light, and may boast not in themselves, but in the Lord, as apostolic words frequently testify in Scripture.

—Canons of Dort, III/IV: Art. 10.

Regeneration's Effect

However, just as by the fall man did not cease to be man, endowed with intellect and will, and just as sin, which has spread through the whole human race, did not abolish the nature of the human race but distorted and spiritually killed it, so also this divine grace of regeneration does not act in people as if they were blocks and stones; nor does it abolish the will and its properties or coerce a reluctant will by force, but spiritually revives, heals, reforms, and—in a manner at once pleasing and powerful—bends it back. As a result, a ready and sincere obedience of the Spirit now begins to prevail where before the rebellion and resistance of the flesh were completely dominant. It is in this that the true and spiritual restoration and freedom of our will consists. Thus, if the marvelous Maker of every good thing were not dealing with us, man would have no hope of getting up from his fall by his free choice, by which he plunged himself into ruin when still standing upright.

—Canons of Dort, III/IV: Art. 16.

Reformed Christians have always stressed that salvation comes from God alone. Why this insistence, late and soon, so loud and clear? Perhaps because a firm grasp of salvation comes only against the backdrop of sin.

John H. Leith summarizes recent Reformed reflection on this matter—but first let's read the classic statement Jonathan Edwards made on this point in a lecture before the smug citizens of Boston in 1731.

From "God Glorified in Man's Dependence," by Jonathan Edwards:

There is an absolute and universal dependence of the redeemed on God. The nature and contrivance of our redemption is such, that the redeemed are in every thing directly, immediately, and entirely dependent on God: They are dependent on him for all, and are dependent on him every way.

The several ways wherein the dependence of one being may be upon another for its good, and wherein the redeemed of Jesus Christ depend on God for all their good, are these, *viz*. That they have all their good of him, and that they have all through him, and that they have all in him: That he is the *cause* and original whence all their good comes, therein it is *of* him; and that he is the *medium* by which it is obtained and conveyed, therein they have it *through* him; and that he is the *good itself* given and conveyed, therein it is *in* him. Now those that are redeemed by Jesus Christ do, in all these respects, very directly and entirely depend on God for their all.

—*Published in* Jonathan Edwards:
Representative Selections, p. 92.

From *The Reformed Imperative,* by John H. Leith:

The plight of human life is that we cannot save ourselves, even though the achievements of the physical and social sciences have been great. The evidence for our human "lostness" is very convincing in at least four dimensions of life. (1) We are sinners, who sin not only in our worst deeds but in our best deeds, which are flawed by our own self-interest. (2) We cannot guarantee the future even when that future involves us on the deepest personal levels of life. (3) We cannot complete human life by our own efforts. (4) We cannot escape the frustrations and defeats which are rooted in the pathetic, tragic, and ironic dimensions of human life. As created and "fallen" human beings we cannot live either in private or public life with serenity, dignity, and poise apart from the grace of God. Our question is still the question of Jeremiah: "Is there no balm in Gilead?"

Four hundred years ago, Martin Luther was tormented by the question, How shall a sinful person stand in the presence of a righteous God? Using all the means of medieval Catholicism, he sought to guarantee for himself a place in heaven. He became a monk; he confessed his sins; he went on pilgrimages. But he could never guarantee his place in heaven. He could always imagine himself a better monk or a more faithful confessor or a more diligent pilgrim. Today, there are not many people who feel guilty before Almighty God. Our culture, which is very different from that of the sixteenth century, or the first century, precludes such a possibility. But everywhere, in middle-class American society, people feel guilty—guilty that they have not been good parents, guilty that they have not been financially successful, guilty that they have not been socially accepted. Even in the church we feel guilty, or at least the best people do, that the church is not really what it says it is, the people of God.

The fragile character of human existence is nowhere better revealed than in our inability to guarantee the future. None of us knows what the future holds for us or for our world. We do not know what we ourselves shall do under pressure or temptation or even in the midst of apathy. Yet we are under constant pressure to guarantee the future of a marriage, of a job, of financial transactions, of a social revolution. We live in a merit society, where success pays great rewards and failure is frightfully painful. Yet we cannot guarantee the future. There is no assurance in advance that this marriage will turn out as we had hoped, that the race problem will be resolved, that the vision we have of life at twenty will be fulfilled at fifty. This is our predicament. We sing, "We shall overcome," but we may not overcome. What then? . . .

Two basic characteristics of all human behavior signify that human life cannot complete itself either by its own efforts or through the support of the various communities to which modern people belong. First, the human spirit has the capacity to go beyond the best we have done. We always know there is something more. Every human achievement opens up new possibilities of further achievement. Every act of love opens up new possibilities of love. Human life has been so created that we cannot exhaust its possibilities in our own achievements or in our communities. There is always something more. This fact about human life is confirmed in the biographies of the most successful. Not infrequently, those who have accomplished the most are most aware of the unfulfilled possibilities of their lives. Human life has been so made that it can only be completed in God. As Augustine put it long ago, "Thou hast made us for thyself and restless is our heart until it comes to rest in thee."

Our problem is not simply that the human spirit goes beyond our highest achievements; it is also that our highest achievements are corrupted by self-love. Martin Luther knew better than anyone else in human history that we sin not simply in our worst deeds, we sin in our best deeds. Or, as Reinhold Niebuhr in our times has taught us, our causes are never as righteous as we think they are, and our participation in them is never as devoid of self-interest as we claim. . . .

There are brief moments in life, especially when we are young, when we feel no need for a God who forgives our sins or redeems our life from destruction. Our personal endowments enable us to exult in the freedom of the secular city; our psychological defenses easily convince us of our own righteousness. But these moments are brief. For health breaks; hopes are unfulfilled; the limits of our will-power become painfully clear. Finally we become aware that the achievements in which we invested so much of our lives were possibly not worth the cost, or that our involvement in them is not so noble as once we imagined. Sooner or later we also discover that life is an uphill battle, which in the end every person loses. We know finally that no one ought to underestimate the vicissitudes of life or the precariousness of the human enterprise.

Human life, as Reinhold Niebuhr so astutely pointed out, is pathetic, tragic, ironic. The pathetic and pitiable dimensions of life are seen most vividly in the case of a deformed child or of a human being overwhelmed by forces over which he or she has no control. Other aspects of life are tragic, as when we have to deny one loyalty for the sake of another loyalty, and when we have to do evil for the sake of good, or when the only choices open to us are evil. Some aspects of life are ironic, as when a man's wisdom becomes his undoing because he did not know its limits, or when a woman's strength becomes her downfall because she trusted it too much. The final human predicament is the irony that our finest achievements have human flaws for which we are responsible.

Once we reflect upon the pathetic, the tragic, and the ironic aspects of human life, it becomes clear that we grossly oversimplify life when we make unqualified distinctions between the good people and the bad, between the successful and the failures. One of the great failures of "fundamentalism," in theology as well as in politics, is its inability to recognize the pitiable, the tragic, and the ironic dimensions of human existence. Fundamentalism, in any of its various forms, whether on the left wing or the right wing of the ideological spectrum, makes too simple a distinction between people. On the one hand there are good people who work hard and who have money, who obey the laws and who go to heaven, who are identified with the right causes and make the right pronouncements about society. On the other hand, there are lazy people who do not work hard and who do not have money, who disobey God and who do not go to heaven, who have wrong ideas about the issues of our day. The people who make these distinctions always think of themselves as the hardworking who deserve money, as the good who are going to heaven. There is no gospel in this, only a self-righteousness that is self-deceiving. The gospel is hidden from those who in their self-righteousness cannot see the sorrow and the tragedy in the worst life. The gospel is hidden from those who do not understand that success is not even a possibility for those who have a poor biochemical inheritance or an impossible social environment. The gospel is hidden from those who in their self-righteousness are proud of their moral achievements, who know that they are righteous by their identification with the proper causes, who are vindictive toward the failures, who have only one solution for failures—to discard them, to electrocute them, to destroy them.

There is no gospel for the "righteous." In the New Testament the basic cleavage between human beings is not between rich and poor, the powerful and the oppressed, male and female, the free and the enslaved, but between those who believed they were righteous and those who knew they were sinners. The gospel is for the poor in the biblical sense—that is, for those who know they cannot save themselves, who know their defense is God. As Jesus, who ate with sinners, put it, "Those who are well have no need of a physician, but those who are sick. Go and learn what this means, 'I desire mercy, and not sacrifice.' For I came not to call the righteous, but sinners" (Matt. 9:12-13).

44

Two important truths about life are set forth in these words. First, Jesus could only help those who knew they were sinners. Second, only those who know they are sinners, only those who have received mercy, can show mercy.

The Christian gospel is directed to the sinfulness, the incompleteness, the pathetic, tragic, and ironic dimensions of life. This gospel is the Christian community's witness to the question, Is there a grace which forgives our sins, which gives courage before an unknown future, which enables us to live with poise and dignity in the presence of the pathetic, the tragic, and the ironic, which enables us to accept the incompleteness of our lives with hope?

This Christian gospel is God's salvation, God's good pleasure. It is dependent neither upon our goodness nor upon our achievements. This gospel finds in the New Testament its foundational statement in the simple assertion of Jesus, "My son, your sins are forgiven" (Mark 2:5). This gospel of forgiveness is not the whole of the Christian faith, but everything else presupposes it.

—*pp. 58-61.*

....

Not only does salvation come solely from God, Reformed believers insist, it comes through God's electing love. Election has become Calvinism's most (in)famous teaching. To its critics, Calvinism and election are equivalent and equally ugly. Given what the Reformed can do with the doctrine, the protest is sometimes deserved.

But, as Lewis B. Smedes argues, election does belong to the heart of the gospel, where all the themes we have raised thus far are tied together and secured: the glory of God, the comfort and proper humility of the believer, the corporate and organic nature of human life, and the redemption of the whole creation.

From *Union with Christ*, by Lewis B. Smedes:

Elect in Christ

> Blessed be the God and Father of our Lord Jesus Christ, who has blessed us in Christ with every spiritual blessing in the heavenly places, even as he chose us in him before the foundation of the world, that we should be holy and blameless before him. (Ephesians 1:3, 4)

No other sentence that Paul wrote carries more mystery into our union with Christ than this doxology. And the doxology can easily be spoiled by trading the mystery for a crisp formula. The Christian faith is better off when it bows before the mystery of antecedent love than when it carries off the prize of a precise formula. Still, the words are in front of us. And words are meant to help our understanding as well as to kindle our devotion.

What does the doctrine of election tell us about our life in Christ? This is the reverse of the question that one ordinarily asks of this text: what does the fact that we are chosen in Christ tell us about the doctrine of election? But the two questions are interwoven. And, in a sense, we are forced to ask them both at the same time. For each question, if asked separately, implies that we already have the answer to the other. So we had better ask again about "*election* in Christ" and also ask if it illumines the reality of our *being* in Christ.

First we must observe that Paul sings his song to electing love from within the reality of life in Christ. He begins from where we are—in Christ. We are, he says, blessed in Christ and are present with Christ "in heavenly places" (1:3). "Heavenly places" points to the new creation that is really, but not comprehensively present. So it is the language of hope: the "heavenly places" point ahead to a future reality—the reality of "all things" united in Christ. The surprising fact is that we are already included in the new reality.

Only a sense of wonder and the experience of surprise inspire songs. A person is not moved to sing by commonplaces. The inevitability of a syllogism does not inspire a doxology. We sing when we wonder; our songs are born of mystery. And the wonder here is that people *like us* are "in the heavenly places with Christ." How does one account for this reality, this "being in Christ"? There is no accounting for it. There is no *reason* in heaven or earth why we should be so blessed.

It is a gift. Paul ran from Christ; Christ pursued and overtook him. Paul resisted Christ; Christ disarmed him. Paul persecuted Christ; Christ converted him. Paul was an alien; Christ made him a member of the family. Paul was an enemy; Christ made him a friend. Paul was "in the flesh"; Christ set him "in the Spirit." Paul was under the law; Christ set him in grace. Paul was dead; Christ made him alive to God. How does one give reasons for this? He does not give reasons; he sings: "Blessed be God who blessed us . . . even as he chose us in him."

The reason for saying this is to remind us that Paul is not philosophizing about the eternal plan of an absolute deity. He is stricken by grace, overwhelmed by love. And he sings. What he says of election in Christ is a song, a confession, a hymn of wonder. Love is not a *reason*; it is a mystery to sing about.

We must now turn to the fact that our election was *in Christ* from before the worlds were made. This means that Christ, *too*, was elect. And to say this is only to repeat what the New Testament says again and again. . . . [Luke 9:35; John 17:24; Acts 2:23; 4:28; 1 Pet. 1:20; Heb. 1:2; 7:16].

He was elect as the *concrete* individual doing the specific task that He was chosen to do. But we must also note that His election was not only as the *concrete* individual Jesus Christ; He was also elect as the *comprehensive* Christ. Paul is always concerned with Jesus in His total significance, in His grand context.

The context, is, first of all, the election of Israel. Israel is God's chosen; out of all the nations of the earth, she was God's unique concern. "You only have I chosen out of all the families of the earth," says Jehovah (Amos 3:2). Israel may have distorted and twisted the meaning of its own election, but it could not undo the fact of it.

The essential meaning of Israel's election is: God and His people in vital community. Community is the purpose or end of election. But it crystallizes the meaning as well as the goal: "I will be their God, and they shall be my *people*" (Jer. 31:33). Jeremiah's conviction is echoed by prophet after prophet. And it is echoed in new forms in the New

46

Testament until, in the vision of the Apocalypse, John hears the great voice from the throne crying, "Behold, the dwelling of God is with men. He will dwell with them, and they shall be his *people*, and God himself will be with them" (Rev. 21:3).

Israel was elect as Jehovah's servant for the blessing of the nations; Jesus is the culmination of Israel's election, for He is the "suffering servant of Jehovah" for the salvation of the world. His cross and resurrection are what Israel's election was all about. He established a covenant "in His blood" that cannot fail. And the core of His covenant is the same as the core of Israel's covenant—God and humanity in reconciled partnership (Isa. 42:1).

This thought must be brought back to our election in Christ, God's election is His "plan for the fulness of time, *to unite all things in him*" (Eph. 1:10). Christ was elect as the Christ "to reconcile to himself all things, whether on earth or in heaven, making peace by the blood of the cross" (Col. 1:20). He is elect as the one in whom a new creation is brought into being through the reconciliation of men with God at the cross. He is elect as head of His body, the Church, which is the harbinger of the coming new creation. This is the comprehensive sense in which we must think of the election of Jesus Christ. Christ the concrete individual, the Man for others, is elect. But *His election, like Israel's, and with Israel's, is the decision of God to create a new world of people in partnership with Him. When we think of election, we must think of God's comprehensive decision to have a "new creation."*

Thus, when we think of ourselves as elect in Christ, we must think of ourselves as elect in the *comprehensive* Christ. When Paul says "Christ" he includes His universal goal and its universal achievement. We are in God's decision to unite "all things" in Christ. The Christ of the cross is God's elect Christ. So is the Christ within whom all things are recreated. And we are elect within that concrete and comprehensive Christ.

If we reflect on our "election in Christ" in this way, we will be spared from the frightening abstractions that have so often plagued the doctrine of election. We will never think of election as a grace-less, love-less decree to select some individuals for heaven and to reject other individuals for hell. The election in Christ is not a matter of numbers. Paul is talking, as we said, as a man dumbfounded that *he* and *we* were included in God's election. He is singing of the mercy of God that included us; he is not speculating on why certain others are not included.

We are elect *in* Christ. How hard it is to *say* what this means! Christ and Christians, the Lord and His subjects, the King and His kingdom, the Reconciler and the reconciled, the Leader and His followers, the Head and His body are elect together. [Herman] Bavinck says: "The community and Christ are together in the one decision; they are, as one community, the elect." Perhaps this is what we should be content to say. God wanted a new creation with people in it who were His people, and *this* was His election. He elected a kingdom *with* a King, a body *with* a Head, a people *with* a Leader, a universe *with* a Lord, and sinners *with* a Savior. He elected us in the comprehensive Christ, the Christ who was—in faith—first defined as "Lord of All."

Being chosen in Christ means that we can no more be the object of God's agapic desire apart from Christ than a fraction can exist without an integer, a part without a whole. He is the circle in which we are included. He unites the whole of which we are individually parts. He is the elect Head of whom we are the body. To confess that we are chosen is, then, to confess that our new being is in Christ fundamentally and eternally; and that is to say that we are included in the new creation in Christ only through God's agapic, free decision of love. To make the discovery that one is in Christ is, at the same time and with the same wonder, to confess that one is in Christ because God in love freely desired a new creation in Christ.

What, then, does election by God's free agapic decision tell us of union with Christ? It tells us that the new order begun at the cross and resurrection, which sweeps into the here and now under His lordship and in the power of His Spirit, and which will culminate in a new earth where all things are reconciled, is rooted, not in time present, but in God's own eternal desire in love to give Himself in partnership with men and to restore a situation where we will be "his people" and He will be "our God" and Christ shall be all and in all.

—*pp. 85-91.*

....

With a mighty Power its agent, sovereign election its means, and the whole cosmos its object, "salvation" can seem a distant, imposing business, leaving people passive if not helpless. While Calvinists are not famous for exuberant questing after God, they are known for earnest searching before and relentless activity after conversion. Richard J. Mouw sketches the dual principle that accounts for this pattern.

From *Called to Holy Worldliness*, by Richard J. Mouw:

In his collection of sermons, *The Shaking of the Foundations*, Paul Tillich offers some interesting reflections on Peter's confession in Mark 8. Tillich notes that Peter's stirring confession regarding Jesus, "Thou art the Christ," is followed by a puzzling observation by the writer of the gospel account: "And [Jesus] charged them to tell no one about him." But the point of Jesus' warning soon becomes clear. When Jesus goes on to tell the disciples that the Son of man must suffer at the hands of the authorities and must be killed by them, Peter rebukes him. Peter does not think that Jesus should have to suffer and die; he does not properly understand the mission of the one whom he has identified as "the Christ."

Tillich observes that it may be that if Jesus were to speak directly to the church today, he would also charge *us* not to tell anyone about him. This is a shocking suggestion in a day in which great emphasis is placed on evangelism, on "telling others about Jesus." But the suggestion ought not to be ignored. "Evangel" means "good news," and there can be no doubt that we are called to "evangelize"; we are commissioned to be bearers of the good news. To take Tillich's suggestion seriously is not to detract from the importance of this commission. Indeed, it is precisely because the commission is of such great impor-

48

tance that we ought to consider seriously the possibility that Jesus might well try to silence the church today.

We are not called to say just anything that happens to come into our heads about Jesus. It is not our job to speak loosely or flippantly or imprecisely about him. We are called to proclaim *the* good news. The gospel has a specific and rich content. To distort or to trivialize that message is a serious matter. Consequently, we must be constantly returning to gaze on, to reflect on, to reconsider, the one who commissions us to speak in his name. We must constantly ask the question, "Who is this?"

Unfortunately, we lay Christians have not always been willing to engage in that process of reflection and renewal. We have not always been willing to explore the full dimensions of a proper answer to the question, "Who is Jesus?" We have often preferred to have the gospel reduced to simple formulas and clich_s; we have preferred to trim the person and ministry of Jesus down to a "manageable" size.

The proper alternative to these all-too-frequent patterns is to permit ourselves to stand in awe before the complex and puzzling Jesus of the gospels. To do so is to encounter a Jesus who does not always conform to our expectations. When Jesus stilled the angry waves, he was doing more than bolstering his reputation as a Savior of individual souls. He was not engaging in a bit of preevangelistic gimmickry. He was not attempting to attract the attention of his audience, in order suddenly to pounce on them with "four spiritual laws." He was not offering an object lesson in "possibility thinking" or "positive thinking."

When Jesus commanded the waves to be still, he was exhibiting his power as the Lord of creation, come to redeem a fallen world from the grip of sin. He was exercising the authority described so triumphantly in Isaac Watts's carol: "He comes to make his blessings flow/ far as the curse is found/ far as the curse is found!"

Jesus directly confronted the complex cursedness of the creation. The Gospel of Mark, in which this version of the story is found, also portrays Jesus as casting out demons, forgiving sins, healing broken bodies, changing the economic attitudes of tax collectors, and even raising the dead. And over and over again, those who witnessed these deeds asked: "Who then is this?"

Jesus conducted a cosmic mission. He was not, and is not, merely a personal Savior, or a therapist, or a healer, or a social critic, or a victor over demons and death—although he is surely at least each of these things. But he is also all of them and more. His mission was as large as the creation. His redeeming power reaches to wherever the curse is found. He has come to rescue the entire cosmos, in all its dimensions and activities, from the bonds of sin.

Passive and Active

The people of God—of whom the vast majority are laity—must relate to that cosmic mission of Jesus in at least two ways. First, we must give evidence that we are a community of persons who are ourselves *experiencing* the healing, calming, reconciling work of Jesus. This is the "passive" dimension of the relationship. We must be acted *upon* by the power of Jesus.

Our lives need to be calmed. We need to hear the word of peace. We are threatened by the forces of chaos and destruction. All around us we see evil at work, and our lives too are touched by disintegration and death. . . .

The forces of chaos are at work in politics, in academia, in the worlds of business, entertainment, and the arts. They threaten marriages and schools, churches and nations, basketball teams and neighborhood associations.

But Jesus has entered into his creation in order to reclaim it. He successfully challenges those forces that threaten to pervert and distort all those things the Creator once pronounced "good." Because Jesus is in our midst, the forces of evil are doomed. And as Christians we experience that power. We sense the victory in a personal way. We know Jesus as one who brings peace to troubled lives. His power is present in our very personal struggles and dealings. But it is also a presence we know and celebrate communally, as a people whom God has visited as Savior and healer.

Second, we are called to *promote* his healing work in the world. Having experienced the firstfruits of his healing mission, we must *become* vehicles of his power in the larger society. This is the "Active" dimension of the relationship. Having been acted *upon* by divine grace, we become *agents* of that grace.

The disciples who stood in awe of the mighty deeds of Jesus became, in the book of Acts, performers of mighty deeds, which caused others to stand in awe of *them*, asking, "Who are these people?" The transition comes in the words Jesus speaks to his disciples in John 20:21: "As the Father has sent me, even so I send you." The disciples become apostles. The ones who are acted upon become the agents. And so it is with us. We who have seen the power of Jesus become instruments of that power. We who have stood in awe become practitioners of the awesome.

This is not to suggest that we can divide these two dimensions into neatly separated time segments. It is not as if the disciples were, for a time, acted upon by Jesus, only to enter into a period in which they were forevermore "pure" agents of his power. They had to return frequently to the posture of observers and receivers of God's grace in Christ. And so must we. We—all of us—must be acting while we are being acted upon. We must be continually giving while we are at the same time receiving. We must be healers who are still in the process of being healed.

—*pp. 137-40.*

3. How do we respond to the gift of salvation?

Q. But why are you called a Christian?

A. Because by faith I am a member of Christ
   and so I share in his anointing.
        I am anointed
        to confess his name,
        to present myself to him as a living sacrifice of thanks,
        to strive with a good conscience against sin and the devil
            in this life,
        and afterward to reign with Christ
            over all creation
            for all eternity.

—*Heidelberg Catechism Q & A 32.*

"**S**alvation must lead to service." Of all their classic tenets, this one more than any other has been drilled into contemporary Reformed believers. I. John Hesselink traces its theological roots.

From *On Being Reformed,* by I. John Hesselink:

Doctrine with a Purpose

It is commonly recognized that the Reformed tradition is theologically oriented. Presbyterian and Reformed believers, not to mention theologians, have always taken theology very seriously. In the classic words of the great German historian, Karl Holl, "The Calvinist knows *what* he believes and why he believes it." A result has been a great concern for doctrinal clarity and purity. What may not be so well known is the classical Reformed concern for doctrine that is useful and profitable, and for truth that produces holiness. There is, in short, a practical, utilitarian bent in the Reformed fascination with theology, an active, ethical thrust of Reformed thought. . . .

Concern for truth, pure doctrine, and sound theology is important, but it should not be an end in itself. If this concern does not result in godliness and the edification of the church it has been perverted. If the approach of the *Heidelberg Catechism* is followed, there will be no problems here. This catechism, very much in the spirit of Calvin, after defining a doctrinal position, invariably asks what "advantage" or "benefit" comes from believing this truth (see Questions 28, 32, 36, 43, et al.). Note, moreover, that already in Question 1 the catechism "contains an ethics in embryo" when it concludes that Jesus Christ "by his Holy Spirit makes me wholeheartedly willing and ready from now on to live for him."

This beautiful blending of belief and action, doctrine and ethics, finds classic expression in a phrase found in the "Form of Government" of *The Constitution of the Presbyterian Church, U.S.A.* (1928), Chapter I, Paragraph 4: "That truth is in order to goodness; and the great touchstone of truth, its tendency to promote holiness. . . . There is an inseparable connection between faith and practice, truth and duty. Otherwise, it would be of no consequence either to discover truth, or to embrace it." . . .

Two manifestations of this approach are seen in the Reformed accent on sanctification (in contrast to the Lutheran emphasis on justification), and the more general interest in ethics. Both these concerns stem from the so-called third use of the law. In contrast to Lutherans, who see the law largely in a negative light and stress its function in deepening our awareness of our sinfulness, in the Reformed tradition the "principal use" of the law is a positive one. That is, for the person already redeemed it serves as a stimulant and guide in living the Christian life. . . . This emphasis on the law, when perverted, produces a legalistic mentality. But properly understood, it produces a concern for obedience to the will of God in every sphere of life.

Moralism is avoided, however, by recognizing that a Reformed ethic is an ethic of gratitude. This is impressively illustrated in the structure of the *Heidelberg Catechism*. Only in Part III, which treats man's thankfulness and obedience (gratitude), do we find the exposition of the Ten Commandments and the Lord's Prayer. Ethical behavior is thus not so much a burden or obligation as an opportunity to express our gratitude to God for such a great salvation.

A corollary of this ethic is a desire to do good works, a stress on growth in the Christian life, and a quest for holiness (both personal and corporate). Whereas a favorite Lutheran phrase is *simul iustus et peccator* (justified and a sinner at the same time), the Reformed emphasis is on progress in the Christian life. "No man will be so unhappy," wrote Calvin, "but that he may every day make some progress, however small" ([*Institutes*] III.6.5). The same interest is found in the *Heidelberg Catechism* which constantly exhorts believers to "*more and more* strengthen their faith and improve their life" (through partaking of the Lord's Supper [Q. 81]. This "more and more" is also found in Questions [70,] 89, 115, and 123).

Good works and the quest for holiness, however, must never be confused with a Pharisaical type of works-righteousness. Ethics and election are inseparable. This is the secret of the dynamic of Reformed activism. We are chosen in Christ "before the foundation of the world, that we should be holy and blameless before him" (Eph. 1:4).

A Life and World View

Calvinism can never be accused of having a God who is too small or a vision that is too narrow. From its powerful concept of a sovereign God whose will determines the destiny of humankind and nations to the vision of the glory of God which is manifest and acknowledged throughout the ends of the earth, Calvinism is a faith of the grand design. In contrast to Lutheranism's quest for a gracious God, pietism's concern for the welfare of the individual soul, and Wesleyanism's goal of personal holiness, the ultimate concern in the Reformed tradition transcends the individual and his salvation. It also goes beyond the church, the body of Christ. The concern is for the realization of the will of God also in the wider realms of the state and culture, in nature and in the cosmos. In short, Reformed theology is kingdom theology.
　　　　　　　　　　　　—pp. 101-103.

....

The Reformed life of service, however, has always been laden with paradox: a "passive" salvation exploding into activism; the premise of human helplessness ending in titanic exertions; a theoretical salvation by grace producing what for all the world looks like salvation by works. Beneath these tensions lies a mixed-mindedness about the world and the Christian's proper role in it. John Bolt probes this tension by examining the relationship between creation and redemption, between enforcing God's law and imitating Christ's sacrifice.

From *Christian and Reformed Today*, by John Bolt:

The Imitation of Christ in the Reformed Tradition

For the purpose of contrast the problem has been stated categorically as creation (law) or cross; Reformed thought linked with creation, Anabaptist thought [i.e., that of the Amish, Mennonites, etc.] with the cross. In actuality, the matter is not so simple. In Reformed thought too, at least in Calvin himself, the cross and the imitation of Christ do receive considerable attention. Because this emphasis upon the imitation of Christ, self-denial, and cross-bearing as essential ingredients of a *Reformed* understanding of life in the world are relatively unfamiliar to many Reformed people, . . . it is worthwhile to summarize briefly Calvin's understanding of the Christian life as it is portrayed in Book III.vi-x of the *Institutes*, the so-called "Golden Booklet of the Christian Life."

There are basically three dimensions to the Christian life according to Calvin: 1. Self-denial and cross-bearing, 2. Meditation upon the future life, and 3. Use and enjoyment of this present life. In this Christian walk of life, Christ Himself is the example we are called to follow.

Calvin begins his discussion of the Christian life by noting that the goal for believers is conformity "between God's righteousness and their obedience." He then adds:

> The law of God contains in itself that newness by which His image can be restored in us. But because our slowness needs many goals and helps, it will be profitable to assemble from various passages of Scripture a pattern for the conduct of life in order that those who heartily repent may not err in their zeal.

And in the next chapter, in a similar vein, Calvin notes:

> Even though the law of the Lord provides the finest and best-disposed method of ordering a man's life, it seemed good to the Heavenly Teacher to shape His people by an even more explicit plan to that rule which He had set forth in the law.

The beginning of this "pattern" of the "more explicit plan" Calvin finds summarized in the words of Romans 12:1 where "the duty of believers is 'to present their bodies to God as a living sacrifice, holy and acceptable to Him.' " The Christian is called to deny self and be ruled by the Spirit of Christ, to put off the old nature and to put on the new. It is in this process of mortification and vivification that Jesus Christ in His death and resurrection is the example and pattern for the believer. In Calvin's words, while it is true that Scripture

> enjoins us to refer our life to God, its author, to whom it is bound; (in other words to orient our life to creation, j.b.) but after it has taught that we have degenerated from the true origin and condition of our creation, it also adds that Christ, through whom we return into favor with God, has been set before us as an example, whose pattern we ought to express in our life.

Here we have the real reason for the *imitation* of Christ—we live in a sinful world. And here we come to the limits of a creation theology and an ethic based on creation and law. As *sinners* we are incapable of keeping the law and living in the creation as we should apart from the regenerating power of the Spirit. Because they rooted their theology in the Father and creation (not in the Son and redemption), Calvin and the Reformed tradition after him always insisted that life in creation is good, under the blessing of God. When God created man, male and female, He blessed them and gave them a position of rulership in the creation. Thus the Reformed tradition has always insisted (over and against the Anabaptist) that the *legitimate* exercise of power (dominion) in business, politics or church life is not to be rejected in principle but to be affirmed. The good creation of God and man's dominion in it are to be accepted and enjoyed as gifts of God. Having and raising a family, starting and operating a successful business, running for and obtaining political office are all proper and valid Christian *vocations* in which one can and is called to glorify God.

However, unlike some of his spiritual descendants, Calvin was also acutely aware that we no longer live in the Garden of Eden but in a fallen, sinful world where sin distorts and power corrupts. And it is for that reason that Calvin stresses the need for self-denial and the struggle to put our inner life under the control of the Word and Spirit of God. The law of creation is thus not enough—we must die with Christ, our old self must be crucified. It is the *new* creature, whose old nature has died with Christ, who can truly obey the law.

For Calvin, however, the example of Christ and our need to follow Him goes further. . . .

The Christian is one who not only patiently accepts God's discipline in the common suffering of mankind but who also, in imitation of Christ and for the sake of Christ's kingdom as well as for his neighbor's good, *voluntarily* suffers or sacrifices by denying himself what may otherwise be rightfully his. While Calvin himself does not reach this specific conclusion, we should note that his emphasis implies, for those of us who live in the affluent sector of a world where God's gifts are inequitably distributed, a willingness to sacrifice that which in itself is legitimate and good. . . .

According to Calvin, even Adam in Eden did not find the full meaning and purpose of his creation in this present life but "was meant rather to use this life with its opportunities and its glory for meditation for the better and heavenly life which was to be his final destiny." In a sinful world, however, this meditation on the future, heavenly life is accentuated and accompanied by a *contemptio mundi* (a contempt of this world). Calvin puts it this way:

> Then only do we rightly advance by the discipline of the cross, when we learn that this life, judged in itself, is troubled, turbulent, unhappy in countless ways, and in no respect clearly happy; that all those things which are judged to be its goods are uncertain, fleeting, vain, and vitiated by many intermingled evils. From this, at the same time, we conclude that in this life we are to seek and hope for nothing but struggle; when we think of our crown, we are to raise our eyes to heaven. For this we must believe; that the mind is never seriously aroused to desire and ponder the life to come unless it be previously imbued with contempt for the present life. Indeed, there is no middle ground between these two; either the world must become worthless to us or hold us bound by intemperate love of it.

If Calvin can be considered a Calvinist, then Reformed Christians should not be altogether uncomfortable with speaking of "this life as a constant death" (the old Dort baptismal form) or of this world as a vale of tears or of being pilgrims and strangers on earth. It must be remembered, however, that Calvin's *contemptio mundi* is a consequence of, and is qualified by the reality of sin. Calvin warns: "But let believers accustom themselves to a contempt of the present life that engenders no hatred of it or ungratitude to God." It is "the *perverse* love of this life" that leads to "the desire for a better one." For that reason this present earthly life "is never to be hated except in so far as it holds us subject to sin; although not even hatred of that condition may ever be turned against life itself."

Calvin goes even further. It is striking that, taking chapters six to ten of Book III as a climactic order, Calvin follows his discussion on the meditation of the future life (chapter 9) with a concluding chapter on the use and enjoyment of this life. It is also worth noting that Calvin, in this chapter on using this present life, affirms the liberty of the Christian believer to use the creation for *delight* as well as *necessity*. He contends that those who advocate ascetic austerity by insisting that men are permitted to use physical goods only in so far as necessity requires are far too severe. "For they would fetter consciences more tightly than does the Word of the Lord—a very dangerous thing." He then adds: "Let this be our principle: the use of God's gifts it not wrongly directed when it is referred to that end to which the Author Himself created and destined them for us, since He created them for our good, not for our ruin." Thus a pipe organ in church, piano lessons for one's children, an original painting on the wall, attractive as well as functional homes, furnishings, table settings, even an occasional restaurant meal, steak, or glass of wine ought to be a matter of free conscience for a Christian. The three rules Calvin suggests in this regard to guide our conduct are moderation, contentment, and stewardship. Calvin's unsurpassed treatment of Christian liberty in Book III, chapter 19 of the *Institutes*, especially on the *adiaphora*, on things "indifferent" is also instructive here. . . .

This exposition of Calvin helps us come to understand and hopefully to resolve some of the tensions that have risen within the Reformed community of late. Specifically, when Anabaptists (including those now within the Reformed community who favor the Anabaptist vision) accuse the classic Reformed position of inevitably tending to a triumphalistic preoccupation with creation, dominion, power and thus to a defense of the capitalist and economic establishment, and that it fails to take into account the temptations of power, the limits of creation theology, the need for the cross—they simply have not read Calvin. Similarly, when certain self-consciously committed Calvinists in the Reformed community view *all* critical suspicion of political and economic power, all concern with the cross as an integral aspect of any truly Christian ethic, as Anabaptist heresy—they too have not read Calvin. There is an unmistakable tension in Calvin's ethics between an affirmation and enjoyment of this world (the creation pole) and a necessary detachment or even renunciation of this world because of sin

(the cross pole). A fully Reformed or Calvinist ethic does not choose between the cross and creation but affirms both.
—pp. 135-41.

....

Following these two principles at once is no easy task, nor is serving a righteous God in a sordid world. Nicholas Wolterstorff wonders whether the uneasy conscience of early Calvinism is not both inevitable among the faithful and urgently needed in our time.

From *Until Justice and Peace Embrace*, by Nicholas Wolterstorff:

I have been speaking of the social thought of the early Calvinists, but of course what was remarkable about them was that this did not remain with them a pattern of thought, but became a component in their praxis. A new way of life came into being, its thought and practice interacting. Along with it a typical psychological formation emerged—call it "the Calvinist social piety"—at the heart of which was the awareness of a tension between demand and reality. The Calvinists knew that they ought to be exercising their obedient gratitude in their occupations and in their social roles in general, but the very Word of God which told them this also showed them that the social roles presented to them were corrupted and not fit instruments for obedience. In some people this double awareness produced a restless impulse toward reformism along with the self-discipline that [the German sociologist Max] Weber so strongly emphasized. In others it produced a feeling of guilt. These are the people who found themselves in the aching situation of being persuaded in their hearts that they ought to be working for reform but stymied by a will too weak to bring themselves to do so. One does not apprehend the contours of the characteristic Calvinist social piety until one discerns the pervasive presence of this form of guilt. Some will say that it is not guilt at all, but a peculiar form of hypocrisy: people saying that they ought to work at reform but not believing it and happily filling their social roles in the ordinary way. Perhaps in some cases this acquiescence is the result of hypocrisy, but my own experience suggests that it is more often otherwise.

There is nothing in the Calvinist system to assuage this form of guilt—nothing other than the general word of pardon for our human failings. By contrast there is a special word of consolation for the persons who have done their best to secure reform but failed: to them the Calvinist says that in this fallen world of conflicting demands there is nonetheless (often) a *best* thing to do, and that this best thing is the *right* thing to do. Those who do the best thing can live with an easy conscience. This stands in contrast to the typical Lutheran formulation that the best of one's options is often nothing more than the lesser of two evils, and that one must accordingly pray to be forgiven for doing the unavoidable evil. The Calvinist does not demand that a politics appropriate to heaven be practiced here already on this fallen earth.

Restless disciplined reformism, or guilt for not being restlessly reformist: these are the characteristic components of the Calvinist social piety. When these are missing, one can reliably surmise that one is confronted with a person who has some other understanding of his or her social role than that characteristic of early Calvinism—with one exception: sometimes one is instead confronted with that most insufferable of all human beings, the triumphalist Calvinist, the one who believes that the revolution instituting the holy commonwealth has already occurred and that his or her task is now simply to keep it in place. Of these triumphalist Calvinists the United States and Holland have both had their share. South Africa today provides them in their purest form.

Original Calvinism represented, then, a passionate desire to reshape the social world so that it would no longer be alienated from God. Thereby it would also no longer be alienated from mankind, for the will of God is that society be an ordered "brotherhood" serving the common good. Once this passion to reshape the social world entered Western civilization, it remained. Later it would be energized by the desire to make the world expressive of one's "self"—to overcome the alienation between the desires of the self and the world. Originally it was energized by the passion to place on the world the stamp of holy obedience.

Is not the passion as relevant and imperative today as it was then? Admittedly, when we hear this word "obedience" we think immediately of the repressiveness of early Calvinism. Though the Calvinists spoke of justice, they failed to think through how they could live together in a just society with those with whom they disagreed. That was their great and tragic failing—though a failing scarcely unique to them. And a second failing, closely related, was their recurrent triumphalism. But is our need today for a society of justice and of peace not just as desperate as it was then? And when we struggle for such a society, do we not stand in continuity with the prophetic tradition of the Old Testament— and with Jesus Christ, who in the inaugural address of his ministry said that in him the words of the prophet Isaiah were fulfilled?

> The Spirit of the Lord is upon me,
> because he has anointed me to preach good news to the poor.
> He has sent me to proclaim release to the captives
> and recovering of sight to the blind,
> to set at liberty those who are oppressed,
> to proclaim the acceptable year of the Lord.

There are those in this world for whom the bonds of oppression are so tight that they cannot themselves work for a better society. Their lot falls on the shoulders of you and me. For I write mainly to those like myself who live in societies where the space of freedom is wide. To us I say: the Word of the Lord and the cries of the people join in calling us to do more than count our blessings, more than shape our inwardness, more than reform our thoughts. They call us to struggle for a new society in the hope and expectation that the goal of our struggle will ultimately be granted us.

—pp. 20-22.

·······················

The theme of service, then, leads us back to the notes of sin and suffering on which section 1 began. Reformed believers try to comprehend this circular structure as testimony to God's glory. John H. Leith tells how this works in theory, and Sietze Buning wonders how it might work in practice.

From *An Introduction to the Reformed Tradition,* by John H. Leith:

The glory of God and his purposes in the world are more important than the salvation of one's own soul. Personal salvation can be a very selfish act. . . . Those Calvinists who asked candidates for the ministry if they were willing to be damned for the glory of God were trying to root out the last element of self-seeking in religion. Human beings are religious, the Calvinist asserts, not to satisfy their needs or to give meaning to their lives but because God has created them and called them to his service.

—p. 69.

The Sea of Forgetfulness: Lake Michigan

With style Dominie and I brought *huisbezoek*
to Willem's Holland Home bedside.
I read Psalm 46.
Dominie praised his regular attendance.
I took note that his budget was all paid up:
"More than a tenth of your old age pension, Willem."
Dominie urged him to join a grow group in the Home—
one that would meet right at his bedside.
I praised his weathering Nelly's death with such courage.
Dominie was arranging the time to bring Willem Communion on Sunday,
a sign *huisbezoek* was almost over.

"Dominie, you don't need to bring no Communion.
I feel the communion of the saints right here in bed.
I'll pray for you during the service.
But you can't move it away from where the saints are,
all together and Jesus with them,
and still keep it Communion.
Thanks for the idea, but don't bother."

He turned to me.
"And about the budget.
I pay, sure, but I envy them Israelites.
Priests ate a little of them unblemished lambs,
but the rest got burned up, useless to everybody but God.
All my budget money is an investment.
My Nelly was in our hospital and I'm in our Home.
All five children went to our Christian Schools,
four to our college.
Pete got a job with the Mission Board because he knows languages.

Bert took up business. Now he's on Synod's budget committee.
Lenore teaches philosophy at our college.
Jake is a preacher.
Now their children are in college and guess what?
They all want jobs like it.
I try to give my money to God, but none of it seems to get through.
Some year our churches ought to collect our money as usual,
put all the money on a boat in Muskegon Harbor,
set out for the middle of the lake,
and while Synod sings a psalm and prays on a boat near by,
sink the boat with the money on it
right to the bottom of Lake Michigan."

We left abruptly.
Dominie could think of nothing to pray
but the Lord's Prayer.

On Sunday at Communion
I remembered Willem was praying for us.

The cash in the offering of thanksgiving never looked greener
or colder.
Would the offertory prayer bury the green and cold of the cash
in the green and cold ocean of God's forgetfulness?
Would the offertory prayer transubstantiate the cash
into warm and living offering?

My style shattered,
I craved Willem's class.

—*Sietze Buning. From* Style and Class,
pp. 43-44.

Viewpoints on Being a Member of Christ's Church

4. How shall we worship?

**Q. What is God's will for you
in the fourth commandment?**

A. First,
    that the gospel ministry and education for it be maintained,
    and that, especially on the festive day of rest,
    I regularly attend the assembly of God's people
        to learn what God's Word teaches,
        to participate in the sacraments,
        to pray to God publicly,
        and to bring Christian offerings for the poor.

Second,
    that every day of my life
        I rest from my evil ways,
        let the Lord work in me through his Spirit,
        and so begin already in this life
    the eternal Sabbath.

—Heidelberg Catechism Q & A 103.

Christ elects the church
    to proclaim the Word and celebrate the sacraments,
    to worship God's name,
    and to live as true disciples.
He creates a community
    to be a place of prayer,
    to provide rest for the weary,
    and to lead people to share in service.

—Our Song of Hope, st. 15.

For most believers, the Christian life begins in worship. There, more than in any private meeting with God, they learn and are confirmed in the faith. Yet Calvinists have a reputation for a rather stuffy, intellectual liturgy—many words and little spirit—implying a like manner of Christian living. Dissatisfied with that, some Reformed congregations recently have turned toward more expressive, enthusiastic styles, winning many smiles—and almost as many frowns.

What can we say about the essential traits of *Reformed* worship? James A. De Jong's answer links liturgy to theology: for the Reformed, worship begins with God's centrality and ends in our everyday service.

From *Into His Presence,* by James A. De Jong:

Reformed worship may be defined simply as "a prescribed, corporate meeting between God and his people, in which God is praised and his church is blessed." Explaining this definition piece by piece should help us better to understand our Reformed worship.

Worship Is a Meeting

As a meeting, worship is distinct from meditation, contemplation, and other private, reflective, spiritual activities. A believer may muse on a sinful act and the pain it causes others, or ponder the mystery of God's sacrifice on the cross. But in such preoccupations, he or she is not addressing God. Meditation may be a high religious art. But while important in the Christian faith, it is surpassed by worship. Worship is a face-to-face meeting and exchange. When Christian worship is so trivial, so novel, so cluttered, so mechanical, or so traditional that it lacks any awareness of meeting with God, it has failed the first and basic test of true worship.

All of life is either an obedient or a disobedient response to God. Reformed thinkers have often emphasized the need for a worshipful attitude throughout the believer's existence. Such general, comprehensive worship is the context of worship as a meeting, but the two are not identical. Worship as a meeting is a conscious, deliberate, and explicit encounter with God. Like a business luncheon or committee meeting, it is scheduled into the rhythm of our lives.

Worship Is a Corporate Meeting

Individual, private, devotional exercises are a kind of worship vital to our spiritual well-being. They ought to be daily events in a believer's life. Such devotions should include both the opportunity for God to address us in his Word and for us to address God in prayer. But personal devotions are not corporate worship.

Even family devotions, worship with a group of friends, and chapel exercises are not, strictly speaking, corporate worship. For while these bodies of people may be intimately and organically bound together, they lack the universal, comprehensive character of the church as the office-led body of Christ. Our definition of worship as a corporate meeting refers precisely to the officially called and supervised worship of the one, holy, catholic, and apostolic church. These four adjectives can, in a sense, be applied to other Christian groups, but they are usually reserved for the organized, instituted congregation of believers.

We mean by worship, therefore, the worship of the church on the corner of Fourth and Main. We are talking about worship in church!

Worship Is a Prescribed, Corporate Meeting

Prescribed means not that worship occurs at a designated time and place or by the command of Jesus Christ, although these are significant dimensions of worship. It means that worship follows a prescribed order or format with prescribed components. This order is commonly called the liturgy.

A liturgy is like a recipe. Every good cook has a favorite recipe that makes her potato salad unique. Similarly, each church has its own liturgy. The variation between the liturgy of churches within the same denomination may be minute; between widely separate traditions, immense.

It is essential that liturgy serve worship. It should be a vehicle to enable worship, not impede it. A good understanding of the history of the liturgy and of the rationale for its components will enhance worship. It may even help improve the liturgy for the sake of better worship. While liturgy and worship are distinguishable, they are never separable.

Worship Is a Prescribed, Corporate Meeting between God and His People

Worship is often characterized as a dialogue. In any liturgy there are places where God speaks and other places where the people respond. There are several exchanges between God and the worshipers.

Yet the idea of dialogue has certain deficiencies. Dialogue is usually between equals. In worship God convenes the meeting and remains in charge through his appointed delegates. Like invited dinner guests, God's people attend worship by divine invitation. Dialogue may ramble. Worship does not; its exchanges are prescribed.

The interaction occurs primarily between God and his people as a group. While aware of each other, Christians do not worship to visit with one another. They remember Suzie's broken leg and John and Sally's wedding in prayer, but they address God, not each other. Worship's fellowship is first of all with God. Our sense of oneness comes from our common address to God. We speak to him in unison. He addresses us as his church. Worship that directs attention on individual members risks becoming banter with and about people. Meeting with each other may be enjoyable, informative, even uplifting, but it is not worship.

Defined as a meeting between God and his people, worship is necessarily restricted. It is not for everyone. It is for the community that knows God by faith and approaches him through Jesus its Lord. "His people" refers not to all humans—his by virtue of creation, but to the body of believers—his through re-creation by water and the Word.

Thus, when some people, say, "I would never take anyone to our church in order to interest them in the Christian faith," they may be right! Interesting people in the faith is not the task of worship but of Christians equipped through worship. Worship is not designed to win converts, but to strengthen the converted. In daily contacts with others Christians witness and evangelize. On Sunday Christians approach God as the body of believers. This is not meant to disparage evangelistic preaching, just to distinguish it carefully from liturgical preaching. Like

Peter and Paul, the Wesleys and Whitefield, modern evangelists should preach in shopping malls, parks, beaches, and neighborhoods. But in worship God meets his people.

A very important, often overlooked, implication of this definition is that worship must be meaningful for children. As members of the church by virtue of God's covenant confirmed in their baptism, children are God's little people. They, as well as adults, must be participants in worship.

Worship Is a Meeting in Which God Is Praised

Praise is the central intent and dominant tone of worship. The Psalms use this term *praise* as the basic word to characterize worship. And then the Psalms and other Scriptures bid us to glorify, magnify, extol, adore, rejoice before, bless, sing hallelujah to, and make a joyful noise to the Lord. These words all capture the exuberance with which the worshipers praise God for his greatness and goodness.

But praise can be stretched to include also the reverence, the awe, the holy fear the worshiper feels; the contrition, the penitence, the confession of sin, the appeal for forgiveness the worshiper brings; and the thanks, the gratitude, the dependence the believers show to God. All these aspects of the worship service are different forms our praise takes.

Worship Is a Meeting in Which the Church Is Blessed

Not only do people give in worship; they also receive. God's blessing, given to his people, is the effect which worship has on the church.

The Word of God is the source of blessing in the service. According to one expert on Reformed worship, this occurs at four points. First, God speaks his Word of greeting at the beginning of the service—he reassures the congregation of his presence in their lives. God's second Word is a word of forgiveness following the confession of sin—he blesses the church with pardon and reconciliation. Third, God speaks his Word of instruction—reassurance, understanding, instruction, correction, inspiration, and guidance are all forms of God's blessing in the sermon. At the close of worship God speaks his fourth Word, the Word of benediction—he blesses his people with the promise of well-being through the week.

Even in the parts of the liturgy in which the people address God, they are blessed. Like the genuine giving of a birthday present, the believer finds that in worship also, "it is more blessed to give than to receive" (Acts 20:35). . . .

[The writer later turns to a consideration of week-day work as another form of worship, concluding that "the best thought in the Reformed heritage . . . is that all work done in faith and in obedience to God is worship."]

Living the Liturgy

We should not conclude . . . that we can dispense with churches and preachers. Sacraments and sermons have not become obsolete. Christianity has not, as a modern current of theological opinion says, become "religionless" after the death and resurrection of Christ. Quite the opposite is true. The Christian worship service clarifies the meaning and reinforces the purpose of our existence.

Another way of explaining this is to say that we must live the liturgy. What we do in worship echoes and reverberates through all the activities and responsibilities of the Christian during the week. The themes of the service are amplified and varied in the symphony of our whole life. A holy harmony exists, then, between the public, official worship of God's gathered people and the work of families and individuals in their everyday praise.

A walk through the liturgy should illustrate this point.

God's greeting on Sunday morning teaches us to hear him addressing us throughout the week. His grace, mercy, and peace are spoken to us without words, in the spirit of Psalm 19. When the TV anchorman announces the ceasefire to a particularly bloody, victimizing conflict, God's grace salutes us. When we narrowly miss a kitchen accident, he greets us with his mercy. He speaks his peace in the birds' evening song. But it is the liturgy that has conditioned us to hear these continuous greetings from our heavenly Father.

Praise, thanks, and adoration are genuine only when they are dispositions of life. To "give the Lord wholehearted praise" in the opening anthem on Sunday, and then to curse the work and the responsibilities he has assigned us during the week is to take God for a fool and to make liars of ourselves. Such praise will not get past the ceiling, and the curse will backlash on the worship services. On the other hand, the woman who is grateful for her jobs, including the one at home, and the man who thankfully accepts his children and his duties toward them can sing heartily in church.

We must live our religion!

Because we never consistently do, life, like the liturgy, must contain times of genuine contrition and penitence. And real penitence is more than words. If we are genuinely sorry for misrepresenting a product in the salesroom, we not only vow to change our "pitch," but we call the bamboozled customer and tell him the truth. James told us, "Confess your sins to one another" (James 5:16). The closer and more intently we live with others, the more crucial his instruction becomes. The depth and quality of our relationships is directly proportional to our willingness to confess wrongs and to accept forgiveness.

Living our religion is hard! That is why God speaks his Word of grace and forgiveness. Spoken from the pulpit, read in the Bible, it is transmitted through a mother's arms around a rowdy child who has just broken a piece of china. It comes through the words of a counselor who has brought an alienated couple through a period of reconciliation. It is conveyed in the clasped hands of long-hostile brothers. The week is not long enough to contain the reconciliation and assurance needed in our lives. But the ministry of reconciliation, begun by Paul in his apostolic message (2 Cor. 5:18-19), is continued by all believers in their lives with others (Matt. 5:24).

Through the liturgy God shapes us to live expectantly. The Christian life is a life of great anticipations. They rest on God's promises. They are expressed in our prayers for help and divine blessing. Looking for God's provision and assistance from one day to the next, whether we are scanning the sky for rain clouds or the want ads for work, becomes a spiritual reflex for believers. As we live and breathe, we pray.

We also listen. We hear God's counsel, warnings, encouragements, and instruction in inner-city social conditions and in political developments in Ottawa or Washington. While we may never be spooked by "divine providences" as the Puritans often were, we must discern the signs of our times. The word preached on Sunday illumines and interprets the news on Thursday. Reinhold Niebuhr's advice to his students is good for all Christians: "Your two indispensable sources for understanding the world must be the Bible and the *New York Times*." Always in that order!

The liturgy might as well be chiseled in granite if its dedication and commitment do not take on the warmth and flesh of our lives. The author of Hebrews says,

> Through him then let us continually offer up the sacrifice of praise to God, that is, the fruit of lips that acknowledge his name. Do not neglect to do good and to share what you have, for such sacrifices are pleasing to God.
> —*Hebrews 13:15-16*

Whether it is in an offering, in our confession of the creed, in our public vows, or in a prayer—sung or spoken—our affirmation of service to God and others is on the line all week.

The liturgy, then, is not ritual magic which works a protective spell over our existence. It is the sum and substance of our lives. It is the presentation of ourselves to the Lord for his benediction. It is also the pattern by which we cut the cloth of our experiences. Another way of putting it, turning things just around, is to say that life is the incarnation of the liturgy.

To be genuine worship, the liturgy must be lived.

—*pp. 13-16, 119-20.*

....

Out of a lifetime's reflection on Reformed liturgy, Howard G. Hageman explains the very lofty conception Calvinists have had of preaching and pleads for a recovery of an equal place for the sacraments, especially the Lord's Supper.

From "The Need and Promise of Reformed Preaching," by Howard G. Hageman:

Preaching has been to . . . a large degree the life of the Reformed Church. We may argue academically about Calvin's insistence on the unity of word and sacrament in the liturgical life of the people of God, but the historic fact is that it is the proclamation of the word that has provided the primary, almost exclusive nourishment for the people of God in the Reformed Church. When the preaching is bad in Anglicanism or in Roman Catholicism, there are other factors to compensate for it, at least in part. When it is bad in the Reformed Church, the loss is almost fatal. The result is that the whole question of preaching has a much more crucial importance for us than for some other branches of the family of God.

As I see it, preaching in the Reformed Church has failed both on the left and on the right. The failure on the left is too obvious to require extensive demonstration, but let us say a word about it. Once the biblical moorings have been slipped, anything can happen—and usually does! Essays or addresses on interesting topics, political, economic, psychological, or even "spiritual" with illustrations a la *Reader's Digest* hardly qualify as preaching in the Reformed tradition, but they have been the Sunday fare in all too many situations. In some cases the charisma of the speaker has been sufficient to cover up the basic deficiency, but the deficiency is there all the same.

The failure on the right has been much less noticed because in outward appearance the biblical basis has been there. But the mere recitation of biblical material, especially when used as proof for theological propositions, is not preaching. Biblical or theological instruction is an aspect of the life of the church which is by no means to be despised, but its place is not in the pulpit, authentically orthodox as it may sound. Until there has been some honest wrestling to discover what it is with which this living Word wishes to confront us . . . in our specific situation, we are still in the category of lecturing or speaking; we have yet to discover what it means to *preach*.

Basic, therefore, to any recovery of preaching is an understanding of what the Reformed Reformation, at least, thought was involved. In another connection Bard Thompson has put it this way:

> With the other great Reformers, Calvin shared the view that true preaching is God speaking. The preached Word was a veritable means of grace by which God elected to address his people and to offer them his gifts of forgiveness, sonship, and a place within the family of faith. Therefore true preaching held the inevitable possibility that the ancient words of scripture and the human words of the minister might, by the action of the Holy Spirit, spring alive in the hearts of the hearers and be heard as the real, alive, effective Word of God.

. . . Perhaps we need to remind ourselves that Calvin was not afraid of the equation, *Predicatio Verbi Dei est Verbum Dei* (the preaching of the word of God is the Word of God) or to read what the Helvetic Confession of 1566, the most ecumenical of all the Reformed confessions, had to say:

> Wherefore when this word of God is now preached in the church by preachers lawfully called, we believe that the very Word of God is preached, and received of the faithful; and that neither any other Word of God is to be feigned, nor to be expected from heaven; and that now the word itself which is preached is to be regarded, not the minister that preached; who, although he be evil and a sinner, nevertheless the Word of God abides true and good.

. . . Perhaps my short critique of both left and right will now be easier to understand. So long as we conceive of preaching as a discussion about a third object, whether that object be biblical, theological, political, psychological, or whatever, we have completely missed the point. A sermon on "Does God Exist?" or "Can We Still Believe in Reprobation?" is no more preaching than one on "How to Be Happy though Religious," or "Should We Buy Non-Union Lettuce?" So long as we are talking about something or even someone who is not present, we are not preaching, at least not in the Reformed understanding of the term.

For in that understanding we must believe that through the uneven humanity of the words of the preacher the Holy Spirit is making Christ present to his people. Out of the ancient Word, contemporary words become the channel through which the living Lord warns, challenges, and comforts his own. Of course, the claim is one of the miraculous! Who ever claimed otherwise? In fact, compared with this claim, the miracle of the medieval mass pales into insignificance; bread and wine are stable objects compared with the humanity of a preacher whose digestion may be poor, whose study habits may not be of the best, who may, in fact, have all kinds of personal problems when he stands to proclaim the Word of the Lord. But all that does not matter, if he (and his people) believe the promise, "Whoever listens to you, listens to me" (Luke 10:16).

This is where the need and promise of preaching begin. Long before we begin to talk about techniques, the implications of cybernetics, the use of the media and a host of other significant things, we need some theological convictions about what we are doing; both ministers and people need them. A man talking about anything, even holy things, will not do. The voice of the living Lord speaking directly to his people in their specific need—if we believe that this is the meaning of preaching, then we have a firm base from which to begin to examine other questions.

—Published in Reformed Review,
Winter 1975; pp. 75-78.

From *Pulpit and Table*, by Howard G. Hageman:

It is the Biblical factor itself which today is asking the Reformed churches whether they have not perverted the Biblical witness in their worship. Our basic perversion goes back to the beginning of our history. It was present in the thinking of Zwingli, but it was fully developed in later centuries. In all of its phases, orthodox, liberal, and pietist, Reformed church worship has at least flirted with an unbiblical dualism, an attempt to oppose the spiritual to the material in worship. For centuries the favorite liturgical proof text in the Reformed churches has been St. John 4:24, exegeted, as the scholars agree, in a most unfortunate way.

Whatever appealed to the mind, whether an orthodox dogmatic discussion or a liberal ethical essay, was *spiritual*. Whatever appealed to the senses—color, light, line, movement, or physical object—was *material*. Almost from the beginning, Reformed worship has been intellectualized. It is not surprising that many people in the Reformed churches are attracted by the Quaker way of worship. It is only the logical conclusion to a tendency which has always been marked in

Reformed worship, a dichotomy between the spiritual and the material, the exaltation of the spiritual and the debasement of the material. . . .

The reconstruction of Reformed worship must begin here. We must recognize that this dualism is false and unbiblical. Not only is it inconsistent with the Biblical view of man, it is still more glaringly inconsistent with that cornerstone of the Christian faith, "the Word became flesh." Leaving to one side the fact that in any commonsense attitude there is as much of the material involved in preaching as there is in the Sacrament, a purely *spiritual* worship, in the common Reformed sense of the term, is impossible in a religion centered in the Incarnation.

The recovery of this Biblical insight, stimulated by a renewed scholarship of the New Testament congregation, should bring us back to the conviction which we would never have lost had Zwingli not conquered Calvin in our liturgics. In the act of Christian worship, Word and Sacrament belong together. Any attempt to set up an antithesis between them is completely false to the Biblical witness. They belong together not as successive or even complementary acts. They are aspects of a single whole. Word and Sacrament are only different media for the same reality, Christ's coming into the midst of his people. . . .

But, it may be asked, if this be true, if Word and Sacraments are both the same, coming of the same Christ, why are we not justified, as the Reformed churches have generally done, in taking one and, if not rejecting the other, relegating it to an obscure corner? . . .

We have to admit that in their violence in restoring the Word to worship the reformers came perilously close to eliminating the Sacrament. They did not intend to. There were all kinds of historical reasons and justifications for what they did. But practically speaking, what did the Reformed Reformation come to but the elevation of the Word as the norm of worship, the removal of the Sacrament to a place of neglect and insignificance? . . .

We have to ask ourselves whether by our neglect of the Sacrament we have not lost as much as the medieval church did by its neglect of the Word. For one thing, that loss of a real understanding of the Word which is such a threat to the life of the Reformed churches is in part the result of our neglect of the Sacrament. Could we so easily have dissolved the Word of God, that concrete and real event, into a set of general abstractions true for all times and places if every proclamation of the Word had been followed by the concrete and real event of the breaking of the bread?

And there are further questions to be asked. Would the preaching in the Reformed churches have become so loosely connected with the gospel, as it has in some places at least, if every Sunday it had been followed by the proclamation of the Lord's death till he come? Or could the Reformed churches have proved such fertile soil for the growth of sectarianism, producing one schism after another in their history, if every week they had reminded themselves that "we being many are one bread, and one body: for we are all partakers of that one bread"? It cannot be denied that of all the confessional groups in Christendom, we Reformed have shown the greatest tendency to fissiparity; the one thing about which we have had no conscience has been schism and secession. But we have been slow to explore the connection between this unhappy tendency and our intellectualization of the gospel, symbolized by our neglect of the Sacrament.

The question which the Biblical factor asks is simply this. A church that loses the Word must finally lose the Sacrament. But is it not equally true that a church which loses the Sacrament must finally lose the Word? . . .

When we bring our liturgical practice under the judgment of Scripture we cannot escape the fact that Word and Sacrament together form the way in which Christ meets his people in worship, that it is dangerous to seek to dispense with either the pulpit or the Table.
—*pp. 111-12, 114-15.*

....

From his experience as a pastor at Madison Square Christian Reformed Church, Grand Rapids, Michigan, David Beelen shows how a contemporary charismatic worship style fits with Reformed tradition, and in a fictional vignette James Calvin Schaap describes how the two clash. In the poem "Holy Water" Sietze Buning tries to pinpoint the principle behind the traditional Reformed worship style.

"A Thirst for Expressive Worship," by David Beelen:

Any sensitive observer of the church's worship will have noticed that during the past decade or two our worship patterns and customs have been changing. On the one hand we see a kind of return to what we might call the liturgical traditions (such as observances of the church year, use of banners and liturgical colors, etc.); on the other, a new openness to the more free-flowing and emotion-releasing "charismatic" style.

Though I am copastor of a church that has been drinking from both these streams, my comments on these pages flow mainly from the second of the two. The charismatic renewal movement has helped our congregation express—both verbally and physically—a deep and intense emotion in our worship. . . . That is something our people long for and need.

As a pastor, I am called to interpret both the Scriptures and the life of the people I lead. I will attempt to interpret . . . four statements and give you a peek into the heart and mind of one who is called to lead a multiracial, multicultural, prismatic, charismatic, Christian, and Reformed people in worship of God.

> As the deer pants for streams of water, so my soul pants for you, O God.
> —*Psalm 42:1*

We long to worship with intensity and abandon because we are created to worship God. The first and greatest commandment is not to serve others but to minister to God. This priority activity in our lives is to be done with a full surrender: with our whole heart and mind and strength.

In this image of the panting deer, the psalmist expresses the God-created thirst and hunger we have for the only One who satisfies. We have been looking for love in all the wrong places. Our heart's deepest longing is to be in God's presence and to open a dialogue with our Lord and Maker.

This truth is expressed confessionally in the famous opening of the Westminster Confession: as image-bearers of God, our ultimate goal is to glorify God and enjoy him forever. Our hearts are restless until they find their rest in God alone. As Isaiah says, "Why spend money on what is not bread, and your labor on what does not satisfy? Listen to me, and eat what is good, and your soul will delight in the richest of fare" (Isa. 55:2).

The kind of desire and longing expressed in these passages is similar to the passion that young lovers communicate. God, as our divine lover, desires our company. We, his bride, need time without limit (a hallmark of worship services of the "charismatic" bent) to enjoy God's presence. The worship time before the sermon, then, is not relegated to insignificant "preliminaries" but becomes a precious and holy time to enter into the bridegroom's chambers. The Lord's Supper becomes a time to linger over dinner with our beloved.

> "I long to worship with freedom, singing songs of joy, clapping my hands in exuberance and worshiping together as we get lost in the presence of God."
> —New Member of Madison Square

Recently I attended a worship service that was so silent it seemed oppressive to me. I noticed very little movement among the people; they sat stone-still while one man did all the talking. Then there were several minutes of silence so complete that I could hear my breathing. Control and quiet seemed to be the guiding values of that worship service.

I know that a full and intimate silence can center our diffused lives and contribute to a more disciplined listening to God's voice. In fact, many so-called "charismatic" worship services could benefit greatly from including more times of quiet and reverent listening. We are noisy people, easily distracted.

But there is also a quietness which is simply oppressive. The Madison Square member who made the statement about clapping hands and singing with joy came to us from an oppressively silent congregation. She felt that her church had suppressed her human need to worship freely—to express praise with childlike exuberance. She also spoke of a desire "to get lost in the presence of God"—to lose her self-consciousness in God-consciousness.

At Madison Square, we sometimes sing a call to worship that goes like this: "We have come into this place and gathered in his name to worship him . . ." In the second verse we urge each other to ". . . forget about ourselves and concentrate on him and worship him." True worship focuses not on self but on God, not on singing to our neighbor but on praising God. When that self-forgetfulness and holy remembering come together, we are in ecstasy (Greek: *ekstasis*, "to stand outside oneself"). This is entering the holy of holies, a re-creating experience.

73

This is knowing God's love and grace. This is enjoying God in a holy, corporate, covenant, family embrace.

Ecstasy has its parallels in non-worship settings. Have you ever observed a crowd of basketball fans celebrating a game-ending slam dunk? That's ecstasy. Do you know the abandon and sweetness of the intimate act of marriage? That's ecstasy. Have you ever watched a three-year-old at play in a sandbox? That's ecstasy.

In fact, that last picture of ecstasy reminds us of Jesus' words to us: ". . . unless you change and become like little children, you will never enter the kingdom of heaven" (Matt. 18:3). During worship we must lose some of our self-consciousness, our adult habit of constantly watching ourselves. We must learn to worship playfully, losing ourselves in the presence of God . . . or we will miss the rich experience of God's presence. We have a human need and desire which is met by God's gift of ecstasy. Let us have ecstatic worship!

> "It was so great to worship with you Sunday night. The songs were great, and the band helped me to worship God. I appreciate the way you recognize people's emotions and include an appeal to emotions."
> —Visitor to Madison Square

There is a new warmth of emotion, freedom, and expressiveness in much worship today which is too often challenged as "insincerely casual and superficial." We live in a society that has been characterized as "the information age," a culture of high-tech and low touch. However, the sophisticated technology and the application of the scientific method to solve our troubles and shape our worldview has produced a cold, barren, one-dimensional life. The human need to feel and express emotion, the deep human capacity to know and experience awe and mystery, has been given too little attention—even in the church. Worship services in the Protestant tradition, for example, have often been overly didactic and verbal, a mostly left-brained experience.

God's children are wonderfully complex creatures. We possess both bodies and souls, thoughts and emotions, left and right hemispheres in our brains. Our theology, in the Reformed tradition, is characteristically holistic; so ought our worship services to be expressive of all aspects of our redeemed humanness.

> "I really enjoyed worship today. It was so beautiful. The time that we spent singing in the Spirit was so cleansing for me. I believe we worshiped God well today."
> —Madison Square Elder

These words were spoken to me recently by a sixty-five-year-old leader in our congregation. He often comes forward after worship services to give elderly direction and commentary. On this particular morning, after a set of songs that had extolled the holiness and majesty of God, our band continued to sustain the final chord of our last song as I led the congregation in a time of free praise, exhorting all worshipers to sing the same note I was singing, then to branch out from that baseline chord. As our tongue-speakers began to sing in tongues, all others joined in English, using their own words to sing a simple song of love to God: "I love you, Lord . . . Glory to your name, Lord . . . I praise you, Jesus."

The song was highly improvised and included individual praise in a corporate expression. We discovered a new way to sing praise to our Lord ("Sing to the LORD a new song," Psalm 98:1), a new way to tell God of our adoration. The power of the Spirit washed over us that day as we became aware of the gentle presence of the third person of the Trinity.

I have noticed over the years that just as people have unique and characteristic personalities, so do congregations. And one way in which congregations differ is in the attention that each one tends to give to the persons of the Trinity.

Some churches seem to pay closest attention to God the Father; their worship often stresses God's power and greatness and our creatureliness.

Others major in God the Son, placing their emphasis on the issues of incarnation, our sin, and the grace of salvation. Worship in these churches is often more informal: Jesus is described as flesh of our flesh and bone of our bone—our Friend. As the incarnate Word is central, so the preaching of the Word is often central. The call to conversion and discipleship is usually the climax of the service and the goal of worship.

Then there are churches that focus mainly on God the Holy Spirit. Such congregations often emphasize the power to overcome in our new life and the ongoing battle between the forces of God and the forces of evil. Worship in these churches is often open to what we often call "extraordinary gifts of the Holy Spirit." Prophecies, tongues, and prayers for healing are common.

Of course, we should never serve just one person of the Trinity. One of the strengths of the Reformed tradition is its careful balance and recognition of God as One who comes to us in three Persons. Pastors and worship leaders who are theologically balanced and biblically sound will seek to give expression to the full range of the image of God found in us and direct worship to all three persons of the Trinity.

However, our churches don't always succeed in providing that balance. The elder quoted above had spent most of his early life in a church that majored in God the Father, minored in God the Son, and only gave lip service to the Spirit. He is now giving expression to his gratefulness for the opportunity to redress the imbalance.

He has recognized, as many of us do, that the Spirit of God is renewing us through new models and patterns of worship. A well-balanced and firmly rooted church has little to fear, much to learn, and much to give to the work of God in the charismatic renewal of worship.

—Published in Reformed Worship 20,
June 1991; pp. 6-8.

"Lord, Have Mercy: Lakeside Church Wrestles with Raised Hands," by James Calvin Schaap:

The council, very much on edge as they talked about it, concluded that the turmoil began when Lizzy Sibbelink visited her sister Heather up north and worshiped at Heather's church on Cutler Avenue.

"Not a real wild place either," Elder Swart claimed, remembering his father's pastorate there when he was a boy. "Not known for anything outlandish," he told the others. "Fine place—quite soft-spoken. Not usually on the cutting edge." On that basis they concluded that what the Sibbelinks saw and experienced had to be quite widespread already up north.

Lizzy had brought her husband along to Heather's this time, and the both of them came back with a fever. What they'd seen at Cutler Street Church, the consistory already knew, was people with their hands raised, during singing especially and sometimes even during prayer. "A whole church of them—" Elder Wilmot wondered—"like a herd of Texas longhorns?"

What had happened was clear: in a church full of arm-raisers, you start to feel apostate if you don't chuck them up yourself. "Okay," Arn must have thought, looking around at a congregation of armpits; "when in Rome"—and up both hands went. That made Lizzy the odd woman out.

Elder Swart said he heard from others who had been there that Lizzy had hesitated for a while. She looked around at all the others in Cutler Street, including Arn. She shifted her weight from foot to foot, obviously undecided. But, finally, reluctantly—after two verses of "Our God Reigns" and a swarm of compelling smiles from those already uplifted around her—she pulled up her arms too.

That's where the problem began, the consistory said. Arn they could have dealt with, coming as he did from a family given to displays of spirituality, the kind of people who pray well in public and shed tears the way some people do dandruff. But Lizzy was something else. Once she raised her hands—something no one could believe, Lizzy being Lizzy—she began to like it. That's right. Arn smiled at her and pointed two fingers in the air as if, in tandem, the two of them had just won the Cotton Bowl. Lizzy nodded back politely, people said, cutting a wholesale smile out of whatever was left of her quickly dissipating cynicism.

On their trip south the two of them argued, back and forth, about how to present their new form of worship to their home church. After all, wasn't it painfully obvious that Lakeside was in dire need of some kind of change, some kind of "revival"? (It was Arn who said the world *revival* actually—or that's what the consistory had heard—and when the word fell, innocently, from his lips, Lizzy swallowed hard, as if he'd let out something profane. But then she said, "Sure, why not?")

That was the beginning.

When Lizzy got back, she went to work. "I mean," she told people, "what's wrong with expressing your faith like that?" "I mean," she said, "how can anybody try to quench the Spirit?" "I mean," she said, "how long has it been since there's been even a glowing ember in First Church of the Ice Box?"—meaning Lakeside, the consistory understood. Lizzy and Arn Sibbelink came back from their trip up north converted and dedicated their summer to getting Lakeside Church to raise its hands.

And now the council, a whole room of worried elders and deacons, had to decide what to do about the matter . . .

Swart leaned back, looked up at the picture of his father with the former pastors, and wished he could have one of those fat black cigars old-time consistories used to savor in silence right in this room. Of course, now there were women, he thought—but then who knows? Maybe they'd be frustrated enough to join him in a stogie.

"I don't like it," Wilmot said, breaking the silence. "It puts people in a swoon. Why last week I saw Herman Fry almost pass out, I swear, his eyes closed tight. There he stood, like he had grown antennae." He tossed his eyes up in the air. "You know, Pastor," he said, "you got to cut down on numbers of verses, or people'll drop like flies."

"Nonsense," Ferris said. "You can't tell people how they can or can't express themselves. If the Spirit's in them, then they're going to raise their hands. We've got no business trying to stanch what the Spirit's up to." Silence. (Ferris and her husband raise their hands.)

"What I want to know," Swart said finally, "is why the Spirit works like a virus." He put both elbows up on the table. "We'd never have had a problem here if the Sibbelinks hadn't visited up north." At that moment he raised both hands himself. "Go ahead—tell me it's the Holy Spirit. If it is, I think he's working a lot like a hula hoop. Smells like a fad to me."

"Whatever the reason," Ludinga said, "we can't tell people they can't do it. We have to face that fact." She twisted her pen between her fingers as she spoke. "I'm not excited about it myself," she said, "but we're not about to ask the ushers to remove people who lift their hands."

"Of course not," Wilmot said, and the way he moved his jaw reminded Swart that the old man had a pinch of tobacco tucked behind his lower lip. "But that doesn't mean I like it," he said. "It sets up a hierarchy. That's what we're seeing now. Some do it, some don't. Those that do are blessed, sure—and those that don't are either full of guilt because they can't do it or mad as heck at those who do for creating all this stink. We got war, boys," he said, forgetting about Ludinga and Ferris. "We got war here, and we got to do something about it."

Prickly silence fell around the table.

"What do the Scriptures say?" Swart said, finally.

Pastor Andrew took in a deep breath. "The Bible tells us in several places," he explained quietly, "to lift up our hands to the Lord in praise.

"Well, then," Swart said, as if the case were closed.

"It also says we're supposed to pour on oil when we visit the sick," Wilmot said, "and it commands us to greet each other with a holy kiss! And the book of Timothy, I think, says women aren't supposed to speak. So what does the Bible have to do with it?"

Swart felt as if he and the whole room were aboard a toboggan hurtling down some river-valley hill toward an inevitable crash.

Pastor Andrew hadn't said much, allowing them all, as he often did, to throw their opinions out over the table. Finally, when the silence had dragged on long enough, he said, "I'm going to raise my hands myself on Sunday. That's what I've decided. I'm going to do it myself."

Wilmot threw up his hands. "Now that's Spirit-filled all right," he said, sarcastically. "Go on and plan it ahead of time. I like that—write it into the liturgy, the way we do 'Amens.' 'All together, like a mighty army. On cue,'" he said. "Why don't you put an asterisk in the bulletin—'Congregation standing—please raise your hands.'"

"I'm serious," Pastor Andrew said. "I know what's going on. I know what it's caused. You can't believe all the calls I'm getting. So-and-so's mad at so-and-so . . ."

"If *you* do it, then we all got to do it?" Wilmot asked stonily.

The preacher sat back and brought his hands up behind his head. "No," he said. "What'll happen is that I'll make it legitimate. That way, Lizzy and Arn won't be to blame anymore. They won't be black sheep. I mean, I'll make it okay—do you know what I'm saying?"

Wilmot didn't say a thing.

"I think it's a good idea," Ferris said.

"You would," Wilmot screamed. "You already raise your hands. Now you got the Reverend on your side."

"Is this a war?" she said. "Are we enemies here?" She bounced her pencil on the eraser. "I mean, aren't we all 'one in the Spirit,' here?—you know 'they'll know we are Christians by our love'?"

"Pollyanna," Wilmot muttered.

Swart looked down at his watch and saw that it was already past eleven. They'd got on the subject because it came up constantly at family visiting. Item three on the agenda—three out of fourteen. With the point of his pen, he ran down the list—reports to classis, angry overtures, then, finally, benevolence, missions. Maybe they'd just quit early, he thought. It was going nowhere. Frustration sat thick as fog.

"Maybe we ought to pray," Ludinga said, finally.

"Right now?" Wilmot said.

"Yes, right now," she told him.

He looked up at the clock. "Okay—but do we raise our hands or not?"

"We can do with less sarcasm, Fred," Pastor Andrew said, and Wilmot pushed himself away from the table. "Prayer is a good suggestion," the pastor continued quietly. He looked around. Ferris was seething, and Wilmot pouting, jawing that chew. "Gene," the pastor said, pointing at Swart. "Would you lead us?"

Pray, Gene Swart thought, now? He shook his head, then looked down at the missionaries whose photos were pressed beneath the glass of the consistory table. Once, years ago, he'd made profession in this room. Now he was forty-four and he had spent more hours than he could count meeting around this table with elders and deacons . . . .

"Gene?" Pastor Andrew asked again, as if he'd not been heard.

Pray?—pray tell, for what?—Gene thought, the air thick with the dusty stench of a battlefield, anger rising from the trenches on either side of the table. Aside from college, Lakeside had been Gene Swart's home church from the time he was twelve. He loved sitting there in silence before the service, waiting and worshiping with the people he'd known for a lifetime.

The council stared, waiting for him to pray.

For whom?—he wondered. For the Sibbelinks? For Wilmot? For the whole bunch? He turned toward each of them, folding his hands as he met their anxious eyes. There was only one real prayer, he thought, one need worth pressing right now. He smiled, stood, and raised his hands. He shook from his shoulders when the rest of them didn't respond, and jerked his hands up again like a maestro until they were all on their feet. And then he prayed, as requested. "Lord," he said in a faint tremolo, "have mercy."

That's all. Three words. Then silence.

The twelve stood, waiting, all of them with their arms raised, until Wilmot finally said it, when no one else did. "Amen," he said, with vehemence born-again.

—*Published in* Reformed Worship *19,
March 1991; pp. 32-33.*

Holy Water

It was style in Middleburg church for Albert van Dongen,
the janitor, to sit alone in the front pew.
He had to pump the organ.

It is style in all Reformed churches
for the janitor to put a glass of water
inside the pulpit in case the dominie gets thirsty.

One Sunday just as Dominie was starting his second point
his mouth turned dry and he reached for a glass of water
that was not there.
Albert had actually forgotten.
Having no rock to strike,
Dominie turned to Albert and rasped out:
"Mr. van Dongen, I would like some water."
Albert was, in fact, sleeping as soundly as a rock.
It was his style after Dominie's first point.
An awkward pause.
"Mr. van Dongen."
Another awkward pause.

Dad,
clerk of the consistory
and seated at the end of the consistory pew,
had a choice: get the water and let Albert sleep,
or do what he did—
walk up to Albert,
shake him awake,
and order water for Dominie.
Nobody should be asleep,
so it was not a difficult decision.

Albert all but ran out:
"Water?
Water, ja. Water."
But alone in the consistory room
the purpose for the water was unclear.

And so Albert appeared with water all right,
but it was in the baptismal basin.

Fortunately we Reformed aren't stuck on holy vessels
or Dominie would have had to send him back for a glass.

As it was, Dominie turned his back to the congregation,
leaned forward, and sucked out of the middle of the basin
like a horse.
The brim would have been too wide.
Water would have streamed all over his clothes.
Baptism is just as effective out of a casserole, isn't it?
So why not drink out of a baptismal basin?
Any Reformed dominie would have done the same,
so that was only style,
as were Albert's sleeping, Albert's mistake,
and Dad's waking him up.

Whose then was the class?
The congregation's.

That congregation witnessed Albert caught asleep,
and Dad's waking him;
the baptismal basin in Albert's hand,
and Dominie's drinking from it—
legs spread wide and leaning forward
like a giraffe.
Yet the first sound
in addition to the clock's suddenly deafening tick
was Dominie's resuming his sermon at point two.

Of course,
after the benediction
we young folks burst out of the church doors
doubled over and stamping our feet.

At dinner
when Dad thought of it
midway through a spoonful of pea soup,
he sprayed great green blotches
all over Mother's white tablecloth.

Even today,
all I need to do to make my brother yelp with laughter
is to take Dominie's pose, sucking up that water.

If anyone had tittered when it happened
the whole congregation would have been beside themselves.

But nobody did.

Everybody was a king or queen.

At state occasions, royalty is not amused.
                    —*Sietze Buning. From* Style and Class,
                    pp. 19-21.

5. How do we view the Bible and the creeds?

The Written Word of God

We confess that this Word of God
was not sent nor delivered by the will of men,
but that holy men of God spoke,
being moved by the Holy Spirit,
    as Peter says.

Afterwards our God—
    because of the special care he has
    for us and our salvation—
commanded his servants,
the prophets and apostles,
to commit this revealed Word to writing.
He himself wrote
with his own finger
the two tables of the law.

Therefore we call such writings
holy and divine Scriptures.

—Belgic Confession, Art. 3.

The Authority of Scripture

We receive all these books
and these only
as holy and canonical,
for the regulating, founding, and establishing
of our faith.

And we believe
without a doubt
all things contained in them—
    not so much because the church
    receives and approves them as such
    but above all because the Holy Spirit
    testifies in our hearts
    that they are from God,
    and also because they
    prove themselves
    to be from God.

For even the blind themselves are able to see
that the things predicted in them
do happen.

—Belgic Confession, Art. 5.

I n former times, a book such as this one might well have *begun* with a section on the Bible. The individual's faith, the church's theology, the proper way of worship—all should be derived, Reformed people have often thought, strictly and expressly from the Bible.

Our placement of discussion about the Bible here, however, does not mean Scripture has been demoted. Rather, this section occurs near the center of the book: five units have come before, and seven will follow. As all our selections assume, and as the four here particularly argue, Scripture must form the heart of the believer and of the church, being at once the source and the object, the measure and target, of the entire life of faith. Thus, our positioning of this section matches a Reformed theological position on Scripture.

Another reason for re-ordering things is that the Bible has not, in fact, been able to do the job some have assigned it: to settle disputes in doctrine and life beyond question. The endless fragmentation of modern Christianity testifies to the great many readings people can make of Scripture. The Reformed recognized this early on and so committed themselves to a particular reading, a definite and communal interpretation of Scripture. Not just any interpretation, to be sure, but the best they could make, guided by the Spirit and subject to further refinement and clarification.

These communal interpretations are called creeds and confessions, and further elaborations of them are, in Reformed jargon, synodical pronouncements. The following two readings define these communal interpretations' relationship to Scripture.

From *Acts of Synod 1975* of the Christian Reformed Church:

SYNODICAL PRONOUNCEMENTS AND THE CONFESSIONS
Scripture and Confession
The confessions are subordinate to Scripture. The Christian Reformed Church confesses "its complete subjection to the Word of God and the Reformed creeds as a true interpretation of this Word" (Church Order, Art. 1). In the Belgic Confession the church confesses the Holy Scriptures "as holy and canonical, for the regulation, foundation, and confirmation of our faith; believing without any doubt all things contained in them" (Art. V). Scripture alone is acknowledged as the "infallible rule" (Art. VII). Thus the confessions—the Belgic Confession, the Heidelberg Catechism, and the Canons of Dort—are subordinate to Scripture and are embraced as "a true interpretation of this Word." Hence, the confessions function as "forms of unity" in which the church confesses its faith. All office-bearers are required to "signify their agreement with the doctrine of the church by signing the Form of Subscription" (Church Order, Art. 5). Furthermore, "members by baptism shall be admitted to the Lord's Supper upon a public profession of Christ according to the Reformed creeds, with the use of the prescribed form" (Church Order, Art. 59a). The criteria for membership of persons coming from other denominations are the same (Art. 59c).

The confessions of the Christian Reformed Church are, of course, held in common with many other Reformed churches throughout the world. The creeds or confessions of the Reformed churches are first of all *confessions* in which the church gives expression to its faith in response to God who revealed himself in his Word. In the confessions the church also presents a *public testimony* to the world concerning her Christian faith. Within its own communion the confessions function as *forms of unity* in which the common faith of the members of the church is expressed. The confessions also serve as *instruments for the instruction* of the youth in the church in order, by God's grace, to bring them to confess this faith also. As forms of unity the confessions also serve a *juridical function* in guarding the purity of the church in doctrine and life. The confessions also serve *a missionary purpose* as instruments for witnessing to the world with the full Gospel of Jesus Christ. Although the confessions are subordinate to the Scriptures, they have a strategic and varied role in the life of the Christian Reformed Church and in the life of those other Reformed churches throughout the world holding the same confession. . . .

The authority of the confessions is subordinate to the Scriptures. The authority of synodical decisions is subordinate to the confessions and the Scriptures as the authority of the confessions is subordinate to the Scriptures. Subscription to the confessions is required of all office-bearers, and agreement with the confessions is expected of all members of the church. *Synodical decisions* are "considered settled and binding, unless it is proved that they conflict with the Word of God or the Church Order." They must be in harmony with the Reformed creeds which the Christian Reformed Church accepts "as a true interpretation of this Word" (Church Order, Arts. 29 and 1). Thus there is a difference in the nature of the authority of the confessions and synodical pronouncements. . . .

Synodical pronouncements of a doctrinal and ethical nature serve the purpose of further *expressing* the church's understanding of Scripture and the confessions. Synodical decisions sometimes interpret Scripture and the creeds; some synodical decisions augment or supplement what is confessed in the creeds; some synodical decisions make biblical applications to issues arising in historical circumstances that were not contemplated or specifically addressed in the confessions; some synodical decisions are juridical in nature dealing with deviations from Scripture or confession or adjudicatory in nature in resolving issues in dispute. Thus there are distinctions as to the purposes served by the confessions and synodical pronouncements.

—*pp. 596-97, 601.*

From *Creeds of the Churches*, ed. John H. Leith:

Still another need that was served by the creeds was the Church's concern for hermeneutics. Originally, the Church had to declare how it would understand the Old Testament and what the substance of the Apostolic tradition was. After the Apostolic witness was put into writing, the Church had to have some measure by which to determine which books were canonical, that is, genuinely apostolic. After the canon of the New Testament was fixed, it was still necessary to provide some principle of interpretation to distinguish the centrally important from the peripheral and to put together in some coherent way the diversity of the New Testament testimony. As Oscar Cullmann has put it, every interpreter has to distinguish between the central principle and what is derived from it. Hence every theology presupposes a rule of faith.

The creed is simply the Church's understanding of the meaning of Scripture. The creed says, Here is how the Church reads and receives Scripture. The whole history of theology is the history of the interpretation of Scripture, even though the theologians do not always cite Biblical references. In general, the victories in the great theological debates have gone to those who have been the most convincing interpreters of Scripture. The creeds are the record of the Church's interpretation of the Bible in the past and the authoritative guide to hermeneutics in the present.

The rise of heresy was still another situation that created the need for creeds. Heresy is so important a factor in the origin of creeds that it tempts the commentator to exaggerate its role. As was said long ago, creeds are signposts to heresies. The task of the creed was to defend the Church against heresy. The creed has the negative role of shutting the heretic out and setting the boundaries within which authentic Christian theology and life can take place. These functions of the creed account in some instances for the choice of words and also for the items of theological affirmation. Yet it is a mistake to attribute creeds simply to heresy, for there would be creeds even if there were no heretics. In fact, theology can become the subject of debate apart from heresy. It may well be that the creeds, without the heretics, would not be as good as they are; for the heretics made their contributions. They required the Church to think through theological issues when it did not want to do so. They made the Church exercise care in theological language so that the language of theology would say what the Christian community wanted to say. Creeds are not due simply to the heretics, but they would be much poorer creeds without the heretics.

Creeds are also a standard, a battle cry, a testimony and witness to the world. In the Ancient Church persecution afforded an occasion for a Christian confession. In the twentieth century the paganism of National Socialism challenged confession from Christians. Communism likewise calls for a declaration of belief. These radical situations illustrate a need that is always present, the need for commitment. Christian faith is not only the gift of God's grace; it is also a command, a task. It is a battle against the "world, the flesh, and the devil." The creed is a marching song, a battle cry. In this fact resides some of the truth in the assertion that creeds are to be sung. . . .

The word creed suggests authority, but the exact nature and extent of creedal authority is a difficult question. There is no one answer that satisfies all Christians. On one extreme the creed is almost identified with the Word of God. On the other extreme creeds are minimized and dogmatic Christianity is regarded as a mistake, or at best an unfortunate necessity.

The attempt to dispense with dogma and to minimize creeds has never been successful. As has been indicated, there has never been a nontheological period in the history of the Church. Even when the Church has been held together only by a common life in the Spirit, a creed has always been implicit. The endeavor to have no creed but the Bible is successful only so long as there is common agreement as to what the Bible teaches. In the long run, organizational necessities demonstrate the need for creeds, and organizational integrity requires some kind of creedal subscription. The attempt to minimize creeds and to magnify Christianity without dogma runs aground either on the theological nature of Christian faith or on the nature of man, who is body as well as spirit, and who cannot get along without organizational structure.

The attempt to assert intentionally or unintentionally the absolute authority of creeds is predicated upon particular views of truth, of man, and of community. The creedal absolutist is likely to believe that propositional statements are fully adequate vehicles for truth. He must also believe that men, at least some men, are both good enough and wise enough, at least in certain situations, to know the truth in a final and definitive way. He is also likely to believe that community can exist only on the basis of full agreement as to truth propositionally stated. Over against the creedal absolutist, there is a considerable body of Christians who insist that, however useful and indispensable propositional statements may be as the embodiment of truth, the ultimate and final embodiment of the wisdom of God is the Person of Jesus Christ. Man's apprehension of the Word of God is never ultimate and final, for every man's theology is limited by his finiteness and his sin. Finally, the Christian community existed prior to the formulation of Christian faith in exact and precise creeds. None of this means that creeds are not indispensable pointers to the wisdom of God and necessary boundaries for Christian living, but it does reject every effort to absolutize a human achievement as idolatry and as, in the end, destructive of community. When creeds have been made absolute, someone always rises to protest in the name of the Word of God, which stands in judgment on every human word.

—pp. 8-11.

....

Though subject to varying interpretations and pronouncements, the words of Scripture still stand above and beyond human exposition. How does that work? Herman N. Ridderbos links Scripture's authority to its purpose, a purpose that is specific yet all-encompassing, requiring careful, practiced reading.

From "The Inspiration and Authority of the Holy Scripture," by Herman N. Ridderbos:

All attributes which the Scripture ascribes to itself stand in close relationship to its purpose and nature. And so our way of thinking about Scripture and our theological definitions must also be related to this purpose.

It is obvious that Scripture is given us for a definite purpose. Paul says that it "was written for our instruction, that by steadfastness and by the encouragement of the scriptures we might have hope" (Rom. 15:4). The famous pronouncement of II Timothy 3:15-16 is to the same effect: the sacred writings "are able to instruct you for salvation through faith in Christ Jesus." Not only are the nature and force of the Scriptures to be found in their providing instruction for salvation, so are the means and key for understanding them—faith in Jesus Christ. Only by the light of such faith is the treasure of wisdom and knowledge of the Scriptures unlocked. . . .

The purpose and the nature of Scripture lie thus in that qualified sort of teaching and instruction which is able to make us wise to salvation, which gives God's people this "completeness" and equips them for every good work.

That we cannot speak about Scripture and its qualities apart from this scope, purpose, and nature should also be the point of departure of every theological evaluation and definition of biblical authority. This authority is not to be separated from the content and purpose of Scripture thus qualified, nor can it be recognized apart from this content and the specific character of the Scripture. No matter to what extent we reject the dualistic doctrine of inspiration, which holds that only the religious-ethical sections of Scripture are inspired and authoritative, this does not remove the fact that, in Herman Bavinck's words, "Holy Scripture has a thoroughly religious-ethical purpose (designation, intention) and is not intended to be a handbook for the various sciences." We may not apply to Scripture standards which do not suit it. Not only does it give no exact knowledge of mathematics or biology, but it also presents no history of Israel or biography of Jesus that accords with the standards of historical science. Therefore, one must not transfer biblical authority.

God speaks to us through the Scriptures not in order to make us scholars, but to make us Christians. To be sure, to make us Christians in our science, too, but not in such a way as to make human science superfluous or to teach us in a supernatural way all sorts of things that could and would otherwise be learned by scientific training and research.

What Scripture does intend is to place us as humans in a right position to God, even in our scientific studies and efforts. Scripture is not concerned only with persons' *religious* needs in a pietistic or existentialistic sense of that word. On the contrary, its purpose and authority is that it teaches us to understand everything *sub specie Dei* ["under God's view"]—humanity, the world, nature, history, their origin and their destination, their past and their future. Therefore the Bible is not only the book of conversion, but also the book of history and the book of creation. But it is the book of history of salvation; and it is this point of view that represents and defines the authority of Scripture.

But when one connects the theological definition of authority and infallibility as attributes of Scripture so closely with Scripture's purpose and nature, does one not run the danger of falling into a kind of subjectivism? Who will establish precisely the boundaries between that which does and that which does not pertain to the purpose of the Scripture? And is the way not thus opened for subjectivism and arbitrariness in the matter of the authority of the Scripture, as has been so detrimental to the authority of the Scripture in the history of the church? I should like in this connection to point out the following:

First, the misuse of the Scripture does not abolish the good and correct use. The Scripture is not a book of separate divine oracles, but is from Genesis to Revelation an organic unity, insofar as it is the book of the history of God's redeeming and judging acts, of which the advent and work of Christ is the all-dominating center and focus. The testimony of Jesus is the spirit of prophecy (Rev. 19:10), and Scripture has the power to save by faith in Christ Jesus (II Tim. 3:15). This is the center to which everything in Scripture stands in relationship and through which it is bound together—beginning and end, creation and recreation, humanity, the world, history, and the future, as all of these have a place in the Scripture. Therefore, there is also a correlation between Scripture and faith, namely, as faith in Jesus Christ. If you take that unity away from Scripture and this correlation of Scripture and faith, you denature Scripture and faith in it; and the authority and infallibility of the Scripture also lose their theological-christological definition and become formal concepts, abstracted from the peculiar nature and content of Scripture.

But in the second place, that does not mean we are permitted to apply all sorts of dualistic operations on Scripture and make distinctions between what is and what is not inspired, what is and what is not from God—to say, for instance, that the content but not the form, or the essence but not the word, was subject to the might and inspiration and authority of God. God gave us the Scripture in this concrete form, in these words and languages. The confession applies to this, and not to specific sections or thoughts, that it is the inspired word of God, that it is given to us as the infallible guide to life, God's light on our path, God's lamp for our feet. But divine inspiration does not necessarily mean that the men who spoke and wrote under inspiration were temporarily stripped of their limitations in knowledge, memory, language, and capability of expressing themselves, as specific human beings in a certain period of history.

We have to be very careful, I think, not to operate as though we know ahead of time to what extent divine inspiration does or does not go together with the human limitations mentioned above. Inspiration does not mean deification. We cannot say everything of Scripture that we say of the word of God, nor can we identify the apostles and prophets during their writing with the Holy Spirit. The word of God exists in eternity, is perfect. But Scripture is neither eternal nor perfect. Inspiration consists in this, that God makes the words for his divine purposes. As such the human words stand in the service of God and participate in the authority and infallibility of the word of God, answer perfectly God's purpose, in short, function as the word of God and therefore can be so called. And it is not up to us; it is up to the free pleasure of God to decide what kind of effect divine inspiration should have in the mind, knowledge, memory, accuracy of those whom he has used in his service, in order that their word really can be accepted and trusted as the inspired word of God. If we deny or ignore this, we dispose of the very nature of the Scriptures as the word of God, and also of the nature of his authority and infallibility. The best way not to fall into such a danger is to study Scripture itself from this point of view.

—*Published in* The Authoritative Word, *pp. 185-88.*

....

As Article 5 of the Belgic Confession indicates, the Reformed say it is not a magical property in Scripture itself but the Spirit's testimony in the reader's heart that makes the Bible ultimately important and convincing. Johanna W. H. van Wijk-Bos testifies to this principle out of her childhood experience under Nazi occupation, and she spells out the riskiness involved in reading Scripture.

From *Reformed and Feminist,* by Johanna W. H. van Wijk-Bos:

No one ever forced me to attend church; there was no lively youth group or other entertainment to attract me. There was only the Scripture. My mother and I kept going, and eventually my father joined us. What exactly happened there in the small, ancient building that could keep a restless youngster interested Sunday after Sunday? There was, to begin with, the beauty of the building and the music of the Genevan Psalter, which even a poor organ and a less-than-perfect organist could not dim. Beauty is a luxury absent in a war-torn world, and our eyes and ears were starved for it. There was the aesthetic pleasure of watching the ceremonial ascent of the pulpit by the minister in his flowing robes, and there was the stark and familiar ritual of the liturgy.

More than anything, however, I learned something there that I could not learn anywhere else, and it had a direct influence on my life. By the time I turned twelve, I had begun to attend a preparatory school in a nearby town that provided me with enough intellectual challenge for the next six years. I read the classics of literature from different cultures, and my school provided learning for mind and heart, spirit and imagination. In church, however, I found a learning that moved me to a commitment. And that made all the difference.

With the fervor of youth, I made my commitment to the Christian faith, a commitment that was formalized when I was eighteen years old, as was the custom in our Netherlands Reformed Church. My commitment was first of all to God. That this commitment also involved a turn toward humanity did not become a reality for me until later. The shape of my early commitment was one of learning. I became a pupil in the weekly class of religious instruction conducted by our minister. This class had a curriculum organized around the fundamental principles of the Reformed heritage as set forth in the Heidelberg Catechism, a document we studied in detail, guided by the lively and intelligent insights of our minister. I took my first tentative steps on the path of theology in this class. In church I learned most of all about Scripture. A compliment that sometimes comes my way is that I "make the Scripture come alive." It never occurred to me that the Scripture can be anything but alive, for so it was presented to us Sunday after Sunday. The biblical text was unfolded in all its vividness, with all its connections to our lives, directly from father Abraham and mother Sarah, from Jacob and Rachel, and from Jesus and Mary to this twentieth-century community. The text of the Scripture was never just an old story; it always held something new, a surprise to be anticipated during its reading. Above everything else, the Scripture was allowed to have a voice. What I heard was not always easy to appropriate or to accommodate, but I was always caught by it. I learned not to expect to know ahead of time what a text of the Bible has to say. The text was treated with respect; stories were read in their entirety, not presented in snippets—digestible "sound bytes." . . .

One hears sometimes of the stereotypical Dutch Calvinist being somber and dour. There must be a grain of truth to that stereotype, but I do not recognize it. Dourness and somberness would not have suited me in my adolescence. The exposition of Scripture that I heard every Sunday was intelligent, profound, and often witty. Perhaps because no one demanded that I go to church or believe, faith was never a burden to me. The Christian faith provided me with guidance, order, and a sense of goodness and hope in the public sphere, something that had been missing in my very early years. This faith and its text liberated me from the fear of brutality's logic and presented a universe of hope. . . .

The Bible offered hope. All human beings are sinful and, for all, forgiveness is possible. To the conviction of sin and the promise of forgiveness, the biblical text gave a vivid witness. The parade of people that came before us on Sundays from the pages of the Bible were far from ideal models of humanity. They showed, rather, all the human frailty of which we had seen such extreme examples during the war. There was Sarah, who was jealous of Hagar and treated her cruelly; Jacob and Rachel, who cheated and lied; King David, who stole and murdered to whitewash his crime; and Naomi, who expressed great bitterness toward God. These were people like my neighbors and me. These were the people to whom God came in Jesus Christ. In Jesus sin and death are not the last words spoken in creation. Here, too, my experience found a point of connection: Liberation from the war *had* taken place; the last word was freedom. . . .

The Bible in the Center

Recently one of the former presidents of our seminary, in his commencement speech to the graduating class, pointed out that a denomination declining in numbers needs to look to what makes it distinctive. In doing so, he maintained, the denomination would gain vitality and strength. If he is right, as he may well be, then the denominations that include themselves in the Reformed stream must examine the position they accord to Scripture. The most distinguishing feature of the churches in the Reformed stream should be that they hold the Bible to be central and finally authoritative. There is deep concern these days in many so-called mainline denominations over a loss of members that many consider to be a threat to the life of these communities. Apparently, the majority of people who leave do so not in order to join another denomination of their choice but to become uninvolved; they leave the church for the world. A common complaint of those who leave is that the church "has nothing to say," that it has no distinct voice. A restoration of the Bible to its central place might go a long way in restoring the distinct voice of these Reformed congregations.

On the other hand, lest we feel that a return to this principle of the Reformation would offer a safe return to the past, a type of retreat, let us remember that the Reformers placed the authority of the Bible over against the authority of the Roman Catholic Church and its clergy.

Thus, while serving to regain a distinct voice, the centrality of the Bible and its authority may at the same time create an awareness of the impermanence and derived authority of the church as a human institution. As in the days of the Reformation, the Bible may point to a need for a radical reformation of what has become misformed in the church. The authority of the Bible may prevent the faithful from worshiping an institution, even a Reformed institution. Also, by their emphasis on the Bible, the Reformers did not intend to put a book in the center of belief and practice. Rather, they intended to focus belief and practice on God. In itself, the Bible is a book of some historical interest, but with no more power than any other such book; it becomes alive, and its power is experienced, only as the Holy Spirit makes it alive to believers as God's word. As it did at the time of the Reformation, biblical authority may prevent the faithful from worshiping custom and tradition, even Reformed tradition. The Bible as the word of God provides at the same time support and a critique of particular forms of Christian communities.

If the Bible is the living Word of God, it might be as surprising and unmanageable as God. There are different ways to flee into safety from the idea that the Bible provides believers with God's Word, different ways to tame its power. . . .

Putting the Bible in the center of belief and practice means that one trusts God to provide a word for our time and perplexity. It may also mean that this word is different from what one expects it to be. We remember the anxious questioner who was confused by the existence of different versions of the Bible. Her anxiety arose because she surmised that there might be rules she was not following in these unknown books of the Bible. In addition, she wanted to know which version was the "true" Bible, the "Bible God wrote." One way to manage the Bible is to view it as a book that consists mainly of rules; another way is to believe that every word in it is factually true. The anxiety of the person confronted with different editions of the Bible arose because of her view of the Bible as both a rule book and as inerrant. One version, therefore, had to be wrong, the other right. God could not have written two different versions.

Neither approach is what the Reformers practiced. They believed that the Bible is the self-revelation of God. Contradictions and errors are to be found in the Bible because this book was, from the beginning, the revelation of God in the Word as that word is accommodated to human nature. The Bible was not written in the sense that modern books are written. It was not written by one author. It was not even written by a group of authors. For most of the Bible the word "written" is inappropriate; we might more accurately use the word "composed." The Bible is a composite of many different speakers and writers, secretaries and notetakers. . . .

Calvin, as has already been pointed out, was little troubled by errors and inconsistencies in the Bible. Errors were a result of the fact, in Calvin's terms, that God had accommodated to human frailty in the process of self-revelation. The image Calvin used was that of the lisp or stammer used when speaking to infants. Calvin derived the category of accommodation from his study of classical Latin rhetoric. Accommodation meant the adaptation of a verbal message to an audience, keeping in mind the particular situation, station in life, character, emotional state, and intellectual gifts of those making up the audience. Interpreters before Calvin used the principle of accommodation to explain difficulties in the Bible; Calvin was the first to expand the concept not only to explain errors and inconsistencies but to explain the relationship between God and human creatures. Calvin used, for example, the principle of accommodation to explain the different ways that God administered grace in Old Testament times compared to New Testament times. According to Calvin, God accommodates to human capacity, a capacity that is beset by limitations and sin. The very fact that God's revelation comes to human creatures in the form of the word is a sign of God's accommodation to human capacity. It does not come as a surprise that the principle of accommodation was lost in the post-Reformation emphasis on the verbal inerrancy of the Bible. . . .

The Authority of the Bible

If the Bible's authority, as the Reformers posed, derives from the fact that this book is the self-disclosure of God, it is a temptation to view this book as a container: To get at God's revelation, all one has to do is to reach in or dig deep enough. But the revelation of God happens through the power of the Holy Spirit. On the human side, there need to be certain conditions to make the climate favorable for God's Word to happen. There is, first, the condition of expectant listening on the part of the believing community or the individual, the kind of listening that assumes there is a word in the text that cannot be heard elsewhere. The second condition is that believers come to the text with something to ask; questions need to be posed, concerns and interests voiced. Without the condition of listening, the agenda of the text will not be heard; it will be drowned out in the concerns and questions of the day, or it will correspond to whatever the community or the individual wants it to say. Without the condition of questioning, the Bible will be static, frozen in time; it has something to say, but not to us, not for today. The word that is there will always sound the same if the contemporary situation does not impinge on the text. . . .

I suggest that the authority of the biblical text works . . . in that *God* addresses us through this text at the deepest level of our questioning. For me and many others in my native country, the deepest level of questioning concerned the experience of systemic oppression perpetrated on human beings by other human beings. It was precisely there, at that level, that God met me in the biblical text. Because this is God's word, the text becomes not only authenticating but redemptive. The biblical text witnesses not only to human relations but to God's involvement with these relations, God's involvement in the abyss of inhumanity that humanity creates. Because of this involvement on God's part, the cycle of violence, the flip-flop of oppressed into oppressor, is not inevitable. God's universe is not closed; it is full of possibilities, even for extremely flawed human beings, those with murder in their hearts, those who have committed murder. It was not strange, then, that when I identified women as victims of systemic oppression later in my life, I looked in the direction of the biblical text for both the authorization of the experience and for the redemptive word that opens

possibilities for ways of being other than those provided by systems that lock us into the domination of one sex over the other.
—pp. 18-21, 36-40, 42-43, 45-46.

6. How do we organize the life of the church?

The Officers of the Church

We believe that
ministers of the Word of God, elders, and deacons
ought to be chosen to their offices
by a legitimate election of the church,
with prayer in the name of the Lord,
and in good order,
    as the Word of God teaches.

So everyone must be careful
not to push himself forward improperly,
but he must wait for God's call,
    so that he may be assured of his calling
    and be certain that he is
    chosen by the Lord.

As for the ministers of the Word,
they all have the same power and authority,
    no matter where they may be,
since they are all servants of Jesus Christ,
    the only universal bishop,
    and the only head of the church.

Moreover,
to keep God's holy order
from being violated or despised,
we say that everyone ought,
as much as possible,
to hold the ministers of the Word and elders of the church
in special esteem,
    because of the work they do,
and be at peace with them,
    without grumbling, quarreling, or fighting.

—Belgic Confession, Art. 31.

Nothing is touchier in church life than the exercise and acceptance of authority. Perhaps that's the reason nothing is more prone to run by custom, nothing provokes more resentment, and nothing has occasioned more argument in the thick annals of Reformed splintering and separation than the conduct of ecclesiastical rule.

As M. Eugene Osterhaven notes, questions of church authority loomed large at the very start of the Reformation and led the Reformers to propose a new structure of offices.

From *The Spirit of the Reformed Tradition*, by M. Eugene Osterhaven:

The Reformation, besides being a return to the religious teachings of the Bible, was a revolt against the religious authority of the Church of Rome. Prince and peasant, landholder and townsman rejected the rule of the Roman hierarchy for a form of government that they felt would bring blessing to Christians. They did not intend to leave the church of Christ, but they sought to correct those abuses within it which threatened to destroy its character. In order to correct them they had to give particular attention to the manner in which the church was governed. The Reformers felt that there was little chance of success at reform as long as the church was dominated by "the Pope, that pagan full of pride," so they devised a form of government for the church in which the pope and his court were absent. In doing this they succeeded to a degree beyond their fondest expectations and their success, in the Calvinistic part of the Reformation at least, was due in large measure to the new organization of the church and its ministry.

Not the least of Calvin's unusual gifts was his talent for organization. A. M. Fairbairn assesses his legislative and organizational abilities and achievements even more highly than his gifts as a theologian, and regards them as a truer expression of the man than his theology. . . .

It is true that all Christians are ministers, *diakonoi*, servants of God. It is also true that there is only "one essential ministry, the perpetual ministry of the risen Lord, present, as he promised to be, where his people are gathered in his name, and renewing to each generation the gifts they need to continue *his* ministry." Yet, as he continues his ministry Christ calls persons to offices that he, the chief officebearer, has given the church. At least, this has been the position of the Reformed Church in its interpretation of the relevant New Testament passages where office as well as function have been found. Paul wrote that Christ's gifts "were that some should be apostles, some prophets, some evangelists, some pastors and teachers, for the equipment of the saints, for the work of ministry, for building up the body of Christ" (Eph. 4:11f.).

In addition to the general office of all Christians to discharge their respective ministries, then, Christ has given the church special offices that some, not all, are called to fill. By offices we mean specific positions of trust, ministration, and authority with specified responsibilities and duties. These offices function within the fellowship of believers through the power of the Holy Spirit, whose anointing qualifies those called by the church and consequently by its Lord. . . .

In the Reformed Church the special offices are usually considered to be three in number: ministers of the Word, elders, and deacons. Each of these offices is derived from Jesus Christ, the only head of the church and the sole lawgiver in Zion. In his name and by his grace the functions of the offices are discharged so that blessing comes to the church and God's name receives praise.

The office that is most fundamental to the policy of the Reformed Church is that of elder. That is why many of its member churches are called Presbyterian, from the Greek word for elder, *presbyteros*. Coming directly out of the Old Testament, where the elders of Israel are mentioned some one hundred times, and out of the New Testament, from where it was taken over by the early church, the office of elder is that of overseer of the church. The Greek word for overseer is *episkopos*, from which the word "episcopal" is derived. The elder is an overseer, an *episkopos*, a ruler over the church of God (Acts 14:23; 20:17, 28; 1 Tim. 5:17; Titus 1:5, 7). He who resists an elder ministering in Christ's name resists God; he who receives the word of an elder ministering in Christ's name receives the word of God. Of this, the reality, the dignity, and the importance of the office, the Reformed Church came to be fully aware. The office of elder is one of the Lord's gifts to his church and it has been the chief advantage of the Presbyterian system of government over those other systems which do not have that office or, having it, do not allow it to function.

Elders are called and ordained to rule the church of God. Some of them are ruling elders only; others have been set aside to preach the Word and to administer the sacraments so that theirs constitutes a specialized office within the body of elders. They are the ministers of the Word.

—*pp. 60, 62-64.*

....

Cynthia M. Campbell, introducing the United Presbyterian Church USA's book of order, gives the theological grounds for the Reformed way of church government.

From Cynthia M. Campbell's "Foreword" to *Presbyterian Policy for Church Officers*:

In what follows, I will suggest several convictions about God and the Christian life which find clear expression in the Presbyterian form of government. Others could have been chosen or added, but these form the core of a theological answer to the question: why are things in the Presbyterian Church the way they are?

The Covenant

The idea of the covenant has long influenced the Reformed way of viewing God and God's relationship with humanity. Out of their conviction that what God began with Israel God completed in Jesus Christ, Calvin and others found in the covenants of the Old Testament the foundation for the Christian life. The covenant image was so powerful because it reminded Calvin that initiative in salvation, as in creation, lay entirely with God: it was *God* who called Israel, *God* who chose Abraham and Sarah, *God* who gave the law through Moses to the people. Each act was an act of grace, not done because any had deserved it; in each case it was God who sought out people with whom to have a relationship.

Such a notion of the primacy of divine initiative and grace lies at the heart of the Reformed understanding of the church. We do not "join" the church of our choosing; rather, we are called by God into relationship. In the language of faith, we are sought before we ourselves find. It is this conviction which undergirds the Reformed emphasis on "infant" baptism. As God made covenant with Abraham and Sarah and their offspring, so God elects or chooses us before we are conscious that there is a God to choose. As church members, then, we do not depend on our agreement with one another in matters of belief or practice to keep us together. We are together because we believe that God has called each of us and that therefore we can and should live together.

This conviction of being called to life together is the second aspect of the covenant theme. The covenants of the Old Testament created the people of Israel; in the New Testament the covenant sealed in the blood of Christ created the church. Individuals are called of God, but they are always called *into* community with one another. However much we would prefer to go it alone, the Christian life is always life together. While this is a conviction shared by almost all Christians, it has led Reformed Christians into particular ways of ordering church life.

Not infrequently you will hear people complain about the never-ending use of committees in the Presbyterian Church; frustrated members and pastors sometimes say, "if you want something done right, do it yourself." The notion that we are called to *be* together has led Presbyterians to conclude that this is how we should make decisions: not independently or unilaterally but together. This is as true within the life of a local congregation as it is for the denomination as a whole. Decisions are shared among the various members or governing bodies for the good of the whole, because *together* we are the body of Christ.

The Law

As noted above, one of the highlights of God's covenant making with Israel was the gift of the law. The Ten Commandments and the laws which flowed from them gave form or shape to the nation of Israel. The law made life together just, humane, and possible. To be sure, the law was abused: not only was it violated, but also the keeping of the law was used to assure individuals of their worthiness or righteousness. Calvin joined Luther in asserting that human beings were made righteous (or set in right relationship with God) by God's grace alone and not by any human works, even keeping God's law. Unlike Luther, however, Calvin retained a rather more positive view of the law itself. He saw it as a gift of grace which could provide an orderly means for people to live together under God. The order of law provided the environment in which people could grow together in grace.

Since an ordered life is crucial for growth, it is small wonder that various forms of government and order have played such a central place in the life of Reformed or Presbyterian churches. The *Book of Order* is *not* a manual of operations. It is a way of making Christian life in community possible. (It is not the only way, to be sure, but one which generations have found conducive to the nurture of faith.) The *Book of Order* is to be studied and learned by those who hold office in the church because of their responsibility to guide and guard that life together.

Included in the *Book of Order* are the "Rules of Discipline." These are procedures to be followed when there is serious difficulty in the life of the church. The intention of these regulations, however, must be carefully noted: discipline in the church is to be exercised for the "building up of the body of Christ, not for destroying it, for redeeming, not for punishing" [D-Preamble]. The same could be said of the entire form of government: these provisions are gifts which can enable orderly and peaceful life together.

Sin

As Luther and Calvin both pointed out, one of the functions of the law of God was to convict humanity of its sin. Compared with that standard of righteousness, no one is innocent. This conviction of the pervasiveness of sin even in the lives of believers stands at the heart of the Reformed faith. . . .

Such a theological affirmation has led to two convictions about the church and decision making which we experience every day as Presbyterians. First, the Reformers assumed that not even the church was immune from the effects of human sin. Because it was made up of human beings and because all humans have sinned and fallen short of the glory of God, the Reformers held that the church could and did make errors of judgment and worse. The Reformation itself was an attempt precisely to reform and purify the church of its more obvious abuses of ecclesiastical and political power. Those same Reformers were not so naive as to assume that the reformed church would not become subject to similar abuses in time. Thus came the motto first used in the Dutch Reformed church: *ecclesia reformata, semper reformanda*—the church reformed, always being reformed. This is a commitment to continual self-examination, to the recognition that good policies do not always produce good results and that "new occasions teach new duties." Reformations are never easy, and change always brings a certain amount of conflict. The *Book of Order* is one means of ordering change and conflict so that minority views are always heard and so that petitions to amend or to redress grievance can always be presented in a civil manner. These procedures for change allow the church to be reformed under the leading of God in each new day.

The second implication of the doctrine of human sinfulness relates to the corporate nature of decision making discussed above. Because it is assumed that all persons will be subject to personal and selfish interest, it is a hallmark of the Presbyterian order that power and decision making are never vested in individuals acting alone. The powers of a pastor acting alone are severely restricted; the power and authority in a Presbyterian congregation rest with the session of which the pastor(s) is a member. The reason that Presbyterians have always been skeptical about the office of bishop is the potential abuse which could result from vesting too much authority in one person. In contrast the presbytery is often called the "corporate bishop" because it is a representative body of constituent congregations and ministers which makes decisions concerning the life and mission of the church in a given area. The conviction that sin is both real and inevitable has led Reformed Christians to the conclusion that the decisions which we make together will most often be better than the decisions which any one of us could make individually.

Called to Serve

Having stressed the reality of human sin, Presbyterians have not found this sufficient reason for withdrawing from the world or from relations with others. Indeed, the effect of the justifying grace of God is precisely to lead persons into relationship with one another and into mission in the world. Those whom God has called have been given grace to amend their lives and the responsibility to serve God and others. Whether in sending evangelists to Korea or Zaire, sharing the poverty of Native Americans on various reservations, or building schools and colleges across the nation, Presbyterians have felt called to act out their faith in God's grace in the world around them. This, too, has led to conflict in the church: what are the priorities for the mission? where does service end and political action begin? how much money should be spent for what?

The presbyterian system of government is intended not only to enable life together in the church but also to facilitate the church's mission in the world. Each governing body has a unique role to play in determining the overall mission of the church as well as in developing its own form of service in the particular place in which it finds itself. Because of the corporate nature of the church, what is done by one is done in the name of all. This has led, to be sure, to significant differences of opinion in the church, but it has also enabled the church to act and speak as one in a world hungry for unity.

The Sovereignty of God

At its heart, any theological question is a matter of our understanding of God. Who God is and how we understand God's self-revelation is *the* issue from which all other affirmations of faith flow. For the Reformed tradition, God's sovereignty and, in particular, the sovereign nature of God's grace have seemed most compelling. . . .

If God is thus sovereign over both the creation and human destiny, God is likewise sovereign over the church. All authority in the church rightly belongs to God, working through the Holy Spirit; all other authority exercised by persons and groups is derivative. All Christians affirm, of course, that Christ is the head of the church, which is the body of Christ. For Presbyterians this affirmation implies that we can invest in no person or church council the kind of absolute authority or honor which belongs to God alone. Along with the conviction that the church, because it is human, will err, this view of God's sovereignty has lead to healthy self-criticism and a general reluctance on the part of church leaders to assume that they are speaking for God. . . .

The sovereignty of God is finally an affirmation of the sovereignty of God's grace. The love, compassion, and mercy of God for humanity can never be frustrated and have already triumphed in the death and resurrection of Christ. In that alone is our hope—for ourselves, for this world, and for the Presbyterian Church. Confidence in the sovereign grace of God enables us to live together and work out our differences while we recall that the hope of the world does not rest on our shoulders. The government and discipline of the Presbyterian Church have at times become demonic: procedures have taken precedence over people; supposed purity has led to schism and rejection of each other; order has been used as a club and not a guide. The only thing which can save Presbyterians from confusing the *Book of Order* with God is grace. Only a constant recollection of who made us and brought us together, only the continual affirmation that it is mercy alone by which we live, enables us to make of our form of government what it is: a way of being the church by the grace of God.

—*pp. iii-viii.*

....

On the other hand, Henry De Moor argues that for church settings the very language of "rule" and "government" may be misleading, just as modern notions of individualism and representative democracy are unbiblical. De Moor's reflections come from reviewing the character and history of the Christian Reformed Church Order.

From "Equipping the Saints," by Henry De Moor:

The essence of ecclesiastical office is and always has been . . . Christ-representation, [the] instrument of God in Christ to do his work in his world. That work is mediatorial, something which cannot simply be equated with the general calling of all mankind to serve the sovereign God in all of life, at the time of creation, now and in eternity. Christ did come to be the "first fruits of those who have fallen asleep"; in principle there *is* a new humanity in him, the *ecclesia*; but "each in his own order: Christ the first fruits, then at his coming those who belong to Christ." On the way to that eschatological reality, that new humanity will require the continued equipment . . . of his Word and Spirit inherent in the apostolic commission, "until we all attain to the unity of the faith and of the knowledge of the Son of God, to mature manhood, to the measure of the stature of the fulness of Christ."

That the task of the believer goes beyond the inner workings of the organized church is clear. . . . But to equip the saints for service in God's world remains the prerogative of those who have been set apart, in their midst, for that specific task. This is not "clericalism." It is the thrust of New Testament revelation, the gift of Christ's grace. . . . Christ has willed them, chosen to use them in his work. Only when that has been carefully acknowledged can we begin to speak of "functional distinctions" the church may choose to make in the kinds of service within the "universal ministry."

The offices were not willed to "rule" an immature congregation. Nor were they meant to "serve" a mature congregation. They were given to equip the Body of Christ on its way toward full maturity. This, clearly, is Paul's message to the Corinthians: it is precisely the most spiritually mature church that will recognize the need to be led by its Lord. Being "eager for manifestations of the Spirit" is not enough. They must "strive to excel in building up the church." That is why "all things should be done decently and in order": so that "the church may be edified." . . .

The focus must no longer be on what we mean nowadays by the "government" of the church, as abstract concept, but on what the Belgic Confession refers to as the "spiritual polity" to which all "ordinances" must be conformed. We should not fail to notice how the CO [Church Order] accentuates the *task*, not the "authority" or "service" of the office-bearers. Ministers are called "to proclaim, explain and apply Holy Scripture," to "administer the sacraments, conduct public worship services, catechize the youth, and train members for Christian service." Together with the elders, they are called to "exercise pastoral care over the congregation, and engage in and promote the work of evangelism." They must also "supervise the congregation and [their] fellow office-bearers, exercise admonition and discipline, and see to it that everything is done decently and in order." Deacons are called to "administer Christian mercy," to "collect, administer, and distribute monies and other gifts," and "serve the distressed with counsel and assistance." Evangelists must "witness for Christ" and "call for a comprehensive discipleship through the means of the preaching of the Word and the administration of the sacraments, evangelism, church education for youths and adults, and pastoral care." In short, the office-bearers are called to equip the saints for ministry, to provide the armor necessary in the fight of faith.

As for "governing" the church as institute or organization, the CO clearly reserves that calling for the assemblies, not for individual office-bearers. In that respect, it clearly follows the lead of the Belgic Confession which reckons that elders and deacons, "together with the pastors, form the council of the Church." It also honors the most basic principle of Reformed church government, verbalized in Art. 95, CO: "No church shall in any way lord it over another church, and no office-bearer shall lord it over another office-bearer." That is the basic reason why the term "ruling elder" causes too much confusion. For the "governing" of the congregation there are no elders who rule in the church. There are only ministers, elders and deacons, organs of Christ, who rule *in concert* by means of deliberative assemblies where the will of the Lord is sought. Thus, a true striving for christocracy is guaranteed.

Is it correct to say that office-bearers have no inherent authority so that, for example, the so-called "headship principle" at stake in the controversy on women in office cannot possibly apply? Our judgment must be that such a position carries the ideal of a christocratic form of church government to an extreme. Office-bearers are more than mere tools or instruments of Christ's authority. They are organs of his leading, just as the writers of Scripture were organs of the Spirit's inspiration. On the other hand, as we have said, whatever authority is inherent is not autonomous. It is *administered* authority . . . which always remains the authority of Christ alone. Crucial, therefore, is not whether one is Jew or Greek, slave or free, male or female, but whether the Spirit-given *charismata* are there, the ones clearly required by the Word to nourish the church of Christ and clearly intended to upbuild his Body.

The offices are organs of Christ in the midst of the congregation called to equip the saints for ministry in God's world. . . .

Reformed church government lacks what every episcopal system does have: the personal unifying element at the denominational level. We have chosen for rule by offices in concert: the assemblies. There is no shame in that, since it is certainly to be preferred to the tyranny of hierarchy. But then the assemblies must function as the "synod" of Jerusalem did: unmistakably led by Word and Spirit.

The tragedy of CRC history is that synodical assemblies especially have been subject to mass psychology. Even worse is the blatant democratization so evident in recent years. It is often the will of the "people back home" that weighs more heavily on the minds of the delegates than the duty to seek the will of the Lord. In the Reformed tradition, assemblies were meant to be truly deliberative. Delegates must ensure that the views of their constituency are brought to the fore in the process of deliberation, but that is the only "democratic representation" demanded of them. Binding their votes beforehand short-circuits what ought to be a Spirit-led process and makes a mockery of the fervent prayers, offered before each gathering, that the Lord may be pleased to lead in the decision-making. Such tyranny of the majority is as deadly as the tyranny of hierarchy. Imagine how Acts 15 would have ended if it had applied in Jerusalem—the consternation rather than the joy in Antioch.

Denying the deliberative character of the assemblies can only lead to schism in the end. If we are incapable of recovering it, more drastic measures may soon have to be contemplated. . . . At this point, the steps to be taken are less important than the diagnosis itself. Communal self-examination on this score is a "must" in every "quarter" of the churches. At stake is nothing less than what the Scriptures force us to ask anew in every age: whether Christ truly rules in the midst of his church. Assemblies have been intended to see to that. . . .

Traveling the paths of compromise has led to a measure of inconsistency. A far more serious consequence, however, has been the accompanying diversion of attention from the real source of all authority. If the debate is limited to finding the "golden mean" between denominationalism and congregationalism so that excesses are avoided, there will always be the tendency to abstract that authority, of consistory or major assembly, from the rule of Christ. In such a climate, one is almost forced to choose between government "from the bottom up" or government "from the top down" or "something in between." Expressions such as the "higher authority" of a synod or the "autonomous authority" of a consistory ignore the Reformed confession that all authority is of Christ, sole Bishop of the church. To silence that confession is to create a vacuum all too quickly filled with democratic or aristocratic notions foreign to the Scriptures.

Consistories, classes and synods are governmental bodies designed to accommodate the rule of Christ through the offices he willed as organs of his rule. They do not have an autonomous authority. They administer his authority. Analogies to political structures must remain just that—analogies. . . . the assemblies are not essentially different in character. The one is not necessarily higher, more important, more assured of the leading of the Spirit, or less prone to error than the other. Every local congregation, every group of churches, every denomination is bound to the Word of Christ and shares in the promise of the Spirit's leading. Those who gather in the assemblies are not representatives of churches but of Christ—office-bearers called to lead and equip the saints of God.

—*pp. 243-44, 265-66, 335, 350.*

....

Beyond the furor over church officers' "rule" and roles, however, stands the crucial matter of church members' attitudes toward them. Richard Robert Osmer recommends John Calvin's concept of "teachability" for contemporary use.

From *A Teachable Spirit*, by Richard Robert Osmer:

Of all persons and movements embodying the Augustinian strain of piety, John Calvin has probably done more than any other single person to describe its fundamental tenets in terms of teachability. At the very heart of Christian piety, he believed, stands a teachable spirit. In its relation to the transcendent, sovereign God, sinful humanity must be teachable, especially those whom God has called to a new life.

In one of the few instances where Calvin describes his own Christian experience, he portrays his conversion as a *conversion to teachableness (conversion ad dociliatem)*. . . . Calvin's use of the phrase "a teachable frame" points to his willingness to suspend old beliefs and open himself to the forgiving and transforming grace of God. The reception of a teachable spirit gave him the zeal to pursue the "knowledge of true godliness" that he might make some "progress therein."

In a closely related fashion, Calvin frequently uses the image of teachability in his commentaries to describe accounts of conversion found in scripture. In describing the call of James and John, for example, he writes that they receive commendation for their teachability (*docilis*) and ready obedience, because they are willing to leave all worldly affairs at the command of Christ. Similarly, the Ethiopian eunuch in Acts is said to show a teachable spirit when he asks Philip to explain the meaning of the scriptures to him, an attitude Calvin recommends to the Christians of his own day. . . .

A teachable spirit is not to be confined to the first stages of the Christian life, however. It is not merely a part of the excitement and zeal that many newly converted Christians feel. Rather, it is an attitude that characterizes piety throughout the Christian life. As Christians develop in faith, they become *more* teachable, not less.

What the Holy Spirit brings in conversion is a fundamental reorientation of the mind and heart away from a preoccupation with the self to a desire to live to God. Persons must now learn to find security not in themselves but in God's providential care, to find the justification of their existence not in their own projects and causes but in God's free gift of acceptance in Jesus Christ, to find the pattern of a new life not in their own insights but in the moral law as found in Jesus Christ and the Decalogue. This is a fundamental, lifelong task, focusing on the renewal of the mind and heart. To have reverence and love toward God is to recognize God as the ultimate teacher, creating an attitude of openness and dependency on God as the One who instructs those whom he has called throughout their lives. . . .

Clearly, there is a wrong sort of docility and submissiveness. Modesty or docility that simply reinforces the social oppression of certain groups is a capitulation to sin, not genuine piety. Such modesty or tameness would represent little more than the internalization of oppressive images that distort the true humanity of individuals or groups whose worth is grounded in their creation by God, not their social definition. Submissiveness to racism, sexism, or social class is not what is meant by docility and tameness. Nor can it be identified with the piety of a warm heart found in much popular religion. Such warm-hearted religion views docility in highly subjective terms, identifying the work of the Holy Spirit with inner peace or an intuitive sense of what should be done in situations of choice. The piety of a teachable spirit as found in Calvin's thought is something quite different. A teachable spirit strives to be docile before God; but God, in Calvin's view, has bound Christians to the ordinary means of grace found in the church's life. These represent objective checks on and helps in the Christian's struggle to hear God's Word and to obey God's will. Teachability before God thus leads to a teachable spirit in relation to the objective means of grace.

Those objective means of grace that Calvin links explicitly to a teachable spirit are scripture and duly constituted leaders in the church. Teachability before God leads to a proper modesty before and openness to the instruction offered by these authorities in the Christian life. The Bible and church leaders, of course, are never to be confused with God. Yet they do have a proper role in the communication of God's truth. . . .

While teachable toward God, thus, Christian piety is bound to objective authorities by which God's Word is revealed. Scripture is preeminent among these authorities in Calvin's view. His understanding of a teachable spirit, however, did not stop here. In ways that stand in sharp contrast to attitudes prevalent in many mainline churches, he also advocated teachability in relation to ministers and theologians. . . .

The fundamental theological affirmation that lies behind Calvin's position here is his belief that God is most likely to be found in the preaching and teaching of the Word. It is the office of the ordained minister to carry out this task in public worship and his or her teaching ministry. The members of the church should approach such preaching and teaching with the expectation that they will find God there. Even a "puny man" who "excels us in nothing" should be approached with openness and a readiness to hear God's Word.

Clearly, Calvin is linking teachability to the *office* of ministry and not to the personality of any particular person. God has established offices in the church as vehicles of divine truth. The legitimate authority of the ministerial office, however, is qualified in many ways by Calvin. Ministers are bound to the teachings of scripture and its communal interpretation by representative bodies of the church. Their authority does not reside in their own opinions. They can be corrected by their colleagues. Their teachings can be tested by the congregation against scripture. Nonetheless, they are normally to be approached with a teachable spirit, for God has bound Christians to the ordinary means of grace, which include the preaching and teaching of the gospel by ordained ministers.

In a closely related fashion, theologians also are to be approached with a teachable spirit. Calvin describes his own purpose in writing the *Institutes* as being "to lead by the hand those who are teachable." He frequently concludes his discussions of a particular doctrine by saying that what he has written will suffice for those who are teachable. Theologians, like ministers, are viewed as possessing special competence in handing on and interpreting the central tenets of the faith. They are not to be ignored or taken lightly.

Once again, the piety of a teachable spirit is firmly linked by Calvin to more objective authorities in the church's life. He is not advocating blind obedience to ministerial leadership or to the theologians of the church. He is, however, arguing that the fundamental attitudes and dispositions of Christian piety should be shaped by a dialogue with ecclesiastical authorities who possess special competence in interpreting the meaning of scripture and theology and relating them to the contemporary situation. These leaders play a special role in articulating the cumulative wisdom of church tradition and the community's interpretation of scripture through the ages. Both of these are desperately needed in mainline Protestantism today in order for it to chart a third way between individualism and authoritarianism.

The emergence of an attitude of teachability toward ministers and theologians, however, is not dependent solely on changes in church members and congregations. It also rests on the demonstration of competence by such leaders, the foundation of true authority. This involves not only scholarly competence but also competence in grasping the basic problems before the church today and addressing them in ways that are genuinely helpful. Calvin viewed his own theology as engaged in the formation of piety and the education of the church. . . .

As a means of divine accommodation, the church's authority can be said to possess four characteristics.

First, the church's authority is *derivative*. The church is an instrument God uses to call and transform the elect. Its authority is that of a means of divine accommodation, not an end in itself. As we have seen, Calvin binds the authority of the church to the teachings of scripture. The church's authority is derivative.

Second, the church's authority is *fallible*. Though God uses human words and agencies to come near to humanity, these means of grace remain finite and sinful. God accommodates to human capacity; God does not eradicate it. The treasure of the gospel is preserved in an earthen vessel. A distinction is maintained between the church and God. No claim to infallibility can be made on behalf of any office or person in the church's life.

Third, the authority of the church is *dispersed*. Since Christ alone is the sole head of the church, Calvin is reticent to place exclusive authority in any single agency or office. He rejects the Roman Catholic argument that the papacy serves as a unifying center of church life, locating authority in a single head of the church universal. Calvin counters on the basis of Ephesians 4, in which church unity is portrayed as residing in Christ alone. As he puts it, "Do you see how he assigns to each member a certain measure, and a definite and limited function, in order that perfection of grace as well as the supreme power of governing may remain with Christ alone?" As the editors of the *Institutes* point out, there is a consistent tendency toward "plural authorities" in Calvin's discussions of ecclesiastical and political forms of government. Authority and power are best dispersed throughout the church in order to protect the prerogatives that belong to God alone.

Fourth, the authority of the church is *real*. In spite of the fact that church authority is derivative, fallible, and dispersed, it is to be acknowledged by the members of the church as a genuine expression of God's love and care for the church. In order to accommodate to human need and capacity, God has ordained certain offices and agencies as the normal means of grace. These are to be taken very, very seriously. Their authority is real, for "although God's power is not bound to outward means, he has nonetheless bound us to this ordinary manner of teaching."

Each of these four characteristics is present in Calvin's description of the visible church's teaching, legislative, and juridical authority. They reflect the church's status as a means of grace by which God accommodates to a sinful, finite humanity. The church's authority is based solely on its ability to function in this role. It should not claim prerogatives properly reserved for God, but it should not refuse to play the important role that it is assigned.

—*pp. 52-58, 113-14.*

Viewpoints on Our Public Life as Christians

7. What is our responsibility as stewards of creation?

Q. **What does God forbid
in the eighth commandment?**

A. He forbids not only outright theft and robbery,
punishable by law.

But in God's sight theft also includes
cheating and swindling our neighbor
by schemes made to appear legitimate,
such as:
inaccurate measurements of weight, size, or volume;
fraudulent merchandising;
counterfeit money;
excessive interest;
or any other means forbidden by God.

In addition he forbids all greed
and pointless squandering of his gifts.

—Heidelberg Catechism Q & A 110.

Q. **What does God require of you
in this commandment?**

A. That I do whatever I can
for my neighbor's good,
that I treat others
as I would like them to treat me,
and that I work faithfully
so that I may share with those in need.

—Heidelberg Catechism Q & A 111.

Calvinists are legendary for having poured their zeal into economic enterprise. Indeed, the "work ethic" that did so much to make the modern world has been called a Reformed Protestant innovation, rooted in the assurance—and anxieties—following from the doctrine of election. While Calvinists certainly did other things besides work, and while others besides Calvinists worked enterprisingly, the association between Calvinists and the work ethic is fitting enough to have stuck. It also has stuck the Reformed with some blame for the defects of modern industrialism, especially its spoliation of the natural environment.

That accusation and the larger problems it points to have prompted Reformed thinkers to reconsider Christian attitudes toward economics. As the following selections show, such reflection quickly leads beyond strictly defined goods and services into the realm of all the resources of life—human as well as natural, time and personal energy as well as land and ore. Just as important, Reformed thinkers are being led to rediscover Scripture's principles for using and managing resources. Chief among these principles is stewardship, which Paul A. Marshall finds at the root of a proper conception of economics. Another is the theology of imitating Christ, which a group of Christian scholars discusses in relation to our attitude toward the natural environment in the book *Earthkeeping*. Still another principle emerges out of Max De Pree's experience as a business executive; in his book *Leadership Is an Art*, De Pree sketches a new attitude toward what his peers usually label "human resources" but which he prefers to think of as people. We begin this section with two poems by Sietze Buning, who ponders here the classic Calvinistic values of his midwestern-farm upbringing and their complex relationships with the earth and with God.

Calvinist Farming

Our Calvinist fathers wore neckties with their bib-overalls
and straw hats, a touch of glory with their humility. They rode
their horse-drawn corn planters like chariots, planting the corn
in straight rows, each hill of three stalks three feet from each hill
around it, up and over the rises. A field-length wire with a metal knot
every three feet ran through the planter and clicked off three kernels
at each knot. Planted in rows east-west, the rows also ran north-
south for cross-cultivating. Each field was a checkerboard even
to the diagonals. No Calvinist followed the land's contours.

Contour farmers in surrounding counties
improvised their rows against the slope
of the land. There was no right way.
Before our fathers planted a field,
they knew where each hill of corn
would be. Be ye perfect, God said,
and the trouble with contour farmers
was that, no matter how hard they worked
at getting a perfect contour, they could
never know for sure it was perfect—and
they didn't even care. At best they
were Arminian, or Lutheran, or Catholic,

or at worst secular. Though they wore bib-
overalls, they wore no neckties, humility
without glory.

Contour fields resulted
from free will, nary a cornstalk predetermined. The God contour farmers
trusted, if any, was as capricious
as their cornfields. Calvinists knew
the distance between God and people was
even greater than the distance between people
and corn kernels. If we were corn kernels in God's
corn planter, would we want him to plant us at random?
Contour farmers were frivolous about the doctrine of election
simply by being contour farmers.

Contour farmers didn't control
weeds because they couldn't cross-cultivate. Weed control was laid
on farmers by God's curse. Contour farmers tried to escape God's curse.
Sooner or later you could tell it on their children: condoning weeds
they condoned movies and square-skipping. And they wasted land,
for planting around the rises, they left more place between
the rows than if they'd checked it. It was all indecent.
We could drive a horse cultivator—it was harder
with a tractor cultivator—through our checked rows
without uprooting any corn at all, but contour farmers
could never quite recapture the arbitrary angle, cultivating,
that they used, planting. They uprooted corn and killed it. All
of it was indecent and untidy.

We youngsters pointed out that the tops
of our rises were turning clay-brown, that bushels of black dirt
washed into creeks and ditches every time it rained, and that
in the non-Calvinist counties the tops of the rises were
black. We were told we were arguing by results, not
by principles. Why, God could replenish the black
dirt overnight. The tops of the rises were God's
business.

Our business was to farm on Biblical principles.
Like, Let everything be done decently and in good order; that is
keep weeds down, plant every square inch, do not waste crops, and be tidy.
Contour farmers were unkingly because they were untidy. They could not be
prophetic, could not explain from the Bible how to farm. Being neither kings
nor prophets, they could not be proper priests; their humility lacked definition. They prayed for crops privately. Our whole county prayed
for crops the second Wednesday of every March.

God's cosmic planter
has planted thirty year's worth of people since then,
all checked and on the diagonal if we could see
as God sees. All third-generation Calvinists
now plant corn on the contour. They have the word
from the State College of Agriculture. And so the clay-

brown has stopped spreading farther down the rises
and life has not turned secular, but broken.

For

God still plants people on the predetermined check
even though Calvinists plant corn on the contour. God's
check doesn't mean a kernel in the Calvinist's cornfield.
There's no easy way to tell the difference between Calvinists
and non-Calvinists: now all plant on the contour; all tolerate
weeds; between rows, all waste space; all uproot corn, cultivating;
all consider erosion their own business, not God's; all wear
overalls without ties; all their children go to the same
movies and dances; the county's prayer meetings
in March are badly attended; and I am improvising
this poem on the contour, not checking it in rhyme.
Glad for the new freedom, I miss the old freedom of choice
between Calvinist and non-Calvinist farming. Only in religion
are Calvinist and non-Calvinist distinguishable now. When different
ideas of God produced different methods of farming, God mattered more.
Was the old freedom worth giving up for the new? Did stopping the old
erosion of earth start a new erosion of the spirit? Was stopping old
erosion worth the pain of the new brokenness? The old Calvinists
insisted that the only hope for unbrokenness between the ways
of God and the ways of farmers is God.

A priest, God wears

infinite humility; a king, he wears infinite glory. He is even
less influenced by his upward-mobile children's notions of what not
to wear with what than our Calvinist fathers were in neckties with bib-
overalls. Moreover, a prophet, he wears the infinite truth our Calvinist
fathers hankered after to vindicate themselves, not only their farming.
Just wait, some dark night God will ride over the rises on his chariot-
corn planter. It will be too dark to tell his crown from a straw hat,
too dark to tell his apocalyptic horses from our buckskin horses or
from unicorns. No matter, just so the wheels of that chariot-corn
planter, dropping fatness, churn up all those clay-brown rises
and turn them all black, just as the old Calvinists predicted.

Lord Jesus, come quickly.

—Sietze Buning. From Purpaleanie and
Other Permutations, pp. 61-63.

Obedience

Were my parents right or wrong
not to mow the ripe oats that Sunday morning
with the rainstorm threatening?

I reminded them that the Sabbath was made for man
and of the ox fallen into the pit.
Without an oats crop, I argued,
the cattle would need to survive on town-bought oats
and then it wouldn't pay to keep them.
Isn't selling cattle at a loss like an ox in a pit?

112

My parents did not argue.
We went to church.
We sang the usual psalms louder than usual—
we, and the others whose harvests were at stake:

"Jerusalem, where blessing waits,
Our feet are standing in thy gates."

"God, be merciful to me;
On thy grace I rest my plea."

Dominie's spur-of-the-moment concession:
"He rides on the clouds, the wings of the storm;
The lightning and wind his missions perform."

Dominie made no concessions on sermon length:
"Five Good Reasons for Infant Baptism,"
though we heard little of it,

for more floods came and more winds blew and beat
upon that House than we had figured on, even,
more lightning and thunder
and hail the size of pullet eggs.
Falling branches snapped the electric wires.
We sang the closing psalm without the organ and in the dark:

"Ye seed from Abraham descended,
God's covenant love is never ended."

Afterward we rode by our oats field,
flattened.

"We still will mow it," Dad said.
"Ten bushels to the acre, maybe, what would have been fifty
if I had mowed right after milking
and if the whole family had shocked.
We could have had it weatherproof before the storm."

Later at dinner Dad said,
"God was testing us. I'm glad we went."
"Those psalms never gave me such a lift as this morning,"
Mother said, "I wouldn't have missed it."
And even I thought but did not say,
How guilty we would feel now if we had saved the harvest.
The one time Dad asked me why I live in a Black neighborhood,
I reminded him of that Sunday morning.
Immediately he understood.

Sometime around the turn of the century
my sons may well bring me an article in *The Banner*
written by a sociologist who argues,
"The integrated neighborhoods of thirty years ago,
in spite of good intentions,
impaired Black self-image and delayed Black independence."
Then I shall tell my sons about that Sunday morning.

And I shall ask my sons to forgive me
(who knows exactly what for?)
as they must ask their sons to forgive them
(who knows exactly what for?)
as I have long ago forgiven my father
(who knows exactly what for?)

Fathers often fail to pass on to sons
their harvest customs
for harvesting grain or real estate or anything.
No matter, so long as fathers pass on to sons
another more important pattern
defined as absolutely as muddlers like us can manage:
obedience.

> —*Sietze Buning. From* Purpaleanie and
> Other Permutations, *pp. 53-54.*

From *Thine Is the Kingdom,* by Paul A. Marshall:

The word 'economics' is derived from the Greek *oikonomia,* which is usually translated in the Scriptures as 'stewardship'. The items we usually think of as economic questions are treated in the Bible as 'stewardship' questions. To be an economist or to be economically productive is to be a good steward. But what does a good steward do? . . .

The steward is one whom the master appoints to stand in his stead, to look after affairs in the way the master wants, and who will give account to the master of what he or she has done. This is why stewardship is one way of describing the task of humankind on the earth. People are God's stewards, standing in God's stead. We do not own the earth, God does. We are to manage it as good stewards who seek to do our master's will and who will give an accounting of our stewardship on the last day. In this vein, Jesus says to Peter 'Who then is the faithful and wise steward, whom his master will set over his household, to give them their portion of food at the proper time? Blessed is that servant whom his master when he comes will find him so doing.' (Luke 12:42-43)

For this reason the 'cultural mandate' [Gen. 1:28] should not be understood as a license for humankind to dominate the earth. We should not read the words about 'subduing', 'conquering', 'filling', and 'having dominion' over the earth as though they were licenses for unbridled exploitation. As we have seen, there are enough examples in the Scriptures of caring for the earth in its own right. The land must be protected, it must be honoured, trees and waters must be protected. The cultural mandate calls us to steward the earth like a good and healthy household. The Christian faith has been criticized for licensing the domination of nature, a domination which has resulted in the resource depletion, pollution and ugliness that desecrates much of the world. But this concept of Christianity is miles apart from the biblical teaching of filling and caring for the creation.

Perhaps it could be argued that what the Bible says is one thing, but that what Christians actually have taught and done is entirely another matter. This argument must be taken very seriously indeed for here we are not concerned with defending this original integrity of the Christian faith but with understanding our own history and situation. Yet even in terms of history this critique of Christian faith is wide of the mark. The theme of the domination of nature appears clearly in the seventeenth century, particularly in such Stoically inclined figures as Francis Bacon. The increasing exploitation of nature since the eighteenth century coincides with the decline of Christianity as a formative force in the West. The economic ideologies which have enshrined such exploitation came into their own in the industrial revolution, just at the time that Christian social teaching became more out-of-date and irrelevant. The twentieth century, the great age of the rape of the natural world, is also the great age of secularity. Rather than looking for the ideological roots of our present exploitation in the Christian faith, one might better look to humanism, whose creed 'Man is the measure of all things' has produced the greatest disjuncture between the human world and the natural world.

Given that our economic activity is to be the loving stewardship of the earth and all that is in it, we must have a clearer idea of what is required by that stewardship. First, it must be said that we are the stewards not only of natural things like land, soil, trees, oceans and minerals. We are the stewards of all things—including time, energy, health, organisation, family life, work styles, buildings—everything that exists in human life. Secondly, to steward all these things is to treat them in the way that God calls us to treat them, being careful to attend to all the ways in which we can express love—through justice, through beauty, through preservation, through use, through faithfulness. To steward something is first of all to be aware of its place in God's creation, to be sensitive to all the ways it can be hurt and to all the ways it can bring benefits to others, and then to preserve it and cause it to be 'fruitful'—to care for it so that what is good is preserved and to use it so that it brings blessing to other things. This is what stewardship is and, therefore, this is what proper economics is.

Such stewardship can be illustrated through the actions of a family. Let us suppose that the husband has a job outside the home, that the wife focuses her work inside the home, and that the husband is offered a new job at higher pay a few hundred miles away. If the family is Christianly responsible then their decision about the job should go something like this. All the family, parents and children, will get together to talk about what will be lost and what will be gained, for them and for others, by taking or not taking the new job.

On the 'loss side' might be such things as: a disruption of the kids' schooling and friendships and neighbourhood; separation from a church community; separation of the wife from her friends and ties; separation from the extended family, grandparents, aunts, uncles, and cousins; leaving a known and happy work situation; depriving a company of a valuable employee; the physical and emotional disruption of the move itself. This list could, of course, be multiplied endlessly but this is enough to point out the *costs* possibly connected with the move.

On the 'gain' or 'benefit' side may be: more money (not to be sniffed at); more challenging work; work which is of better service to the community; the possibility of joining or helping develop a new church community; moving closer to the extended family; widening circles of friendship, and so on. These are some of the possible gains from such a move.

The family should consider all of these effects and try to determine whether any injustice will be done to somebody by moving (justice), whether any promises will be broken by moving (unfaithfulness), and then, if neither of these is the case, the family will weigh the benefits and losses of the proposed move and decide whether overall it is a good thing to do.

In trying to make a decision this way the family is engaging in the activity that the Bible calls stewardship. It is real *economic* activity. Economics should not be understood as referring only to what we now call 'economic' things, such as money, jobs, interest rates, or buying and selling. Real economics is an activity that tries to deal with *everything* in a *stewardly* way. This is true for families, for individuals, for companies, for churches, for governments. All of these must be stewardly in their activities. . . .

In emphasizing stewardship, I am not offering a 'moral' critique of economics. Nor am I saying that 'ethical' questions must be considered *alongside* 'economic' questions, nor that 'social' questions should be considered *alongside* 'economic' questions. I am saying that these costs and benefits are themselves *actual, real, concrete, intrinsic, economic* questions. I am saying that to be anything other than a steward is uneconomic, wasteful, and inefficient. We should not try to add 'Christian ethics' to economics. Instead we should strive for a *Christianly inspired economics itself,* one which is rooted in the biblical view of stewardship. . . .

Our society is committed to economic growth. But there is nothing wrong with growth. We should always desire that what is truly economic should continue to grow. Societies are made to grow—to grow in justice, in stewardship, in care for one another, in needed goods, in fulfilling work, in humane environments. We should not be opposed to real economic growth.

But what we now call 'growth' is often anything but truly economic. Our usual indicator of economic growth is the Gross National Product (GNP) which is the gross sum in pounds of all the goods we produce and all the services we provide involving money. The GNP does *not* measure *all* goods and services but only those that involve money. . . . It focuses on a particular range of costs and benefits as if they were the only ones or, at least, the only important ones. But, despite this narrow focus, our government's economic policies are geared toward making this GNP rise, with little regard for how the GNP actually relates to substantive human wellbeing.

The point is not that the GNP should not rise. It is that such a rise itself indicates nothing about human wellbeing. Many things add to our GNP. Smoking and other forms of pollution do, both in consumption and in the medical services which must follow. Marital breakdown and divorce are good for the GNP because people no longer share TV's or beds and need to buy one each. Shift work is good for the GNP, and not bad for marital breakdown either. Eating out is good for the GNP. Eating at home is not.

116

Clearly the relation between GNP and human wellbeing is not a simple one. If you grow your own food, or make your own clothing, or chop your own wood, or fix up your own dwelling, then very little enters the GNP figures. If you pay someone else to do these things for you, then the GNP goes up. Raising children and doing housework does not enter the GNP, but if it is contracted out then it does. Putting Granny in a home helps the GNP, keeping her at home does not. . . .

Because of the way we collect economic statistics, relevant figures are not available, but it seems to be true that much of our 'economic growth' is not adding new goods and services but merely shifting things away from unpaid, domestic or voluntary activity and into paid activity. This shift is itself neither right nor wrong, but it is certainly wrong to call it growth without further question in that it can be merely a shifting around of activities, or even represent a breakdown of community and neighbourhood spirit, a weakening of family ties, and the increased commercialisation of life. . . .

But this process of boosting 'economic' growth ignores many of the real costs and benefits that we outlined earlier. Families can be disrupted, unemployment can lead to loss of meaning, to crime, to alcoholism, even to suicide. People can find themselves lonelier and their work ever more crippling and deadening. For a long time governments ignored these effects but, to its eternal credit, the welfare state has been an attempt to address these matters, usually under the heading of 'social policy'. So we have had social security plans, the National Health Service, job retraining programmes, and so on. We now have government agencies whose job it is to pick up the 'hidden costs', the ignored effects, of our dealing with economic matters.

The combined result is a 'two-track' government approach. One track is 'economic policy', which is to boost 'economic growth' and, if possible, to keep inflation and unemployment in check. The other track is 'social policy' to deal with all the things neglected by the 'economic policy'. The 'economic policy' is supposed to produce enough wealth so that government can afford a decent 'social policy'. Typically, right wing governments call themselves 'realists' and emphasize 'economic' policy by saying that, in the long run, this is the only way to afford the 'social' programmes. Left wing governments emphasize 'social policy' and, of late, are quite fuzzy on 'economic policy'. . . .

We should emphasize neither 'economic policy' nor 'social policy' at the expense of the other, for they are both essential parts of stewardship. We cannot select either 'realist' economics or 'compassionate' economics, for, if realism is to be true to the real human world then it must be compassionate and, if compassion is to be more than pious exhortation, then it must be realistic. Instead we must avoid the 'two track' framework altogether and try to make our corporate, family, individual and government decisions ones which are stewardly from the word go. We must make decisions about starting factories, developing new technologies, moving families, buying food, and adjusting taxes on the basis of their effects on unemployment, family life, production of genuinely needed things and gentleness to the environment as well as on their effects on incomes, profits and inflation. Right from the beginning we must be stewards and weigh the options before us.

There are no predetermined answers in such a process. Such a weighing of options cannot be reduced to flow charts on econometricians' print outs. Like everything else done in God's world it is always an act of responsibility. Economic acts must be acts of service designed to bring health and wellbeing to our neighbours. Anything else will be not just unethical or uncaring, it will also be wasteful, inefficient, unstewardly, *uneconomic*. While no ethical theory (or theological theory for that matter) can *dictate* what will be a stewardly decision in any given instance, yet we can learn about priorities in costs and benefits. The major economic priority in the Scriptures is the priority of the poor. . . .

The poor in Scripture include those who are poor in many ways. The poor are coupled with the hungry, the homeless, the stranger, the widow, the orphan, the sick, the meek, the oppressed, the prisoners, the blind and those who are bowed down (Ps. 10; Ps. 146). It is certainly true that an orphan or a widow is often in dire financial straits, especially in our society where they comprise most of the poor. But they also suffer from loneliness, isolation and lack of warmth and stability—things not related solely to financial conditions. The command to care for the poor is the command to care for all those who are suffering and sorrowing. We may say that in Scripture *the poor are those who lack the social, economic, political, or spiritual resources to fulfil God's calling for their lives.* Yet, while it is clear that poverty is more than money, lack of food, shelter, clothing, work and money are a large part of it. This is especially true today, for in our society more and more things are available only for money. Access to the law, health, leisure and privacy is becoming as dependent on income as is food and clothing.

—pp. 97-100, 102-106.

From *Earthkeeping*, ed. Loren Wilkinson:

Christ and Dominion

It is, perhaps, an indication of our fallen condition that we humans have not only seized the Genesis commandment [Gen. 1:28] to rule as a permit to use nature only for *human* comfort, but have interpreted the sacrificial death of Christ as being only for *human* salvation. Thus the most compelling argument in favor of any degradation of the environment, whether it be strip-mining a hill, clear-cutting a mountain, or butchering a whale, is always the contribution such an action will make to *human* survival—if not the actual survival of individuals, at least the survival of a certain kind of comfort or security.

The unique message of the Christian gospel, however, is not only the proclamation of the infinite worth of human life (for God, in Christ, died to redeem it); it also is the importance of being willing to give up that life—or at least to forgo one's comfort and material security—for the sake of another. We have tended to interpret that sacrificial Christian *caritas* as directed only toward other humans. Yet our record—particularly in North America—of forgoing some wealth and comfort even for other suffering people is a dismal one. Despite the remarkably explicit teaching of Christ on sharing one's wealth, we still find it very difficult to do anything other than multiply our own comforts and securities. . . .

118

To acknowledge a greater worth to the human than to the natural does not mean that the human is of infinite value and the natural of no value. Since it is clear from Scripture that God values all of creation, and that we are placed in it to care for it, we must work out the difficult choices of nature *or* humanity with care and wisdom, and one case at a time. All our actions should be guided by the *example* of the use of dominion provided by Christ.

The central statement of that divine use of power is in Philippians 2. There Christians are told to have the "mind of Christ." And the verses which follow leave little doubt as to the sort of actions the mind of Christ should impel us to. For Christ was he who,

> . . . though he was in the form of God, did not count equality with God a thing to be grasped, but emptied himself, taking the form of a servant, being born in the likeness of men. And being found in human form he humbled himself and became obedient unto death, even death on a cross. (Phil. 2:6-8)

In the words of Ian McHarg . . . the misuse of nature is attributed to the damaging consequences of the idea of humans as divine: "Show me a man-oriented society in which it is believed . . . that the cosmos is a structure erected to support man on its pinnacle, that man exclusively is divine and given dominion over all things, . . . and I will predict the nature of its cities and their landscapes." Yet Christians place at the center of their faith the example of one who, "in the form of God" and thus on the "pinnacle of the cosmos," gave up the dominion which was a consequence of that position, "did not regard it as a thing to be grasped," and became a servant. The implication is clear: what God became for us, we are to become for nature. But that McHarg (and others) should make such accurate criticisms of what a Christian civilization has done to nature suggests that we have almost totally ignored the application of "the mind of Christ' to our treatment of the natural world.

Christians have not only neglected to apply "the mind of Christ" to their use of nature, but they have also rarely reflected enough on the involvement of Christ in nature. It is easy to neglect care for nature if we see it only as a backdrop for the drama of human salvation. But the Bible is quite clear in affirming that Christ's involvement with creation is not an involvement with humans only.

It is true, as Christians and their critics alike have affirmed, that God the Creator is utterly beyond nature. Thus it is idolatrous to worship nature as divine—whatever the environmental benefits of such nature worship may be thought to be. But it is equally true that Scripture teaches a continual, creative, and sustaining presence of God with his creation. And that creative and sustaining presence is understood as the second person of the Trinity, Christ Jesus of Nazareth, who is the Word without which nothing was made. In choosing to speak of Jesus as the Word, Logos, the apostle John brilliantly clarifies those half understood groupings of the Stoics to comprehend the ordering presence of God in nature.

Another source for this idea of the presence of the Word of God in nature is the Jewish Wisdom literature, in which a passage from

Proverbs is the most striking. There the personified figure of Wisdom speaks:

> The Lord created me at the beginning of his work,
>> the first of his acts of old.
> Ages ago I was set up,
>> at the first, before the beginning of the earth.
> . . . then I was beside him, like a master workman;
> and I was daily his delight,
>> rejoicing before him always,
> rejoicing in his inhabited world
>> and delighting in the sons of men.
>> *(Prov. 8:22-23, 30-31)*

Christians have usually seen this figure of God's master workman, "rejoicing in his inhabited world," as a prefiguring of Christ. And there is abundant Scripture in the New Testament which, in a similar way, describes the involvement of Christ with nature [Heb. 1:2-3; 1 Cor. 8:6; Col. 1:15-17; John 1:1-3]. . . .

In the face of these clear statements of God's involvement in the created order, it is necessary to revise somewhat our understanding of the Christian doctrine of transcendence with a doctrine of immanence. Though God, the Creator, is indeed beyond the world, he is also in it. The historical Incarnation is the center, the exemplification in time, of God's willingness in Christ to create, sustain, delight in, and (if necessary) sacrificially *redeem* creation. . . .

This may sound superficially like Pantheism, but it is the opposite of Pantheism. It is because God stands apart from the world that he creates and sustains it. Likewise, it is because of the specific, historic entrance of Christ into nature that we are able to understand the continual involvement of Christ, the upholding Word, in all of nature.

If we grant that Scripture teaches an involvement of Christ in all of nature, what does this imply for *human* involvement in nature? Without yet considering the pertinent Scripture, we can notice a kind of symmetry between God's relationship to nature and the human relationship to nature. We noticed it first in Genesis, but when we come to the gospel of the Incarnation, its significance for contemporary Christians becomes much more practical. God is transcendent over nature. That is a fact of Christian faith, but it has been scorned, in recent years, because of the supposed indifference to nature which that divine transcendence produces in people. For we have seen also, in the doctrine of the "image of God" and the accompanying task to have dominion over creation, that Scripture speaks of a kind of *human* transcendence.

What a consideration of the Incarnation shows, however, is that in Christ, both as Creator and Redeemer, God is immanent in creation. The "equality with God" enables the creating Word to share the flesh of his creation in an immanence which grasps neither at glory nor survival, but which leads ultimately to death. Likewise, though Christians transcend the world, they also are directed to become a redemptive part of what they transcend. Humans are to become saviors of nature, as Christ is the savior of humanity (and hence, through humans, of nature).

This idea of humans as the saviors of nature is not simply theological speculation. It is implied in all of those many Scripture passages which speak of redeemed humans as "joint-heirs" with Christ. As Christ is Ruler, Creator, and Sustainer of the world, so also is man to be. Being heirs with Christ involves (as Paul saw) being crucified with Christ; it also involves sharing in the sustaining activity in nature of Christ the Creator.

Most specifically, this startling, but orthodox, idea of man as sharing in the redemption of nature is taught in several verses in Romans 8. After a passage which speaks of Christians as fellow heirs with Christ, there follow these verses:

> For the creation waits with eager longing for the revealing of the sons of God; for the creation was subjected to futility, not of its own will but by the will of him who subjected it in hope; because the creation itself will be set free from its bondage to decay and obtain the glorious liberty of the children of God. We know that the whole creation has been groaning in travail together until now. . . . (Rom. 8:19-22)

In this suggestively cryptic passage, it is clear that the fate of creation is bound up with the fate of humanity and that whatever glory comes to humans as a result of their participation in divine redemption will come also to creation. Is this a promise in reference only to some far future millennial kingdom, or are we *now* to be redemptively involved in that groaning and suffering creation? Scripture does not generally put tasks off into some eschatological future, a fact which would point to the present as the occasion for our work with nature. So also does the wording of the final sentence: the "until now" suggests that the childbirth is over and that humans, who have been shown the pattern of their dominion as stewards of the earth, can begin to exercise it wisely, according to the mind of Christ.

—pp. 215-19.

From *Leadership Is an Art,* by Max De Pree:

The first responsibility of a leader is to define reality. The last is to say thank you. In between the two, the leader must become a servant and a debtor. That sums up the progress of an artful leader.

Concepts of leadership, ideas about leadership, and leadership practices are the subject of much thought, discussion, writing, teaching, and learning. True leaders are sought after and cultivated. Leadership is not an easy subject to explain. A friend of mine characterizes leaders simply like this: "Leaders don't inflict pain; they bear pain."

The goal of thinking hard about leadership is not to produce great, or charismatic, or well-known leaders. The measure of leadership is not the quality of the head, but the tone of the body. The signs of outstanding leadership appear primarily among the followers. Are the followers reaching their potential? Are they learning? Serving? Do they achieve the required results? Do they change with grace? Manage conflict?

I would like to ask you to think about the concept of leadership in a certain way. Try to think about a leader, in the words of the gospel writer Luke, as "one who serves." Leadership is a concept of owing certain things to the institution. It is a way of thinking about institutional heirs, a way of thinking about stewardship as contrasted with ownership.

. . . The art of leadership requires us to think about the leader-as-steward in terms of relationships: of assets and legacy, . . . of civility and values.

Leaders should leave behind them assets and a legacy. First, consider assets; certainly leaders owe assets. Leaders owe their institutions vital financial health, and the relationships and reputation that enable continuity of that financial health. Leaders must deliver to their organizations the appropriate services, products, tools, and equipment that people in the organization need in order to be accountable. In many institutions leaders are responsible for providing land and facilities.

But what else do leaders *owe?* What are artful leaders responsible for? Surely we need to include people. People are the heart and spirit of all that counts. Without people, there is no need for leaders. Leaders can decide to be primarily concerned with leaving assets to their institutional heirs or they can go beyond that and capitalize on the opportunity to leave a legacy, a legacy that takes into account the more difficult, qualitative side of life, one which provides greater meaning, more challenge, and more joy in the lives of those whom leaders enable.

Besides owing assets to their institutions, leaders owe the people in those institutions certain things. Leaders need to be concerned with the institutional value system which, after all, leads to the principles and standards that guide the practices of the people in the institution. Leaders owe a clear statement of the values of the organization. These values should be broadly understood and agreed to and should shape our corporate and individual behavior. What is this value system based on? How is it expressed? How is it audited? These are not easy questions to deal with.

Leaders are also responsible for future leadership. They need to identify, develop, and nurture future leaders.

Leaders are responsible for such things as a sense of quality in the institution, for whether or not the institution is open to influence and open to change. Effective leaders encourage contrary opinions, an important source of vitality. I am talking about how leaders can nurture the roots of an institution, about a sense of continuity, about institutional culture.

Leaders owe a covenant to the corporation or institution, which is, after all, a group of people. Leaders owe the organization a new reference point for what caring, purposeful, committed people can be in the institutional setting. Notice I did not say what people can do— what we can do is merely a consequence of what we can be. Corporations, like the people who compose them, are always in a state of becoming. Covenants bind people together and enable them to meet their corporate needs by meeting the needs of one another. We must do this in a way that is consonant with the world around us.

Leaders owe a certain maturity. Maturity as expressed in a sense of self-worth, a sense of belonging, a sense of expectancy, a sense of responsibility, a sense of accountability, and a sense of equality.

Leaders owe the corporation rationality. Rationality gives reason and mutual understanding to programs and to relationships. It gives visible order. Excellence and commitment and competence are available to us only under the rubric of rationality. A rational environment values trust and human dignity and provides the opportunity for personal development and self-fulfillment in the attainment of the organization's goals.

Business literacy, understanding the economic basis of a corporation, is essential. Only a group of people who share a body of knowledge and continually learn together can stay vital and viable.

Leaders owe people space, space in the sense of freedom. Freedom in the sense of enabling our gifts to be exercised. We need to give each other the space to grow, to be ourselves, to exercise our diversity. We need to give each other space so that we may both *give* and *receive* such beautiful things as ideas, openness, dignity, joy, healing, and inclusion. And in giving each other the gift of space, we need also to offer the gifts of grace and beauty to which each of us is entitled.

Another way to think about what leaders owe is to ask this question: What is it, without which this institution would not be what it is? . . .

Leaders must take a role in developing, expressing, and defending civility and values. In a civilized institution or corporation, we see good manners, respect for persons, an understanding of "good goods," and an appreciation of the way in which we serve each other.

Civility has to do with identifying values as opposed to following fashions. Civility might be defined as an ability to distinguish between what is actually healthy and what merely appears to be living. A leader can tell the difference between living edges and dying ones.

To lose sight of the beauty of ideas and of hope and opportunity, and to frustrate the right to be needed, is to be at the dying edge.

To be a part of a throwaway mentality that discards goods and ideas, that discards principles and law, that discards persons and families, is to be at the dying edge.

To be at the leading edge of consumption, affluence, and instant gratification is to be at the dying edge.

To ignore the dignity of work and the elegance of simplicity, and the essential responsibility of serving each other, is to be at the dying edge.

Justice Oliver Wendell Holmes is reported to have said this about simplicity, "I would not give a fig for the simplicity this side of complexity, but I would give my life for the simplicity on the other side of complexity." To be at the living edge is to search out the "simplicity on the other side of complexity."

In a day when so much energy seems to be spent on maintenance and manuals, on bureaucracy and meaningless quantification, to be a leader is to enjoy the special privileges of complexity, of ambiguity, of diversity. But to be a leader means, especially, having the opportunity to make a meaningful difference in the lives of those who permit leaders to lead.
        —*pp. 9-14, 17-19.*

8. What responsibilities do we have for justice in our society?

(version used by the Christian Reformed Church)

The Civil Government

We believe that
because of the depravity of the human race
our good God has ordained kings, princes, and civil officers.
He wants the world to be governed by laws and policies
so that human lawlessness may be restrained
and that everything may be conducted in good order
among human beings.

For that purpose he has placed the sword
in the hands of the government,
to punish evil people
and protect the good.

And being called in this manner
to contribute to the advancement of a society
that is pleasing to God,
the civil rulers have the task,
    subject to God's law,
of removing every obstacle
    to the preaching of the gospel
    and to every aspect of divine worship.

They should do this
while completely refraining from every tendency
    toward exercising absolute authority,
and while functioning in the sphere entrusted to them,
    with the means belonging to them.

They should do it in order that
    the Word of God may have free course;
    the kingdom of Jesus Christ may make progress;
    and every anti-Christian power may be resisted.*

*The Synod of 1958, in line with 1910 and 1938, substituted the preceding statement for the following (which it judged unbiblical):

And the government's task is not limited
to caring for and watching over the public domain
but extends also to upholding the sacred ministry,
    with a view to removing and destroying
        all idolatry and false worship of the Antichrist;
    to promoting the kingdom of Jesus Christ;
    and to furthering the preaching of the gospel everywhere;
    to the end that God may be honored and served by everyone,
    as he requires in his Word.

Moreover everyone,
regardless of status, condition, or rank,
must be subject to the government,
and pay taxes,
and hold its representatives in honor and respect,
and obey them in all things that are not in conflict
    with God's Word,
praying for them
    that the Lord may be willing to lead them
      in all their ways
    and that we may live a peaceful and quiet life
      in all piety and decency.**

—*Belgic Confession, Art. 36.*

**The Synod of 1985 directed that the following paragraph be taken from the body of the text and be placed in a footnote:

And on this matter we denounce the Anabaptists, other anarchists,
and in general all those who want
to reject the authorities and civil officers
and to subvert justice
    by introducing common ownership of goods
    and corrupting the moral order
      that God has established among human beings.

....

(version used by the Reformed Church in America)

The Civil Government

We believe that
because of the depravity of the human race
our good God has ordained kings, princes, and civil officers.
God wants the world to be governed by laws and policies
so that human lawlessness may be restrained
and that everything may be conducted in good order
among human beings.

For that purpose God has placed the sword
in the hands of the government,
to punish evil people
and protect the good.

And the government's task is not limited
to caring for and watching over the public domain
but extends also to upholding the sacred ministry,
    with a view to removing and destroying
      all idolatry and false worship of the Antichrist;
    to promoting the kingdom of Jesus Christ;
    and to furthering the preaching of the gospel everywhere;
    to the end that God may be honored and served by everyone,
    as required in God's Word.

Moreover everyone,
regardless of status, condition, or rank,
must be subject to the government,
and pay taxes,
and hold its representatives in honor and respect,
and obey them in all things that are not in conflict
    with God's Word,
praying for them
    that the Lord may be willing to lead them
        in all their ways
    and that we may live a peaceful and quiet life
        in all piety and decency.

And on this matter we denounce the Anabaptists, the anarchists,
and, in general, all those who want
to reject the authorities and civil officers
and to subvert justice
    by introducing common ownership of goods
    and corrupting the moral order
        that God has established among human beings.

                                    —*Belgic Confession, Art. 36.*

As we stated in introducing this volume, Reformed Christianity is famous for propelling its members out into the world with energy and conviction. Yet history shows this zeal to have been conflicted—if not inconsistent in its purposes, at least ambivalent in its attitudes and uneasy in its conscience.

This conflicted zeal is particularly evident with regard to politics. Calvinists helped fuel resistance and revolutionary movements in the Netherlands and Great Britain and in British colonies that became the United States. And yet Calvinists themselves have established govern-ments—in New England, Northern Ireland, and South Africa—that are legendary for their "law and order." Why this mixed profile? Is the Reformed purpose in government to "rule" or to "serve"? Both at once? How? What is Reformed Christianity's political legacy for us today? By a Reformed standard, is the ideal government "big" or "small"? "Enabling" or "restricting"? And by theory and practice, what is and ought to be the relationship between "church" and "state"?

Rather than answer these questions directly, the readings in this section provide materials for further reflection on the role of Reformed Christianity in politics. Paul A. Marshall traces the biblical principles for a Reformed theory of politics and illustrates its double-mindedness toward modern states. James W. Skillen thickens this tension with a political theology oriented toward Christ's present and future rule. And Eugene P. Heideman evaluates two different positions that closely related Reformed denominations in the United States have taken on church-state issues.

From *Thine Is the Kingdom,* by Paul A. Marshall:

Sometimes much is made of the fact that the political order appears after the fall and is first manifested in response to Cain's sin. Hence it is thought that government is not part of the original creation but is something which only comes into existence because of sin and will only last as long as sin does. This is a complex and vexed question. At this point we should just note that virtually all of the diversity of human actions and institutions are described in the Bible as coming after sin and as being affected by sin. This is true of, for example, music-making—which is also in the line of Cain (Gen. 4:21). But, while we may have our doubts about what comes over the radio these days, it is doubtful that we can say that music only exists because of sin! It depends on the song sung (Rev. 14:2, 3). Similarly, the use of bricks and tar is first described as part of the building of the tower of Babel, a project conceived in sin (Gen. 11:3-5).

Because of these other examples, we cannot conclude from the story of Cain that politics and law are only necessary because of sin. An answer to this question will depend on whether we see the state, and the justice associated with it, as having only a *negative* task (i.e. the restraint of sin) or whether we see it also as having a *positive* task in the *promotion* of justice between people. Such a positive task can be rooted in the way God has made the world and would continue to be part of humankind's cultural mandate even after sin has been kept away. The fact that the book of Revelation says that kings will bring their glory and the honour of the nations into the New Jerusalem suggests that the political enterprise has its own intrinsic merit apart from the effects of sin (Rev. 21:24-26).

What we can say on the basis of the story of Cain is that the institution of law has an intrinsic connection with justice. Law is to uphold the right relations that God calls people to have with one another. It is to provide a response that is sevenfold—one which is right, fitting and complete. . . .

[After reviewing Old Testament developments and New Testament teachings, the author summarizes the biblical concept of political authority.]

Political authority is authority from God. Those who hold political office, even if they are unbelievers, can do so because God has authorised such an office for the governing and service of humankind. Political authority is not an area apart from the gospel, but can be an area of ministry performed by ministers of God. It can be ministry just as much as any office in the church. This authority is not a thing separate from the reign of Jesus Christ but is itself a manifestation of the authority of the 'King of Kings' (Rev. 1:5, 17:14; 19:16) who said 'All authority in heaven and earth is given unto me' (Matt. 28:18). . . .

It is God, not we ourselves who will punish evil and reward good. God's means of doing so, or at least one of God's means of doing so, is the governing authorities which God has provided to exercise precisely that role. Leaving it to God to execute justice also means leaving it to the governing authorities to execute justice. No individual person has the personal right of revenging evil, nor can they give that right to another. But because God, in the course of human history, provides governments with particular authority to execute justice, then those who rightfully hold government authority may and should avenge evil and reward good.

Because of Paul's distinction between personal action and authorised political action, it is not right to counterpose the Sermon on the Mount to Romans 13. It is not right to say that Jesus' reign is one of nonviolence and peace as opposed to the reign of government where force may be necessary. Governments are also under the reign of Jesus Christ and, under that reign, they have the particular task of avenging good and evil. Nor is it right to say that while it may indeed be true that governments derive their authority from God yet they do so only under a separate dispensation, such as 'God's order of preservation', distinct from 'God's order of redemption' which is supposedly manifested only in the church. *The state is what God through Jesus Christ has set up to maintain justice.* Its officers are as much ministers of God as are prophets and priests. The authority of the state is not some sort of separate authority outside of Christ and redemption. It is authority from Jesus Christ to whom *all* authority is given just as much as is authority in the church. 'Thrones or dominions or principalities or authorities—all things were created through him and for him . . . in him all things hold together' (Col. 1:16-17). The gospel itself has its place in political power (1 Pet. 3:22).

Because political authority is an aspect of the authority of Jesus Christ, the first thing that Paul tells the Roman Christians to do is to submit to that authority. This submission is not only to avoid 'wrath' but is 'also for the sake of conscience,' (13:5)—such submission is right and proper. Furthermore 'he who resists the authorities resists what God has appointed and . . . will incur judgment' (13:3). It is plain that submitting to government authority is not an optional thing for a Christian, or for anyone. Government is not a happenstance thing, something to be followed only in so far as we approve of its policies. We cannot claim that as we are followers of Christ then we are obedient only to his and not to the government's authority, for government authority is one aspect of Christ's authority. The Christian realm is not one apart from the governmental realm, for to obey governments is one part of obeying God. . . .

[Next, after showing that the goal of political authority is to establish justice, the author asks us to notice] how much of the Bible is about justice. The word 'righteousness', which we often use instead, seems to have different connotations in the modern world and is often used by Christians to mean 'holiness' or 'morality'. However, if we substitute, as we should, variations of the term 'justice' wherever we read 'righteous-ness', then the Bible begins to sound quite different. We realise that justice appears and is stressed again and again throughout the Scriptures in reference to God, to Jesus Christ, to kings, judges, priests, prophets, the poor and the rich. Yet, despite this overflowing of justice, we often pass over these texts without noticing, much less heeding, their implications. For example, evangelicals have engaged in mam-moth speculations about the eschatological meaning of the more obscure parts of Daniel, often without paying attention to the teaching in the book about what the nations are and how God is calling them to behave. We must stop and realise that the Bible is a book full to overflowing with commands to do justice.

Justice refers, first of all, not to persons or acts but to the fact that there can be a just ordering of things according to God's will. God maintains a just order in the creation. We are to conform our actions to this order and we are to judge all things and all actions in terms of this order. When we say that something is just or unjust we are measuring it in terms of God's requirement for justice. This just order should be upheld by people but, if they do not act justly, God still upholds justice in the world. God is just and judges in a right way. One aspect of this justice is that God shows no partiality and is not a respecter of persons. This means that all people are judged equally before God (John 5:3; 7:24; Acts 17:31; Romans 2:11; Eph. 6:9; 1 Pet. 1:17; 2:23; Rev. 16:7; 19:2).

Because God requires all things to be just then justice is a standard which can be applied not only to people. Even weights and measures must be just, i.e., they must be fair, they must represent what they are supposed to represent (Lev. 19:36; Deut. 25:18). Wages must be just, political arrangements must be just. . . .

[Thus] a Christian answer to the question of what is due to people or anything else must be answered in terms of the place of everything in God's creation. Everyone in the world is responsible to God in their particular place. Each of us has tasks to do and responsibilities to take up. Each of us has a 'calling' or 'callings' to fulfil. We must be faithful husbands or wives, loving and wise parents, industrious and careful workers, caring neighbours, responsible citizens, steadfast friends. What is due to us is related to the callings we have. We can say that due to each of us is what we need in order to discharge our life's responsibilities. If we put this in more modern language we can say that each of us has a right to fulfil the callings that God has given us.

Hence justice means comparing the place, the callings, of everything in God's creation and making sure that they have what they need (whether that be freedom or protection or goods and services) relative to others. . . .

[Having considered the positive, binding purposes of government, the author takes up the critical side of the question.]

Although we can outline the authority, task and place of political institutions in such sweeping terms, we must not become mesmerised by them. Governments must not be thought of as mini-gods that can do anything while our only responsibility is passively just to obey. That this is clearly *not* the case is shown by the fact that in each instance where the New Testament speaks of governing authorities it describes them in terms of the specific task they have to do, in terms of what they been given their specific authority *for*. . . .

With utter realism the Bible portrays governments as both potentially and actually dangerous and as easily perverted. Governments in this fallen world wield tremendous power, the power of the sword, the power to force and coerce. Therefore we must be doubly careful to ensure that this particular servant of God *remains* a servant and does not become a lord or a tyrant. We must know not only what governments are supposed to do but also what they are *not* supposed to do.

We have seen already that God gave authority to priests (the Levites) and prophets as well as to elders, judges and kings. Each of these offices manifests a particular form of God-given authority. Each of these has a particular type of service for which they have authority and responsibility from God. God's authority on earth is not centred in any one type of person or in any one type of institution, be that government or anything else. There are many areas of authority, such as those of husband, wife, parents, employers, bishops and deacons (Eph. 5:21-6:9; Col. 3:18-4:5; 1 Tim. 3). The laws of Israel also were not all of a juridical, political kind. The tenth commandment is 'Thou shalt not covet' which seems to be a command not capable of any legal enforcement. In fact the basic command to love the Lord your God completely defies any political enforcement whatsoever. It is literally impossible to *compel* anybody to obey this commandment. Israel's political authorities were not given the responsibility to enforce all the law. Other authorities had their own place and task.

We each are responsible to God in distinct ways. There is no one body or person on earth who represents *all* of God's authority. Responsibility and authority are not channeled through one single institution. Neither the Emperor, nor the apostle, nor the master, nor the teacher, nor the parent, nor the husband nor wife, can claim to be the only or the ultimate authority. One of these cannot override another in the others' proper sphere of authority. Each and all have the responsibility, and the authority that goes with it, to do a particular task within the creation. . . .

All of this means that we should not think of politics as everything or the most important thing. C. S. Lewis once wrote that Christians make two mistakes about evil spirits: one was to ignore or dismiss them, the other was to be totally fascinated by them. Politics is similar in this respect. We must ensure that we do not make either of these mistakes. To try to make politics the centre of life is as bad as trying to ignore it entirely. The political order is only one sphere of responsibility before God. Christ alone has all authority. The political order has a particular authority for particular things and it should not try to go beyond those bounds. Merely because something is a problem, even a problem of justice, this does not mean that the political authorities can or should try to solve it.

We can delineate part of government's authority by realising that it should not override other authorities such as those of the church, the parent, or the individual person. The authority of government ends where the authorities of others begin. In fact we can say more because, unlike the family or the church, the government is not given any specific zone within the creation where it is to act. Yet, at the same time, government is charged with the responsibility for maintaining an overall order of justice. In the light of these two things, taken together, we may say that the governing authority's task is to *justly interrelate* the authorities, the areas of responsibility, of others within the creation. Government is not to supplant other authorities but it is to make sure that relations, such as those between person and person, between family and family, between church and church or church and state, are ones which conform to God's requirements for a just order.

—pp. 41-42, 46-47, 53, 55, 57-58.

From "Christian Action and the Coming of God's Kingdom," by James W. Skillen:

How should our political action be guided by our faith in the coming of God's kingdom? How does our knowledge of the future impinge upon our political life in the present age? To answer these questions, we must first understand that the biblical revelation calls us to respond to God with our whole life in the service of our neighbors. It does not allow for either "quietism" or "activism." By "quietism" I mean an attitude that has, unfortunately, characterized Christians for centuries, namely, a sense of hopelessness about life in this world. Or, if not hopelessness, at least a strong doubt that Christians can have much effect on life in this world, especially on political life. The consequence of such an attitude is for Christians to hold back, quietly, from serious reforming engagement in the affairs of this world. By "activism" I mean almost the opposite attitude—a conviction that Christians can change the world to such an extent that the primary motivation for their efforts here and now is the hope of transforming this world into the kingdom of God through political, economic, educational, and evangelistic good deeds.

By contrast, the biblical picture of God's people living and working expectantly for the coming of the kingdom is neither quietistic nor activistic. It is a picture of God's people working diligently in all areas of life, including politics, knowing that God will bring all things to completion and fulfillment in His kingdom through His Son, Jesus Christ. Our attitude ought to be one of confidence that in Christ there is an intimate connection between this world and the coming kingdom, that there is no radical discontinuity between our labor in this world and our fulfillment in the next. But the coming kingdom is in God's hands not ours.

The Creation's Sabbath Structure

This is directly relevant for politics, because it is in political life that quietism and activism show up most clearly among Christians. In an attempt to overcome this problem, I would like to consider a particular characteristic of the biblical revelation that begins to unfold in the very first chapter of Genesis. That characteristic is the seven-day, sabbatical structure of the creation. Although the first chapter of Genesis in the English Bible concludes with the end of the sixth day, the whole story of creation in the Hebrew text includes the description, in 2:1-4, of the seventh day, the sabbath rest into which God Himself entered after His labor. This sabbatical pattern as a whole forms the context for God's revelation of Himself to Israel and for the final revelation of Jesus Christ. . . .

We need to keep this revelation in mind in order to understand politics and the future. The coming age is a new age, but it is the completion, the fulfillment of this age. It is the restoration of what was lost in our sin, but also the completion of the creation which has existed from the beginning as a seven-day creation. In Christ we have been given the promise of entering God's rest. Therefore, the final triumph, the final coming of Christ, the new heaven and new earth, the new age—all of those aspects of the future which might seem to suggest a discontinuity, a break with the present world, are really aspects of sabbatical fulfillment of God's single creation. The radical newness of the future is not a symbol of the destruction of God's first creation but rather the sign of perfect fulfillment of what God has been doing from the beginning. A close continuity exists between what we are doing now and what we will be doing then in politics as in the rest of life. . . .

Sojourners and Homesteaders

With this general sabbatical framework in mind, we can look briefly at two important images or metaphors that are frequently used to describe the life of God's people in this world: the metaphors of "sojourners" or "pilgrims" and "householders" or "homesteaders." These metaphors are in fact related, I will suggest, because the Scriptures encourage us to think of our sojourning not as sojourners but as homesteaders, and to think of our homesteading not as homesteaders but as sojourners. Let me explain.

If we have the quietistic idea that this is *not* our Father's world or that we do not really belong here, then the sojourning attitude will be one of looking forward to getting out of this world. We will walk through the world with no intention of participating too seriously in its political life, for example, except in so far as it is necessary to do some minimum amount of work to survive or to look after ourselves. We will walk through the world leaving all kinds of good creaturely things behind, including the full creaturely meaning of political life. We will always be looking forward to another world to live in because this one does not seem very much like home.

It seems to me, however, that the idea of sojourning ought to be one of always moving on toward the fulfillment of what we now have, of what we now are in God's creation. This idea is connected in the Scriptures with sojourning in the midst of sin or in the midst of persecution; it is sojourning in the midst of deformity. But sojourning is for those who know that they ought to break with sin and occupy the land, who sojourn as homesteaders who belong *here* and not elsewhere. It means to take politics seriously as an important dimension of our lives that must be developed, realizing that the final fulfillment of God's perfect kingdom of justice will gather into it all the glories of the earthly kingdoms and all the goodness of our labors for justice in this age. God did not intend that Israel should walk forever in the wilderness. Israel sojourned in the wilderness so that God could teach His people how to leave sin behind and to become responsible homesteaders. They were in the wilderness *not* so that they could adopt a permanent attitude of having no home, but so that they could learn what it would mean to live properly in the city of God when they finally got into the place where they would build their homes.

On the other hand, our homesteading in this world ought to be as sojourners. This age, even in its creaturely goodness, was not designed to remain forever. The sixth day is not the last day; God's sabbath rest is our final destination. If we think of ourselves simply as homesteaders, that is, as those who were put here on earth to remain permanently as caretakers, then we lose sight of our present disposability and our ultimate destiny. That is wrong. From the beginning we were meant to be the kind of stewards and homesteaders who are always anticipating and moving toward the final sabbath. From the beginning there has been an eschatological direction to the creation. From the beginning God has been calling us toward the fulfillment of the works of our hands. In this regard our homesteading in this world is a homesteading that looks ahead for more. We are homesteading as Abraham's sons and daughters, looking ahead to the heavenly city that God is building for us and through us in Christ Jesus. We are homesteading as sojourners.

We have to be both sojourners and homesteaders, but we have to be both at the same time. We must not be divided, thinking of ourselves at one time simply as sojourners in a world that is not really ours and at another time as homesteaders in a world that has no future to it. We are always on the move, looking forward to the creation's fulfillment, but we do so as people who are gathering up all the creation with us as we go; we are leaving nothing behind but are carrying everything with us into the kingdom. We were meant for this world and it was meant for us. There is only one creation. And yet all of God's good creation is intended for a final sabbatical fulfillment. . . .

The biblical revelation assures us that history *will* be fulfilled. This means, among other things, that justice will be accomplished. The prophets announced Christ's coming as the arrival of a righteous and just King. Christ is King! Kingship is a political designation, a political office. He comes as the One who is going to bring justice. The fact that the kingdom was at hand in His first appearance meant that the coming of His justice was at hand as well. As Christians, we can count on the fact that justice will finally be established. The One who makes things right and just has come; He has already begun the harvest of justice. His resurrection, which is the firstfruits of the *one* resurrection, is the firstfruits of the fulfillment of justice. The One who was raised was not just a slaughtered lamb; He was the King. Since the King has come among us, we are those who look forward to the completion of His kingdom of justice.

If the kingdom of justice is *Christ's* kingdom, then it is clearly not a kingdom that *we* design and construct. Our labors for justice will be gathered into it, incorporated into its final shape, but it is Christ who does the gathering and incorporating. He is King of the kings of this world and is going to inaugurate the kingdom to complete all kingdoms. Christ is not the King of some other world. He is the King and Judge of this world. He told His disciples that "All authority has been given to me in heaven and on earth" (Matt. 28:18). At that point He was saying, "This is my Father's footstool" (see Isaiah 66:1); He had put His feet on it. He had dwelt among us, and He was laying final claim to the earth. His final revelation of justice will bring this world to its fulfillment.

Hence we need not have a divided understanding of our life in this world—on the one hand as Christians with a hope of Christ's coming, and on the other, as citizens with earthly political responsibility. Instead, we should have an integral sense of *one* life in *one* world under *one* King. The Christian gospel is not a gnostic escape mechanism. We cannot escape politics, nor should we try to do so. Politics is part of what we are. But at the same time, even in politics, we are not locked up into a closed world of purely human deeds. Politics is not a world solely of human action. All that human beings do, even in deformity, is subject to the judgment and redemption of the King. He never lets us get away from Him. Therefore Christians can live in this world completely, without reservation, without holding anything back, without longing for a means of escape. But we can live in this world with quite a different attitude and approach than those who think that politics is merely a human affair. It is not merely human. This is God's Kingdom; this is God's world. Kings do not rule by human appointment alone; Presidents do not obtain their offices simply because they win electoral races. They hold their offices under the providential judgment of the King. We can count on that. We can do our politics, and think politically, and act politically in that light, in obedience to the King, because we know that this is His kingdom.

Thus, we do not have to give up on politics; we can be hopeful and expectant because the King has come and true justice will be established. At the same time we must really *do* politics. One ought not to say, "I'm expectant, I'm expecting the King to come," and yet not be busy with part of the King's business. A pregnant woman cannot be expecting a baby without being busy with the preparations for her baby's arrival. If we truly expect the second coming of the Lord and the fulfillment of His kingdom, then everything in creation will be caught up in our preparation for the coming of the kingdom. We cannot say, "We have to be busy with evangelism, with Christian education, and with our church work because the King is coming," but at the same time say, "We can leave politics alone since the King does not care much about rotten earthly politics." That would be to act like a cook who doesn't care about a dirty kitchen or a librarian who doesn't care about the order of the books. No, the King is coming to bring His whole creation to fulfillment and to restore it to perfect righteousness. Therefore we must be busy as citizens with all that pertains to political life so that justice might shine through in our preparations.

—*Published in* Confessing Christ and Doing Politics, *ed. James W. Skillen; pp. 88-93, 97-100.*

"The Americanization of Reformed Confessions," by Eugene P. Heideman:

American churches have usually been equivocal about their European roots. In their desire to witness to the truth, they have affirmed that their inherited confessions provide a sure guide for their witness to Christ in their new land. In their need to be relevant, they have been forced to Americanize the confessional statement. Two sister denominations, the Reformed Church in America and the Christian Reformed Church, have inherited the same confessional statements but have taken different routes in the Americanizing process. In this article I sketch briefly the separate roads they have traveled and then conclude that at present these two roads properly should interact as a double helix, neither of them complete without the other.

The Reformed Church in America in 1792 published the *Explanatory Articles*, which Americanized the *Church Order of Dort* and thereby also its understanding of the Heidelberg Catechism, the Belgic Confession, and the Canons of Dort. The Christian Reformed Church completed its confessional move much later, in [1938 and again in] 1958, when it amended the Belgic Confession, Article 36, with a view to achieving the same ends. The two-hundredth anniversary of the *Explanatory Articles* in 1992 can furnish an occasion for joint reflection on the confessional issues involved in the Americanization process.

Americanization of the Confessions after 1792

In 1792, the Reformed Church in America's leadership was still keenly aware of the differences between their circumstances and those that prevailed in the age of the Reformation. The *Explanatory Articles* seek to come to terms with several such differences. First, they insist upon freedom of conscience and of public worship. "In consequence of that liberty wherewith Christ hath made his people free, it becomes their duty as well as their privilege, openly to confess and worship him according to the dictates of their own consciences." Second, the church is a body "wholly voluntary" and a society, "wholly distinct in its principles, laws and end, from any society which men have ever instituted for civil purposes." Third, the American Constitution's view of the separation of church and state is accepted. Therefore, what may be the most important paragraph ever written by the Reformed Church in America reads:

> Whatever relates to the immediate authority and interposi-
> tion of the Magistrate in the government of the Church,
> and which is introduced more or less into all the national
> establishments in Europe, is entirely omitted in the
> Constitution now published. Whether the Church of Christ
> will not be more effectually patronized in a civil govern-
> ment where full freedom of conscience and worship is

equally protected and insured to all men, and where truth is left to vindicate her own sovereign authority and influence, than where men in power promote their favorite denominations by temporal emoluments and partial discriminations, will now, in America, have a fair trial; and all who know and love the truth will rejoice in the prospect which such a happy situation affords for the triumph of the Gospel, and the reign of peace and love.

The *Explanatory Articles* were specifically intended to be an Americanization of the *Church Order of Dort*. They also opened the process of Americanizing the Heidelberg Catechism and the Belgic Confession with the Canons of Dort. . . .

In accepting the American principles of the separation of church and state, of the primacy of the individual conscience, and of the voluntary principle for church membership, the Reformed Church in America in 1792 has moved a long distance from the original context of the Heidelberg Catechism. As a result, the covenantal structure of a Christian faith and baptism (Q & A 74) over time began to recede in the face of a growing emphasis on the need for individual conversion or revival. Where in the time of Frederick [the ruler of Heidelberg who ordered that the catechism be written] faithfulness to the teachings of the Catechism represented one aspect of Christian citizenship, in the United States the Catechism's impact would be on the life of the church and the personal faith of the believers.

The Belgic Confession in Article 36 avoided an Erastian understanding of the relation of church and state. It recognized that within human society, God has ordained civil authorities separate from the church as a means of carrying out the divine will on earth. Civil governments are established "in order that the unbridledness of men might be restrained and all human affairs might be conducted in good orderly fashion." Such governments are not religiously neutral, however. They are called upon not only to be concerned with public policy, but also to maintain the holy worship of the church and to remove all idolatry and false religion.

Moreover, the Belgic Confession clearly wanted believers in Jesus Christ to function as part of the body politic, paying taxes, obeying and respecting the civil rulers, and praying constantly for them. For that reason, harsh words were included against the "Anabaptists and other rebellious people," who cut themselves off from the rest of the citizenry as they separated themselves into their own religious enclaves.

Following their Americanizing of the Church Order of Dort and the Reformed confessions in 1792, the Reformed Church in America only gradually has come to understand the scope of what happened. The nature of individualism and the relation of church and state in the United States in 1792 was still quite different in nature from the present situation. Throughout the next 150 years, the country was still commonly understood to be a Protestant Christian nation with "the soul of a church." The Reformed Church in America joined in the building of the nation, secure in its conviction that the King James Version of the Bible could be read in the public schools and that Protestants could take the lead in shaping personal morality.

Reformed individualism remained more or less covenantal in character through the old ethnic structures of family and church life, and through encouraging individual members to participate in a vast array of voluntary Christian and humanitarian societies working for the evangelization and uplift of society at home and abroad. Although G. J. Diekema, sometime mayor of Holland, Michigan, and a United States congressman, may represent an extreme, his admonition that IN GOD WE TRUST should remain on the nation's coins and "Nation, State, City, and School for God" should be their banner did represent the Reformed Church in America's understanding of the proper Americanization of the confessions.

Americanization of Reformed Confessions in a Neutral State

The Christian Reformed Church, from the time of its origins in the American Midwest, has been highly suspicious of the Reformed Church in America's participation in the building of a Christian nation. The new wave of Christian Reformed immigrants arriving from the Netherlands after the 1880s reinforced this suspicion. Within the Christian Reformed Church, considerable controversy raged concerning issues of Americanization. In contrast to the situation in the Reformed Church in America, which struggled with the issues for almost two centuries (1628-1792) prior to writing the *Explanatory Articles*, the Christian Reformed Church was forced to deal with the issues within a very short time after many of its leaders arrived in the United States.

Given the very recent arrival in America of much of its leadership, the debate within the Christian Reformed Church was for decades shaped at least as much by events in the Netherlands as it was by its American experience. The powerful influence of Abraham Kuyper, Dutch theologian and statesman, undergirded much of the analysis of the American situation. In contrast to the optimistic-attitude of the Reformed Church in America, Kuyper set forth as a principle the concept of a state that was essentially neutral in character. He developed a doctrine of "sphere sovereignty," by which he meant that the various areas of human life, such as family, science, society, state, and church, each had its own law of life and existence, possessing a sovereignty in its own sphere. Rejecting individualism in favor of an "organic" view of society in which the family is the basic unit ordained by God, he understood the state to be "artificial," ordained of God only in consequence of the Fall. The role of the state must therefore be to maintain a neutral position in society, for the purpose of maintaining order and correcting imbalances among the various spheres.

Given the fact that the role of the state had to be confined to its own sphere, one could no longer hold to the language of the Belgic Confession, Article 36, which calls upon the civil authorities to act positively and even aggressively in maintaining the holy worship of the church, removing all idolatry and false religion, and advancing the kingdom of Christ. Within the framework of God's common grace, the state had responsibility to preserve human freedom and to allow various persons (whether regenerate or unregenerate) and organizations to set forth their principles and programs within a democratic environment. In the United States, the Christian Reformed Church followed the lead of Kuyper and the Gereformeerde Kerken in

Nederland. After a preliminary action in 1910, the CRC Synod in [1938] amended Article 36 concerning the civil authorities to read, "Their office is not only to have regard unto and watch for the welfare of the civil state, but also to protect the sacred ministry, that the kingdom of Christ may be thus promoted." [Synod 1958 provisionally adopted a substitute for this statement, and a slightly edited version of that substitute was incorporated into the Belgic Confession in 1985 (see Article 36, CRC version, at the beginning of this section).*] Thus the Synod affirmed the freedom of religion, while sustaining the neutral character of the state.

Having adopted this confessional change, the Christian Reformed Church had to recognize a basis for action in American society other than that of a "Christian America." Its essential solution to the problem was to call upon members of the church to form themselves into Christian organizations with a Reformed confessional stance, in order to establish Christian schools, labor unions, and a variety of other Christian movements, including consideration of a Christian political party. These specifically Christian organizations could fruitfully participate in society in view of God's common grace given to all, even while recognizing the underlying conflict between the regenerate and the unregenerate and between Christian and other movements in public life.

Reformed Confessions in the American Mainstream

In moving toward the two-hundredth anniversary of the adoption of the *Explanatory Articles*, Reformed Christians must address the question, On what basis does one participate in society when society understands itself to be radically pluralistic? In the United States, Reformed participation in society has tended to follow the philosophy of church-state relationships. With the vanishing of "Protestant America," the theological basis laid for the Reformed Church in America in the *Explanatory Articles* has dissipated. The harmony presumed to exist between the faith of the church and the "theology of the Republic" can no longer be taken for granted. As a result, the Reformed Church in America today operates in a confessional vacuum regarding a basis for participation in the life of the nation.

In light of its revision of Article 36 and its tendency to look to the concept of common grace as the basis for action in society, the

---

*[The original statement about civil authorities had included the following phrase (which the CRC judged unbiblical): "and thus may remove and prevent all idolatry and false worship, that the kingdom of antichrist may be thus destroyed and the kingdom of Christ promoted." The 1938 revision, however, did not satisfy the churches, and Synod repeatedly studied and discussed it for the next twenty years. In 1958 Synod approved the following substitute statement for evaluation and reaction by other Reformed churches that accept the Belgic Confession: "And being called in this manner to contribute to the advancement of a society that is pleasing to God, the civil rulers have the task, in subjection to the law of God, while completely refraining from every tendency toward exercising absolute authority, and while functioning in the sphere entrusted to them and with the means belonging to them, to remove every obstacle to the preaching of the gospel and to every aspect of divine worship, in order that the Word of God may have free course, the kingdom of Jesus Christ may make progress, and every anti-Christian power may be resisted." In 1985 Synod finally incorporated this statement, in slightly altered form, into the text of a new translation of the Belgic Confession based on the French text of 1619.]

Christian Reformed Church has moved toward a more clearly defined rationale for participation in society. Nevertheless, it has never been able to define clearly the line between special grace and common grace. The problem with maintaining a clear line of demarcation between the two is that almost all daily and public life falls within the realm of common grace, which restrains sin and the progress of evil and leads to acts of civil righteousness but does not have a salvific quality. It is then common grace apart from Jesus Christ, which makes possible a sense of unity in society, which facilitates cultural achievements, and which undergirds economic and social systems. The grace in Jesus Christ, on the other hand, divides humanity, ultimately denigrates human achievements as mere stop-gap measures, and forces believers to speak in the church on the basis of the gospel while participating and advocating in civic life on the basis of conscience and an understanding of natural and positive law.

The issue here is urgent, not only for the churches, but for the nation as a whole. As the nation becomes more radically pluralistic, one can no longer take for granted, as did the founders of the nation, that the belief in a Creator functions as the underpinning for governmental protection of human rights and of justice. The arena of common grace or of "the theology of the Republic" is becoming as much a sphere of radical division as is that of conflict among the religions.

The two-hundredth anniversary of the *Explanatory Articles* can furnish the Christian Reformed Church and the Reformed Church in America, with their base in Canada as well as the United States and with their missionary experience in many countries, to break out of the specifically American isolation of the issues. Certainly, the experience of Christians in other cultures offers wider possibilities for understanding the relation of church to state and the relationship of the gospel to public life. In their recent attempts at writing new confessions, both denominations have sought to move beyond earlier formulations.

One can simply ask whether the . . . outlook of the Heidelberg Catechism does not in our contemporary pluralistic (rather than "Christendom") culture provide a hint that it is now necessary to ask whether it is the Spirit of Jesus Christ (rather than the spirit of the Enlightenment or of common grace) that works for peace on earth and among governments, and that works in human government for the welfare of the people and for justice among the poor. Is it possible that Kuyper's "principle against principle" now refers to the way in which the testimony of the gospel itself enters into public life as the arena where God seeks to work out Jesus' proclamation of the reign of God for time and eternity? Mutual exploration of questions such as these could enable us (on the basis of the gospel) to internationalize our attempts (on the basis of the "theology of the Republic" or common grace) to Americanize the Reformed confessions.

—*Published in* Perspectives, *June 1991; pp. 13-16.*

9. How do we carry out the task of evangelism?

Q. We have been delivered
from our misery
by God's grace alone through Christ
and not because we have earned it:
why then must we still do good?

A. To be sure, Christ has redeemed us by his blood.
But we do good because
Christ by his Spirit is also renewing us to be like himself,
so that in all our living
we may show that we are thankful to God
for all he has done for us,
and so that he may be praised through us.

And we do good
so that we may be assured of our faith by its fruits,
and so that by our godly living
our neighbors may be won over to Christ.

—Heidelberg Catechism Q & A 86.

One might expect the topic of evangelism to fall under the "private life" or "church membership" categories in this book. In other words, evangelism is usually seen as a matter of "personal witnessing" to unbelievers at work or at the mall, or as a line item in the church budget, duly supervised by a committee.

In placing evangelism among the concerns of public life, we return to a Reformed tradition that has operated out of some good and some bad instincts. John H. Kromminga, president emeritus of Calvin Theological Seminary, Grand Rapids, Michigan, asserts that a misunderstanding of the Reformed emphases on covenant and election has crippled evangelism in the past and that a more biblical grasp of them is essential if we are to reinvigorate the church's mission today.

From "General Overview of the Relationship of Covenant and Mission in the Reformed Tradition," by John H. Kromminga:

In recent years there has been a great deal of attention given to the relation of covenant and mission. Several interacting theological developments have taken place, involving a wide variety of theologians. Biblical studies, particularly those concerned with the Old Testament, have, so to speak, rediscovered the covenant. It may fairly be said that the pervasiveness of covenant elements throughout the Old Testament has never been more clearly seen. At the same time, missiological studies have turned more and more to the exploration of the Old Testament, as a truly missiological book *par excellence*. What has emerged from these studies is the understanding that covenant and mission are inseparably connected with each other.

It is not our purpose to give a thorough review of this subject, but simply to state it with sufficient clarity and detail to lay the groundwork for other considerations which will follow. Old Testament theology has been much occupied with the understanding that throughout the story of God's dealing with His Old Testament people, He has dealt with them in terms of the covenant. The covenant, to be sure, is not the only familiar Reformed doctrinal theme to receive new attention. Closely allied with this concentration is the renewed emphasis on the fact that election plays a role in the definition of the covenant community and that the kingdom of God plays a role in defining the goal of that community. Election, covenant, and kingdom have all emerged as key concepts in understanding the unfolding of God's will and work in the Old Testament. . . .

Now having noted that the Reformed community has been the locus of the greatest covenant emphasis, and that covenant and mission are inseparably connected with each other, it is only natural to assume that the Reformed churches should have taken the leadership in pursuing the task of mission in the world. Such leadership, it might well be assumed, would include both the theory and the practice of mission.

This, however, simply cannot be said to be the case. Despite all the arguments and considerations which can be raised to the contrary, the following generalizations hold true. In the period immediately following the Reformation, it was not the Protestant churches, but the Catholic church which entered into an expanded role in foreign missions. When somewhat later Protestants did join the missionary effort in increasingly large numbers, it was not the mainline churches, whether Lutheran, Calvinist, or Anglican, which took the lead, but rather Pietists, Baptists, and various sects. Up to fairly recent times, the communities which have emphasized election and the covenant have lagged behind communities which have ignored these doctrines in the pursuit of the mission of the church. This is a fact which calls for a little bit of closer definition and a great deal of explanation. . . .

Such is the grip of a selfish appropriation of the covenant that its adherents experience their greatest difficulty in applying it to mission just where those adherents are the most numerous. For the North American community this has a direct bearing on evangelism. Surely not all of the shortcomings of their evangelistic effort can be laid at the doorstep of the covenant doctrine or even their inadequate view of that doctrine. But just as surely, covenant-related ideas play their role in these shortcomings. All honor to the noble few who seek to break through the barriers to evangelism. For the ignoble many, however, there is a them-and-us situation, embodying the sense that we are the covenant people, and that somehow our character ought not to be altered by too great an infusion of other blood. This makes world mission on a distant continent much more palatable than real, all-out evangelistic effort on the home front.

The changed circumstances in the mission situation have made that distinction between foreign and domestic missions less important than it once was. The dispersion of the people of God in the world is not only a fact but is being increasingly recognized. The maintenance of covenant communities out of touch with mission situations is no longer a possibility, and even the fiction of its possibility is increasingly difficult to maintain.

What is evident on the North American scene is even more obvious in South Africa. . . . In both communities, and in the Netherlands as well, the covenant was confused with election and became a source of endless dispute.

But the difficulties escalate when the mission situation is considered, and especially when the mission subjects are not only from a vastly different culture but also near at hand. In South Africa . . . heathen people come into contact not only with missionaries who have dedicated their lives to them, but with many other Christians who are not only not missionaries, but may even be hostile to the missionary task. Here the heathen can see for themselves that great gap between doctrine and life which, alas, is often painfully evident to all who have eyes to see.

At this point we are close to the heart of the dilemma of covenant and mission. The temptation of a self-conscious covenant community is to deepen the covenant, to use it as a mark of distinction from other groups of Christians (leaving in limbo the question whether they are then real Christians or not). But if the mission potential is to be realized, the idea must be broadened to the dimensions included in the call of Abraham, the poetry of Isaiah, and the great commission. There have been, as we have noted, leaders who have called for a truer appreciation of what the covenant is, with whom it is made, and what constitutes obedience to it. But they have always been and still are constrained to work against a resistance composed partly of sheer lethargy and partly of smug self-satisfaction. . . .

The mission experience of dialog with other peoples has driven us to rely more and more on the Word of God for the source of missiology. Because of the strong covenant emphasis of the Old Testament, we may be content to rest with the idea that this going back to Scripture confirms what Reformed people have believed all along. But this is a dangerous half-truth. Going back to the Scriptures must deepen and expand the Reformed view and rebuke its failures.

An extended quotation from [Richard R.] De Ridder is in order here:

> How must the present be assessed, and how ought the church to conceive of itself today? The chief concern of the believing community must be to "make disciples" or what is the same thing, "to preach the kingdom of God." It has to develop a theology concerning itself that is commensurate with the purpose of its existence. This procedure will force God's people to look to God and to the world which He has created, and then to themselves as a people of God in the world, people who are agents of His reconciling work. And if the challenge of mission brings the church closer to the writers of the New Testament than to the Reformers, or forces it to enlarge the vision of its thinking, let it be so, because the challenge of mission was the context in which the New Testament church did its work. The sons of God with the heritage of the Reformation are called to build in today's generation on the foundation laid for them in Christ Jesus.

One must agree with him in the last analysis. But one may also hope, as he undoubtedly does, that the heritage of the Reformation may be brought into useful captivity to the biblical insights which have been or shall yet be made.

The need to think in corporate terms when one deals with the covenant has also received new attention as a result of mission experience. Direct contact with areas such as Asia and Africa has brought Western missionaries into contact with cultures in which corporate life has not been eclipsed by rampant individualism, as in the West. Mission experience, in this respect, has opened up new vistas. The actual participation in missions has given the church a new challenge and thrown it back upon its resources.

But in the process of that renewed drawing upon the Old and New Testaments, some profit can be gained also from the Reformed heritage. Corporate and family emphases have been present even in the restricted covenant thinking of past generations. What is to prevent them from enriching the understanding of how God accomplishes the spread of the gospel of grace to mission peoples? Covenant doctrine, even in the restricted, misappropriated, sometimes misused and misunderstood form in which we are familiar with it, has insights that can be applied to the mission cause. This is the more evident because, as many others are coming to recognize together with the Reformed community, covenant insights are profoundly in keeping with and expressive of the plan of redemption as revealed in the Scriptures.

144

Perhaps enough has been said to cover the subject at least lightly. It is good to see the amount of work which is going into the address to this subject . . . . because the stakes are so high, so very high. These stakes concern not only the world waiting to be evangelized, but also, and especially, the traditional covenant communities. If biblical studies are correct, the church community today is the heir of the promises and obligations given to Old Testament Israel. Failure to obey the demands may well lead to the removal of the responsibility, together with its attendant blessing, so that it may be given to a nation which will bring forth the fruits thereof.

What has been grasped in the Reformed tradition is the fact that God has made a covenant with His people for their salvation. What has not been grasped is that this is not the heart of the covenant relationship, which is rather that God's people are a sign to the surrounding world. A central problem and challenge today is to let this new insight, developed mainly in terms of Old Testament Israel, find its full application in the life and mission of the church of God. It cannot be said that we are anywhere near the completion of this task. We have hardly begun.

—*pp. 5-6, 9, 15-17, 19-22.*

. . . .

As we end the twentieth century, the church's situation is brand-new, yet very old, says George R. Hunsberger. In this context evangelism is nothing special, only the church's entire life; nothing private and individualistic, but a public, corporate way of being.

From "The Changing Face of Ministry: Christian Leadership in the 21st Century," by George R. Hunsberger:

There is a crisis in the life of the churches of North America . . . : the social function the churches once fulfilled in American life is gone. . . .

As Kennon Callahan has put it in more popular fashion, "the day of the churched culture is over." The day when the church was generally valued by the society as important to the social and moral order and when because of that people tended to seek out a church for themselves, has gone. We sail today in a different kind of sea.

If our caretaker days are over and the church is no longer looked to for moral underpinning, we have scarcely begun to live as though that were true, and this explains why we experience these changes as a crisis. The Christendom experiment has run its course, but our images and instincts are still formed by its memory. We play out the church's routine as though the concerns of the church and the quests of the culture go hand-in-glove. We are never quite sure which is the hand and which the glove, but we are certain they form common cause. The rude awakening is that such a connection, whatever it may have been in the past, is vanishing.

That growing disjuncture causes distress in a variety of forms. A lack of focus in the midst of a proliferation of church programs, a loss of meaning in the work of clergy and laity alike, and an uneasiness that our faith does not really fit in the world where we live, all contribute to a certain dis-ease in our congregations. When a pastor is discharged and after all the reasons are given we still are not sure we know what is really behind it, when capable and committed clergy or laity experience "burnout," and when all of us sit together in worship week by week feeling a hunger and readiness for something more, something beyond what we have thought before about ourselves and our programs—then the signs are telling us to look again and see what has shifted to cause such strain. . . .

Pathetically, we have seen and felt all this to be "crisis" only when it has come upon us as "denominational decline" in membership. Massive research efforts have been searching for clues to explain the decline, and in virtually every mainline church high profile emphases on "evangelism" attempt to stem the ebbing tide. But the recovery of evangelism is elusive; our efforts are better described as "member recruitment," and the new churches we start—even if they do keep pace with the number of churches that close—amount to more of a relocation of members than an increase.

Even the myths that prop up this spate of "growth-ism" are crumbling and begging for a much deeper diagnosis and prescription than "doing things more and better." For some, hope has been attached to the notion that mainline churches are losing their members to the conservative churches. The logic suggests that a recovery of a conservative theology and an aggressive program of evangelization will be the solution for declining denominations. But it may not be so simple. As studies conducted by Wade Clark Roof and William McKinney have shown, mainline churches are losing their members not so much to conservative churches as to secular lifestyle. People are leaving to no church at all. Another part of the myth has been questioned by Reginald Bibby, the leading researcher of the fortunes of the Canadian churches. In a major study of twenty conservative-evangelical churches in an urban area, he discovered that their supposed "evangelistic" success (i.e., they were growing while their counterparts in mainline churches were declining) was not attributable to the evangelizing of outsiders but to a better record of retaining their own, retaining both the children of the churches as they reached adulthood and people migrating into the city from similar conservative churches in the smaller towns and rural areas. He concluded that "conservatives are no more successful than the mainline Protestant denominations in reaching people not active in other religious groups."

This is perhaps the most vexing aspect of our self-learning of late. The myth-breakers tell us there is a wider gap between the inner life of the churches and their appeal to companions in the culture than can be bridged by better techniques and more effective technicians. Our church growth strategies waltz all around the problem but never get to the heart of the issue, content instead to appeal to the consumerism of today's religious shoppers. In some particular places and times, that might appear to "work" and reverse the "trend." But in either case, our growth strategies may in fact be detrimentally masking the more serious challenge of a fundamentally new day for the church. The crisis is not first about decline or growth. Those are symptoms. The crisis has to do with the way the church sees itself and forms its life. . . .

Evangelism is all but gone from the life of our congregations. If we are concerned about it at all, we have tended either to "program" it in prescribed (and mechanical) ways, or to transmute it into "member recruitment." Some of this has happened, undoubtedly, because of the sort of intimidation we have noted. Coming to a sense of the validity of claiming to "know" God, and recognizing ways we can speak about that to friends without feeling we are admitting to a serious irrationality, will provide beginning points for evangelism to spring up again. And that may be the most apt expression, it will "spring up." Evangelism wells up in the life of a congregation more than it is manufactured. All that has been said before in this essay about pastoral leadership is proposed as the form of ministry which will prepare the conditions for that to occur. What remains now is to suggest the shape evangelism takes when it emerges from beneath our "church growth" masking of the current dilemmas and as it is rediscovered beyond our consumer-driven membership recruitment.

Donald Posterski has anticipated our need to "reinvent evangelism." In a day in which there has come to be a serious credibility gap regarding the Christianity people have heard or tasted, nothing else will do but a fresh demonstration. The gospel, Posterski says, "will be perceived as a feasible alternative when those who do not know God have some positive, personal experiences with people who do know him." People are questioning the functional relevance of such a claim to knowledge even more than its factuality. If they are looking for the gospel's relevance, they will look at people who claim to bear that faith. Then they will answer the question, Is it plausible to believe and live this way?

This, on a personal scale, is what [Lesslie] Newbigin indicates in properly larger, corporate terms. The congregation, he says, must be understood to be "the hermeneutic of the gospel." The only way that people can "come to believe that the power which has the last word in human affairs is represented by a man hanging on a cross" is through a "congregation of men and women who believe it and live by it." If this is true, evangelism only emerges as the congregation is prepared to give its life away to the world around it. All other evangelistic methods are purely secondary to this and have their power "only as they are rooted in and lead back to a believing community."

It is mistaken to think that this somehow means that evangelism is stripped of its verbal, gospel-articulating character. The congregation is the hermeneutic, the lens through which the gospel will inevitably be read. But it will be the gospel which is read. A believing community gives voice to it. But this understanding of the congregation as hermeneutic does imply something about the style and manner of that voicing. Three images may serve as pointers.

First, a reading of the word "witness" in its courtroom sense. "The function of a witness is not to develop conclusions out of already known data, but simply to point to, report, affirm that which cannot come into the argument at all except simply as a new datum, a reality which is attested by a witness." A return to the simplicity of what our "testimony" entails invites the scrutiny of the congregation by those who want to know whether our testimony has feasibility as a life commitment.

Second, the notion of "docent." The word has a rich heritage in continental European academia. But its use as a description of a certain corps of volunteers at the Atlanta Zoo is what presents an intriguing image for evangelism. The volunteers are trained to be present among the people visiting the zoo and to be available to help them understand the animal behaviors they are watching. They interpret the animals' worlds to the curious.

Third, the image journalist. It is most pervasive in the New Testament and less an "image" of evangelism than it is a description or definition. David Lowes Watson has made a powerful case for employing a journalist model for reporting the presence of the kingdom of God. Such an announcement includes the fundamental news that in the life, death, and resurrection of Jesus, God's purpose to save the world has been revealed and effected. It also includes pointing to the continuing presence of the reign of God now as a pretaste of its full and final future coming.

As the gospel is published, as it provides interpretation of the world's life, and as it testifies to the clue to the world's meaning, a form of witness emerges from the life of the congregation which is subversive. It is so because it is the witness of a community that does not believe the "empire's version" of the way things are. It is subversive first in that it challenges the pretensions, claims, and promises of the reigning blueprint for people's aspirations and trusts. Second, it subverts the "ungood" in the social order by working for the common good in ways that weave into the society's fabric experiences and tastes of God's reigning over life. Third, it undermines the governing principles as inadequate for a true and comprehensive reading of the nature and destiny of things. All of these subversions guard against the danger of forming an aloof, exclusive, and self-absorbed alternative community. Instead, the community that subverts by its witness offers its life as an alternative for the sake of the world. . . .

These approaches may hold promise for developing missionary pastors for missionary congregations. But by whatever means, it will be most essential that we have leadership that possesses and engenders hope. Vital Christian communities live by hope, which the author to the Hebrews calls an anchor of the soul (6:19). But it is not so much an anchor that grips the bottom and holds the ship against the tide and wind. It is more a sea-anchor that orients the ship in the shifting, and at times violent, seas to keep it stable and safe while it rides the waves. Our calling is not to brace ourselves against all currents of our cultural environment. But neither is it our calling to be swept around mercilessly by them. Hope is the genuine and freeing anchor for missionary congregations and their missionary pastors.

—*Published in* Reformed Review, *Spring 1991; pp. 225-27, 239-40, 242.*

....

If Christians are defined by a new way of being, how does being relate to doing? Lesslie Newbigin explores *doing* as both words and action and reaffirms the principle that evangelism will be the natural life of a church that is truly part of our Lord's church. The Heidelberg Catechism has maintained the same view. Question and Answer 86, with its declaration that good works win neighbors to Christ, opens the catechism's famous third section, devoted to our life of service, or gratitude.

From *Mission in Christ's Way: Bible Studies*, by Lesslie Newbigin:

Jesus preaches the kingdom

In the mission of Jesus we see that there is both the *presence* of the kingdom and also the *proclamation* of the kingdom. Jesus himself is the presence of the kingdom; but Jesus also preaches the kingdom. It is present, but it has to preached. But if it is not present, then the preaching is empty words.

How is it present? Look at the first mission charge of Jesus to his disciples as it is given in Matthew 10. At the outset there is nothing about preaching. Jesus called the twelve and gave them authority to heal and to exorcise (Matt. 10:1). Then follow the names of the twelve. Then Jesus sends them out with the instruction: "Preach as you go, saying, the kingdom of heaven is at hand" (v. 7). Clearly the preaching is the explanation of the healing. People are being healed. Why? Is it just that someone with a gift of healing has turned up? This would not be anything new (see Luke 11:19). No! The healing is a sign pointing beyond itself, a sign that the kingdom of God has come upon you. The preaching is the interpretation of the happening. If nothing is happening, then there is nothing to explain and the preaching is just empty words—as ours often is. But, on the other hand, the happenings do not explain themselves. Even the most wonderful healing, or the most sacrificial act of kindness, or the most splendid programme of action for justice does not by itself tell us that the kingdom of God has come. It does not point away from itself to something greater of which it is a sign. It is not a substitute for the name of the one in whom the kingdom of God has actually come among us; it is not a substitute for the name of Jesus.

So words without deeds are empty, but deeds without words are dumb. It is stupid to set them against each other. It is, for example, stupid to say: "The one thing that matters is to go everywhere and preach the gospel; all other activities such as schools and hospitals and programmes for social action are at best merely auxiliary and at worst irrelevant." Why should people believe our preaching that the kingdom of God has come near in Jesus if they see no sign that anything is happening as a result, if they can see no evidence that disease and ignorance and cruelty and injustice are being challenged and over-come? Why should they believe our words if there is nothing happening to authenticate them?

On the other hand, it is equally stupid to say: "Preaching is a waste of time. Forget it and get on with tackling the real human problems of poverty, injustice and oppression." That is to repeat the folly of the people who are fed in the desert. It is to confuse the sign with the thing it points to. Our best programmes are not the kingdom of God; they are full of our pride and ambition—as the world easily sees. But apart from these obvious inconsistencies, we surely know that human beings have a greater and more glorious destiny than even the best of our programmes can offer. To a hungry man a good meal looks like heaven; when he has eaten it he knows that it is not. We know that our true life is beyond our grasp, and we are deceived when we invest all our hopes, and encourage others to invest all their hopes, in programmes that do not reach beyond the horizon of this present age.

I know that some will denounce this language as escapist, but in fact it is simply realist. The best of our programmes are still full of the seeds of their own corruption. We do not establish God's kingdom. That kingdom, that kingly rule, has been given to us in the form of the suffering servant, the wounded healer, the crucified liberator. God's kingdom is a given fact, and our actions for justice and compassion are at the very best only signs, pointers to help men and women to turn round so that it becomes possible for them also to believe in the reality of that kingdom, to have a foretaste of its liberating power, to follow in the way of the cross and to find in it life—a life that death cannot threaten.

Our preaching is mere empty words if it does not have behind it a costly engagement with the powers of evil, with all the powers that rob men and women of their humanity, and if it does not call men and women to share in the same costly engagement. But, equally, our programmes for teaching, healing, feeding the hungry, caring for the sick and action for justice and freedom are futile if they do not point beyond themselves to a reality greater than they—to the great healer, the great liberator, the one who is himself the living bread. In themselves, as a contribution to solving the problems of the nation and the world, our programmes are a mere drop in the ocean. Quantitatively they are insignificant. But as signs pointing beyond themselves they can be powerful indeed, leading men and women to him who is the power of God and the wisdom of God.

So, for God's sake, let us not fall into this game of setting words and deeds against each other, preaching against action for justice and action for justice against preaching. Do not let us set "kingdom" against "church" and "church" against "kingdom". The church is not an end in itself. "Church growth" is not an end in itself. The church is only true to its calling when it is a sign, an instrument and a foretaste of the kingdom. But, on the other hand, talk about the kingdom is mere ideology if it is not tied to the name of Jesus in whom the kingdom is present and if it does not invite men and women to recognize that presence, to do the U-turn, to become part of that company that (sinful as it has always been) acknowledges Jesus as the one in whom God's kingdom is present and so seeks to honour him, to serve him, to follow him.

Mission is not a success story

That leads to the third point, which can be brief. Mission in Christ's way will not be a success story as the world reckons success. There is a kind of ideology of success that fits badly with the gospel.

When I was bishop in Madras I used to get letters about once a month, usually from somewhere in the neighbourhood of Texas, in such terms as the following: "Dear Bishop, if you will kindly arrange for me to hold a series of revival meetings in your diocese I will guarantee to revive your church within a fortnight." Now that I am a pastor of a small congregation in Birmingham I receive literature, beautifully produced on glossy paper, inviting me to write for their course of teaching that will tell me how to double the membership of the congregation within six months. One is tempted to say: "What a pity that Jesus did not have some professionally qualified experts in public relations to help him! He could have avoided crucifixion."

This sort of thing is far away from the mission in Christ's way. Let us never forget that in its first and mightiest conflict against the powers of this world, represented in the imperial might of Rome, the victory of the gospel was won not by the cleverness of its preachers and theologians, and certainly not by its programmes for social justice, but by the blood of the martyrs. And let us not forget that the most notable examples of vital Christian mission today are to be found in places where success in worldly terms has been denied: in the [former] USSR, where one of the most powerful governments in the world . . . tried for seventy years to destroy the church, yet where the sheer reality and joy of Christian holiness continues to draw men and women to the faith; in China, where the church has come through the agony of the cultural revolution mightily strengthened and renewed; in Latin America, where the blood of countless martyrs has been shed in witness to the gospel against cruel and unjust dictatorships.

Success in the sense of growth in the number of committed Christians is not in our hands. It is the work of God the Holy Spirit to call men and women to faith in Jesus, and the Spirit does so in ways that are often mysterious and beyond any possibility of manipulation or even of comprehension by us. What is required of us is faithfulness in word and deed, at whatever cost; faithfulness in action for truth, for justice, for mercy, for compassion; faithfulness in speaking the name of Jesus when the time is right, bearing witness, by explicit word as occasion arises, to God whose we are and whom we serve. There are situations where the word is easy and the deed is costly; there are situations where the deed is easy and the word is costly. Whether in word or in deed, what is required in every situation is that we be faithful to him who said to his disciples: "As the Father sent me, so I send you," and showed them his hands and his side. . . .

Mission is wrongly understood if it is seen primarily as a task laid upon us. It is primarily a work of the Spirit, a spill-over from Pentecost.

That is confirmed in the record of the Acts of the Apostles. The first Christian sermon was preached not because the apostles decided to have a mission, but because the presence of a new reality was so manifest that people came running to ask what it was. In fact most of the great Christian preachings in Acts are responses to questions, not actions initiated by the church. There is a reality present; people enquire about it; the church has to explain, and the explanation has to take the form of telling the story of Jesus. It is not that the church has a mission and the Spirit helps us in fulfilling it. It is rather that the Spirit is the active missionary, and the church (where it is faithful) is the place where the Spirit is enabled to complete the Spirit's work.

It is, is it not, a striking fact that in all his letters to the churches Paul never urges on them the duty of evangelism. He can rebuke, remind, exhort his readers about faithfulness to Christ in many matters. But he is never found exhorting them to be active in evangelism. For himself he knows that he cannot keep silent about the gospel. "Woe is me if I do not preach," he says. There is an inner constraint; the love of Christ constrains him. But he does not lay this constraint upon the consciences of his readers. Mission, in other words, is gospel and not law; it is the overflow of a great gift, not the carrying of a great burden. It is the fulfilment of a promise: "You shall be my witness, when the Holy Spirit comes upon you."

—pp. 10-14, 20-21.

Viewpoints on Our Private Life as Christians

10. How should we use the gifts and abilities God has given us?

Q. What do you understand by
"the communion of saints"?

A. First, that believers one and all,
as members of this community,
share in Christ
and in all his treasures and gifts.

Second, that each member
should consider it a duty
to use these gifts
readily and cheerfully
for the service and enrichment
of the other members.

—Heidelberg Catechism Q & A 55.

The Spirit leads us into Truth—
the Truth of Christ's salvation,
into increasing knowledge of all existence.
He rejoices in human awareness of God's creation
and gives freedom to those on the frontiers of research.
We are overwhelmed by the growth in our knowledge.
While our truths come in broken fragments,
we expect the Spirit to unite these in Christ.

—Our Song of Hope, st. 14.

L ike any category, "private life" is an artificial construct. No hard and fast line separates the "private" or "personal" from the "public." Nor does *private* mean simply "personal" or "individual." Persons are at all times meeting grounds, blending sites, of public and private, communal and individual. But the concept is still useful as a pointer toward the smaller scale, the concrete, daily activities, the more intimate relations of life.

"The earth is the LORD's, and everything in it, the world, and all who live in it . . . ." These opening lines of Psalm 24 give Reformed Christians a charter for making their faith public. But the phrase "all who live in it" also makes their faith deeply personal: not only the world but also the people who live in it belong to God—and in all the facets of their being.

In truth, however, Calvinists have sometimes honored certain facets or talents over others: the spiritual above the intellectual above the material and artistic. Truly valuing all gifts, including our own being, is an imperative that resurfaces from time to time.

Max De Pree, who contributed to the preceding discussion on public life, deftly shows how close the connection is between public and private life in his reflections on the role of people's diverse gifts in the workplace. The following selection begins with De Pree's recollection of a story his father told about a millwright who had been a vital employee in their furniture factory.

From *Leadership Is an Art,* by Max De Pree:

One day the millwright died.

My father, being a young manager at the time, did not particularly know what he should do when a key person died, but thought he ought to go visit the family. He went to the house and was invited to join the family in the living room. There was some awkward conversation—the kind with which many of us are familiar.

The widow asked my father if it would be all right if she read aloud some poetry. Naturally, he agreed. She went into another room, came back with a bound book, and for many minutes read selected pieces of beautiful poetry. When she finished, my father commented on how beautiful the poetry was and asked who wrote it. She replied that her husband, the millwright, was the poet.

It is now nearly sixty years since the millwright died, and my father and many of us at Herman Miller continue to wonder: Was he a poet who did millwright's work, or was he a millwright who wrote poetry?

In our effort to understand corporate life, what is it we should learn from this story? In addition to all of the ratios and goals and parameters and bottom lines, it is fundamental that leaders endorse a concept of persons. This begins with an understanding of the diversity of people's gifts and talents and skills.

Understanding and accepting diversity enables us to see that each of us is needed. It also enables us to begin to think about being abandoned to the strengths of others, of admitting that we cannot *know* or *do* everything.

The simple act of recognizing diversity in corporate life helps us to connect the great variety of gifts that people bring to the work and service of the organization. Diversity allows each of us to contribute in a special way, to make our special gift a part of the corporate effort.

Recognizing diversity helps us to understand the need we have for opportunity, equity, and identity in the workplace. Recognizing diversity gives us the chance to provide meaning, fulfillment, and purpose, which are not to be relegated solely to private life any more than are such things as love, beauty, and joy. It also helps us to understand that for many of us there is a fundamental difference between goals and rewards.

In the end, diversity is not only real in our corporate groups but, as with the millwright, it frequently goes unrecognized. . . .

When we think about leaders and the variety of gifts people bring to corporations and institutions, we see that the art of leadership lies in polishing and liberating and enabling those gifts. . . .

I believe that the most effective contemporary management process is participative management. Participative management is glibly discussed these days in a number of magazines and books, but it is not a theoretical position to be adopted after studying a few journals. It begins with a belief in the potential of people. Participative management without a belief in that potential and without convictions about the gifts people bring to organizations is a contradiction in terms.

Participative management arises out of the heart and out of a personal philosophy about people. It cannot be added to, or subtracted from, a corporate policy manual as though it were one more managerial tool. . . .

Leaders need to foster environments and work processes within which people can develop high-quality relationships—relationships with each other, relationships with the group with which we work, relationships with our clients and customers.

How does one approach the problem of turning the ideals about relationships into reality? There are no guaranteed formulas, but I would propose five steps as a starting point. Surely, you will revise and add to the list.

Respect people. This begins with an understanding of the diversity of their gifts. Understanding the diversity of these gifts enables us to begin taking the crucial step of trusting each other. It also enables us to begin to think in a new way about the strengths of others. Everyone comes with certain gifts—but not the same gifts. True participation and enlightened leadership allow these gifts to be expressed in different ways and at different times. For the CEO to vote on the kind of drill press to buy would be foolish. For the drill press operator (who should be voting on the kind of tool to use) to vote on whether to declare a stock split would be equally foolish.

Understand that what we believe precedes policy and practice. Here I am talking about both our corporate and personal value systems. It seems to me that our value system and world view should be as closely integrated into our work lives as they are integrated into our lives with our families, our churches, and our other activities and groups.

Many managers are concerned about their style. They wonder whether they are perceived as open or autocratic or participative. As practice is to policy, so style is to belief. Style is merely a consequence of what we believe, of what is in our hearts.

Agree on the rights of work. Each of us, no matter what our rank in the hierarchy may be, has the same rights: to be needed, to be involved, to have a covenantal relationship, to understand the corporation, to affect one's destiny, to be accountable, to appeal, to make a commitment. . . .

Understand the respective role and relationship of contractual agreements and covenants. Contractual relationships cover such things as expectations, objectives, compensation, working conditions, benefits, incentive opportunities, constraints, timetables, etc. These are all a part of our normal life and need to be there.

But more is needed . . . [particularly] covenants.

Covenantal relationships enable corporations and institutions to be hospitable to the unusual person and to unusual ideas. Covenantal relationships enable participation to be practiced and inclusive groups to be formed.

—*pp. 6-8, 22-25.*

....

After the heyday of the Reformation, some Calvinists tried to preserve the pure faith by walling it off from "worldly" pursuits, to which they consigned art and literature. In the middle of the twentieth century, Henry Zylstra issued a clarion call for reclaiming these talents—and, by implication, all others—as parts of God's kingdom.

From *Testament of Vision,* by Henry Zylstra:

We are Calvinists. Our Christian conviction is a Reformed conviction. And it is part of that conviction that the religious and spiritual cannot exist in a void, in isolation from life. It is part of the Reformed conviction that the spiritual in us requires human fulfillment, human embodiment. It is part of the Reformed conviction that the religious in us is part and parcel of the rest of us. We maintain that, so far from identifying science, and nature, and culture, and literature, and history with the world, and so expressing the antithesis of Christian and world in ignoring them, we must know, judge and appropriate these all, and express the antithesis of Christian and world through them. We are not Barthians in this sense that we think God's will is unknowable to man, "wholly other," as the phrase is, and virtually irrelevant to history. We are not Manicheans: the world is not the Devil's; the earth is the Lord's and the fullness thereof, the world and they that dwell therein. True, we know the kingdom is spiritual, and not to be identified with any historical cultural product; but we know that we have no means of building for the spiritual kingdom except by cultural means as human beings living on this earth at this point in history. Hence we are not anxious about civilization, as though in this life only we had hope. We are not liberals, identifying the task of the church with, and losing the Gospel message in a preoccupation with cultural concerns. We are not monastic. We neither retire into monasteries, nor into small scale social orders of our own. As a matter of fact, ours is not the facile dualism between church on the one hand, and practical life on the other, the practical life construed then as a way of making some money to continue the work of the church. . . . It is as human beings that we are Christians, in our human nature expressing itself in a natural environment, expressing itself also in cultural activity of all kinds, and further, in a particular historical situation here on earth. Our being called to be saints does not exempt us from being human, nor exempt us from cultural activity, nor exempt us from social and political obligation, nor render reason superfluous, nor permit an indifference to art and literature, nor lift us out of history. On the contrary, it is in and through these things that our moral and religious choice for the spiritual kingdom of Christ becomes concrete, real, and meaningful. . . .

Now this humanness of ours in which we must be educated, through which we must express both our opposition to the spirit of the world and our choice for the kingdom of Christ, includes a lot. It includes, for instance, that part of us which we share with inorganic and organic nature. We are chemical and physical and biological in part, and so is our environment. Thence the natural sciences in our curriculum. We have, further, a nervous organization, akin to that of an animal, and yet differing from it, and so we learn psychology. And at that point the uniqueness of the human creature among created beings asserts itself rapidly. We are conscious. We have mind. We can think. We are moral. We can make choices. We have creative freedom. We can make things out of things, expressive of higher things. You will remember that second chapter of Genesis: "And God formed every beast of the field, and every fowl of the air, and brought them unto Adam, to see what he would call them." There lies the human uniqueness, the gift of reason, the expressiveness of language. And it is in this area of our humanity that most of the subjects lie: science, government, history, mathematics, literature, social studies, and the rest. There are the materials proper of school education. By means of these, religious man enters into scientific man, aesthetic man, social man, practical man, and the rest. All of these are involved in the shaping and maturing of the Christian choice for God. . . .

And this is a further fact: whatever is human is religious. The religious in us is as natural and as real to us as the moral, or the rational, as the scientific and aesthetic, as the biological and psychological, as the social and historical. This religious in us, I say, is a part of our being a creature; it is, I say, natural to us. And this continues so in spite of the pervasive presence of sin. Just as we continue to be human beings now that sin has invaded us, so we continue to be religious beings. We say sometimes that man has become a beast because of the presence of sin, but that is only a way of speaking. Man cannot escape being human; if he could, his approaching the bestial would not be a gross disgrace to him. And so he continues to be religious, though to be sure, except for the intervening grace of God, the religion will be false. We sometimes say of people also that they are irreligious. We understand each other when we say that: we probably mean that they are profane, or pay no attention to the things of the church. But there are no irreligious people. The question is one only of a false or of the true religion. And, again, we sometimes say of a book that it is a godless book, or of a nation that it is a godless nation. There, too, we understand what is meant, and there can be no particular objection to such a way of speaking: we mean of course that the god who is served in the book or the nation is not the one true God. But that is the limit of the figure of speech. The fact is that wherever there is a man, there a God is worshipped. All men require a God for the vindication of themselves, the justification of their thoughts and actions, the justification, too, of their cultural activity. . . .

It is so easy in the name of Christianity to turn one's back to art, to science, to politics, to social problems, to historical tensions and pressures, in one word, to culture, if you will. But once the conviction seizes on you that these all, precisely because they are cultural realities, exhibit a religious allegiance and an ultimate loyalty, that none of them is neutral but rather that all of them are faith-founded, all laid on an altar, all dedicated to a god, then you realize that they are the very least important. Then you realize, too, that the true discernment of the God behind the culture, the assumption underlying the thought, the dogma beneath the action, the soul in the body of the thing, are precisely what it is the business of our schools as schools to disclose and to judge. In that lies the strengthening of the moral sinews of our young Christians. It is so that their choice for Christ and God can become a meaningful human choice. Christianity versus culture: no, it is the fundamentalist heresy. Culture alone: indeed not; it is the liberal heresy. Christianity through culture: the religious in man governing, shaping, determining the scientific, artistic, social in him, precisely; it is the Reformed truth.

—pp. 92-93, 96-97, 99.

....

As Zylstra's statement indicates, the issue of nurturing gifts often arises in the context of education, and education has long been a Reformed strong suit. Yet the tone of duty and the goal of professional success that pervade learning might keep us from enjoying all our skills as responses to God. John Bolt's remarks on this theme conclude with a call to Christ-centered hope that echoes the venerable words of the Heidelberg Catechism and the contemporary strains of Our Song of Hope that began this section on personal gifts and abilities.

From *Christian and Reformed Today*, by John Bolt:

Joy must be a hallmark of good Christian education. Joy is necessary because God created the world to enjoy it. When we ask the question of why God created the world, we can only answer: because of His good pleasure. God saw what He had made and rejoiced in its goodness. The Book of Proverbs (8:30-31) notes that God's wisdom, by which He created all things "was daily His delight rejoicing before Him always, rejoicing in His inhabited world and delighting in the sons of men." Creation is rooted in God's free good pleasure and serves His and man's joy. Joy is also a key characteristic of the new heaven and the new earth as Isaiah (65:17-19) describes it: "For behold, I create new heavens and a new earth; and the former things shall not be remembered or come to mind. But be glad and rejoice forever in that which I create; for behold, I create Jerusalem a rejoicing city and her people a joy; I will rejoice in Jerusalem, and be glad in my people."

This citation from Isaiah is very important because it underscores the need for a trinitarian framework in which the Holy Spirit and eschatology are every bit as *educationally* significant as the Father, creation and culture. If it is true that life in the creation and culture is to be characterized by joy, then a school cannot cultivate joy in its students by merely cultivating the enjoyment of creation and culture. Not in *our* day at least. Our educational systems and institutions today have material, creational and cultural advances as never before, and make them virtually universally accessible. Yet the "products" of our society's schools seem depressingly joyless. Why? Because in *our* age (the age of the Spirit, the last days), creation and culture in themselves are not enough. With the prospect of nuclear war hanging over our heads, with the growing likelihood of being unable to find employment after graduation, with war, poverty and famine on the increase, delight and joy in creation and culture are very difficult for many young people. Creational and cultural excess are joined with cynicism and apathy. While Christians should not be naive about or indifferent to real problems in our world, they do have hope and can be joyful. Joy is a fruit of the Holy Spirit; while we cannot make fruit grow, we do create the conditions in which it either flourishes or withers. If schools and teachers are to cultivate true joy in learning, creation and culture cannot stand alone. Joy needs room or permission if it is to flourish. We know that activities which are prohibited or forbidden prevent genuine enjoyment. Guilt intrudes and saps true joy. Christians who grow up with excessive prohibitions against cultural activities such as theater and dance require some form of permission, even if it comes from a rationalized conscience, in order to participate in them freely. Marriage counselors remind us that we need permission to enjoy our sexuality. For the Christian, joy is rooted in the fact that God the Creator delights in the world He fashioned and that we are thus permitted, given the freedom by Him, to enjoy it. "For everything created by God is good and nothing is to be rejected if it is received with thanksgiving for then it is consecrated by the word of God and prayer" (I Timothy 4:4-5). Joy is possible only when we affirm and say "Amen" to God's creation.

Yet it is precisely here that we encounter the objection briefly considered a moment ago. Christians, reflecting upon the state of our world, could object: "How can we sing the Lord's song in a strange land?" or as a Negro spiritual has it, "How can I play when I'm in a strange land?" Would a real Tevye in a real Russia not sing Psalm 137, weeping by the rivers of Babylon, rather than the light, dancing, joyful strains of "If I Were a Rich Man"? Is it not in bad taste to enjoy dessert when millions are starving? Can we be joyful before we overcome world poverty and malnutrition?

It is indeed true that in a sinful, broken world, joy needs love. We have no right to talk about joy or enjoyment if in our creational affluence and cultural abundance we are indifferent to the plight of the needy and oppressed. We may not abuse joy by making it captive to an ideology which uncritically allows exploitation to continue in the name of enjoying the creation. Joy without love is empty and self-deceiving. However, love and concern with joy is moralism; we do need permission to enjoy God's gifts without guilt. This is our Father's world, and we may find joy as well as rest in that truth. The certainty which arises out of Christian hope makes our joy in creation and culture possible today. This brings us to another dimension of joy.

One of the remarkable affirmations of the New Testament is that Christians who follow their Lord are to find joy in suffering (the cross). Peter tells us (I Peter 4:12) that we are to rejoice when we share the sufferings of Christ. James (1:2) notes: "Consider yourselves happy indeed my brethren, when you encounter trials of every sort." "Blessed (happy) are the mourners." The journey that leads to joy must travel through the valley of sorrow. In the sixteenth chapter of John's gospel, Jesus reminds His disciples that they will be sorrowful, but that their sorrow will turn into joy that cannot be taken away from them.

Two things flow from this: 1) the suffering and sorrows of this present age are not eternal and are not worth comparing with the glory that shall be revealed to us (Romans 8:18). We find joy in assurance of the final triumph of God's kingdom. 2) There is joy in our present life not through avoidance of suffering but *in* it. It is the paradox of the Christian experience that joy is found *in* the cross and in cross-bearing. The apostles rejoiced that they were considered worthy to suffer for the name of Jesus (Acts 5:41).

Learning which cultivates and promotes joy, in other words, must be seen in a trinitarian perspective. Father, Son and Holy Spirit, creation, cross and hope are inseparable also in education. Only that education which begins by acknowledging God's joy (pleasure, glory) as the foundation and goal of reality can truly have joy in learning. It is the task of the Christian school and the Christian teacher to assist students in the joy of discovering that this world is God's world. This means concretely that teachers must delight (take joy) in their subject matter and radiate the joy of the Lord in their own walk of life. Not only knowledge of subject matter but joy in it and enthusiasm for it are essential. It also means that we must not consider subjects whose primary purpose is to cultivate delight (art, music, literature) as secondary luxuries but every bit as crucial as writing, arithmetic and computer science. Christian schools may, in the next few years, especially in the face of a sluggish economy, face a real temptation to go the way of the "world" and to focus programs and curricula on "useful" courses, i.e., those that give students employable, marketable skills. In the crunch, the art, drama, and music courses and teachers might be the first ones considered expendable. This would be a serious mistake. Christian schools must not be tyrannized by what the world considers *economically* useful, at least not if there is to be joy in our learning. Christian students need to learn that there is a life-long joy in studying the humanities that cannot be measured by "how much will it pay me?" On this score too, Christians must resist that spirit of our age.

The joy that comes with the cross also requires of Christian education that it cultivates a spirit of caring and compassion for a suffering world, a care that is directed toward the world beyond our affluent West but also to the suffering within Christian schools. The slow learner comes to mind here. Christians must not apologize for striving for academic excellence in their schools. But a Christian school must not become elitist. If it lacks the compassion for those who find learning more difficult, if it is unable to rejoice with their accomplishments then Christian education has lost its soul. For this reason competition in Christian schools should be focused less on *external* competition between students and more on the *internal* competition that the student experiences with his or her own personal mastery of a subject or activity.

Finally, joy dies without hope. What does it profit Christian day school education if it gains the whole world of culture and loses hope? If the students who graduate from Christian educational institutions lack the joy and confidence that comes from the certainty that the triune God is also in charge of history and will bring it to a glorious conclusion, the educational process has in large measure failed. Christian schools and teachers have an obligation to counter the gloom and despair of our age with the hope of the gospel or else their basic task in cultivating Christian socio-cultural obedience collapses.
—*pp. 117-121.*

11. Why are families important to our lives as Christians?

**Q. What is God's will for you
in the fifth commandment?**

A. That I honor, love, and be loyal to
     my father and mother
     and all those in authority over me;
  that I obey and submit to them, as is proper,
     when they correct and punish me;
  and also that I be patient with their failings—
  for through them God chooses to rule us.

—Heidelberg Catechism Q & A 104.

Since God made us male and female in his image,
one sex may not look down on the other,
nor should we flaunt or exploit our sexuality.
Our roles as men and women must conform
to God's gifts and commands
as we shape our cultural patterns.
Sexuality is disordered in our fallen world;
grief and loneliness are the result;
but Christ's renewing work gives hope
for order and healing
and surrounds suffering persons
with a compassionate community.

—Our World Belongs to God, st. 47.

The Reformation of the sixteenth century gave new luster to family life. The new middle class in the nineteenth century made the nuclear family the center of their society and their sentiments. As heirs to both developments, Reformed Christians in North America have invested an enormous stake in the family, which makes recent strains on family life deeply troubling.

As our selections here show, there are right and wrong reasons for our anxiety, biblical and idolatrous components in the family ideal. James H. Olthuis focuses on the psychological dynamics of family life, grounding these in the Scripture's norm of troth.

From *I Pledge You My Troth,* by James H. Olthuis:

The family is a gift of the Lord to mankind, a "room" in the creation for man's benefit. God did not leave man alone in an uncharted, unstructured world; rather, he so structured the world by his creative Word that man could know how to live. As a human community the family is structurally anchored in the law-order of God and takes its place as one of the central "rooms" in the creation.

Man comes to life in the family; he learns to love in the family. The family is his nursery, his first school, it is his initial world and his launching pad into the big outdoors. As he participates in the family, he experiences the diversity of life without having to bear full responsibility for all that happens. The family is his place of joy and sadness; it is the place where he learns to take and bear responsibility. In the family he learns the meaning of keeping his word. In the family he learns to express his feelings and to know himself; he finds his identity; he experiences intimacy. Without the family the young child stands unprotected against the world. Without a family a child is alone, forced to live before he has even learned how. Nothing is more tragic than children worn out by life just when life should be opening up its riches.

Troth Is the Key

The family ought to be a community of troth between parents and children based on the instinctual biotic drive for motherhood and fatherhood and on the subsequent blood ties. Again, the key word here is *troth*, that is loyalty, trust, fidelity, devotion, and reliability. Troth is a pledged vow; it is the central norm or standard to be worked out in the family. In the measure that troth develops, a family prospers: loyal, trustworthy parents make for loyal, trustworthy children and vice versa. Likewise, unfaithful children and unfaithful parents belong together. Family relations are reciprocal and interdependent in nature. The family is a call to intimacy.

The fact that children are born into a family (or are adopted into it) does not in itself make a family. The arrival of children is only the basis upon which a family must be built. Blood ties provide the foundation for the family unit—but that is all. In contrast to animals, man's bio-psychic structures require unfolding under the leading of other human dimensions. . . .

Blood ties by themselves are not enough to ensure troth in the family, for fathers and mothers can turn on their children. Unless father and mother exercise troth in nurturing their children, they are not really fathers and mothers in the basic sense. If troth is exercised, even if the children are adopted, the parenthood is true. Sometimes a child knows and feels that his real parent is someone other than his "natural" parent.

Becoming a parent is not the trick; it is being a parent. A family must work at developing, strengthening, and conserving the bond of troth between its members. Only then is there a real family. All family activities—balancing the budget, attending worship services, skating, and just plain living—are to take place under the norm of troth. Father, mother, and children are called to intimacy. They are devoted to each other, they help each other, and they pledge their love to each other. In this kind of unity they are a family.

Nurture

In the intimacy of the family, parents must lead, educate, steer, guide, and nurture their children so that they come to see the norms that hold for life and so that they will be able to bear the responsibility of living according to these norms. Although others may point their children to other standards, Christian parents must help their children see the Lord's norms for life so that they can wholeheartedly serve him. Out of love the parents must guide their children so carefully that they will gradually come to accept responsibility for their own lives. Their goal is to prepare their children to live responsible, useful lives as the Lord's representatives. . . .

Establishing families as troth communities is no easy matter. We are helped in this situation to think of the family as a place of rest, adventure, and guidance. The family is first of all a place of rest. The family home is a place of troth, security, and peace, where a child can come to himself and can feel safe—no matter what. He knows that he will always be accepted, even if he does poorly in school, even if he can't do arithmetic and his father wants him to take over the family business, even if he does not want to be a farmer and his father has the best farm in the country. He can count on his parents, and they can count on him. He does not have to worry about being the best at everything or about proving himself. He knows that his parents will love him even if he does not meet their expectations.

The child who is fully accepted at home can grow and discover his own identity without looking for meaning in tests of physical daring or in sexual attractiveness. Consequently, he develops a certain self-confidence and aplomb in doing some things well. Nothing is more important for a child than his parents' acceptance, and there is nothing that he senses sooner than their rejection. He needs to know that his parents will stand by him always. They may not approve, but they will understand. Such unconditional acceptance is the birthright of every child; without it family troth cannot develop as it should.

Regrettably, many modern families make love conditional. The child hears his parents' message: "If you fulfill this goal or accomplish that purpose, you will be wanted and loved." He feels the constant pressure to succeed, to match the accomplishments of a petted high-achiever. Meanwhile he becomes miserable and insecure.

Even permissive parents attach strings to their love; if they do all they can for their children, they naturally expect that their children will indulge their every whim in return. Often the child becomes emotionally insecure because he is overwhelmed with the obligation to fulfill his parents' wishes. Such conditional love is both destructive and contrary to the norm of troth for the family. . . .

Once the child begins the uncertain task of trying to earn his parents' love, he loses the freedom and trust he needs to learn to know himself. He becomes anxious and uncertain of his own worth. He begins to read any critique from his parents as confirmation of the rejection he fears.

In families where intimacy and troth are guaranteed, a child develops roots and matures as a person. He learns to accept critique as constructive rather than a personal attack. No one needs masks in such a home because parents and children are authentic, free to be themselves and express their real feelings and opinions. The rest of the family may not always approve of these feelings and opinions, but they always respect them. Together the family will work through differences and express their joy and sorrow. Troth enables people to live freely, authentically, joyfully before the Lord. Children don't have to struggle for their parents' attention. Their parents tell them openly, warmly about life, about sex and health, about the meaning of troth, about whatever children want to know. Since they can disagree without breaking their trust, the family can discuss anything, knowing that they can count on each other's help, encouragement, and understanding. . . .

Home Is Adventure

The first priceless gift parents can give their children is roots. The second is wings. Safe in the security of his home, the child gains confidence and is encouraged to look to the world beyond the family. Guided by his parents the child tries different activities and learns what he does well and what he does badly. He opens up to the world and discovers that the family is not closed off in itself, but is one part of the kingdom of God. Family projects, everyday adventures, and times of deep family sharing kindle his spontaneity, creativity, and individuality.
—*pp. 78-80, 83-85.*

....

Lewis B. Smedes explores the social implications of family nurture. He begins here with reflections on the fifth commandment—which opens the "second table" of the Law—and moves on to the theme of covenant.

From *Mere Morality*, by Lewis B. Smedes:

The scattered biblical data give us some hints of what honoring a parent meant. A child was early led to understand that he was brought into life and was to find his own identity as a member of a family, not as a mere individual. He knew that he was not an equal in the family alliance, but was expected to defer to his parents as go-betweens between himself and God, mediators of his own past and pointers to his future. He accepted them as his teachers and guides, as well as his trusted protectors and nourishers. When he listened with respect and learned what he was taught, he honored his parents.

It is not hard to see why the commandment speaks of honor rather than love. Love is a natural impulse born of our intense desire to be close to someone we need. The commandment simply assumes that children will love their parents. Love is a natural impulse; honor is a moral choice. These two drives push children in opposite directions, and in doing so create most of the tension and vitality in their relationships with parents. Honor separates them; love draws them together. Honor keeps a distance, maintains a certain reserve; love pulls them close, creates a certain intimacy. When she honors her parents, a daughter stands back a bit, keeps her place, lets the parent keep to himself, with his own mystery. When she loves her parents, a child shares all, invades their sacred places, and enters her parents' private heart. Honor respects the gap between them; love bridges it. Honor is an act of the will that defers and stands back; love is an impulse of the heart that leans on a mother's breast at one stage and gently tucks a feeble mother to bed at another.

Honor and love need each other. Without love honor is frigid, strained, forced, infected with resentment, a hollow shell of polite anger. Without honor love lacks structure and is eventually destructive. Between parents and child, love without honor stands family life on its head, confuses the primal relationship of the human race. Honor is the moral fiber that holds the family together so that all the warm and loving, cold and hateful feelings between parent and child can be enjoyed and endured in a structure of loyalty and respect.

What is there about parents that makes it imperative for children to treat them with honor? We are not asking what a parent needs to do to *earn* the right to honor; parents have a presumptive right to honor simply because they have conceived and cared for a child. The child's duty assumes the parents' right—but why? . . .

If there is a single reason why parents have a right to their children's respect, I suggest it is *authority*. Within the small society called a family, in which joyful and painful human intimacies are experienced in the fundamental human relationship, one of the strong fibers that holds the alliance together is the authority of the parent. Authority is not a popular facet of family life today, and countless homes have deliberately abandoned it, mistaking authority for a kind of tyranny which all who respect the rights of children should overthrow. Nevertheless, I am going to argue that parental authority, rightly understood, is the one quality all parents have which corresponds to the honor that children are asked to give them. Authority, moreover, is the backbone of family life. So important is it to the strength of the human community that the Lord God—in one of the five primal commandments for human life—called us all to honor our parents for their calling to nurture and guide us, the children set in their care.

Fear of authority

Among those who claim to be experts on effective parenting today, authority is generally in bad graces. Such aversion to authority plays on our fears of being manipulated into someone else's control. We are especially afraid of the oppression of the young; we fear parental tyrants who force children to do "good" while holding them in bondage. . . .

Authority has become hopelessly confused with authoritarianism, though in truth they are utterly opposed to each other. . . . authoritarianism and authority are related as sickness is to health. Authoritarianism is a pathological caricature of authority. Authoritarianism is sick compensation for weakness; authority is a healthy expression of strength. Authoritarian people stifle freedom; authority requires freedom to make it work. Authoritarianism works only when people surrender their own wills; authority works only when people give free and critical consent.

Fear of authority is, in our time, actually a fear of authoritarianism, a confusion that cries for cure. . . .

Parents cannot give up authority, however, without robbing their children—and eventually society—of strengths neither can do without. The first thing a child loses in a home without authority is a strong sense of his own identity. We become strong individuals when we spend our childhood in a strong family. The child with a clear sense of place in a family is likely to develop a clear sense of who and what he is outside of it. The fact that suicide is now the second most common cause of adolescent deaths in the U.S. cannot be wholly unrelated to the loss of authority in the American home. Genuine authority, based in parents' belief in their calling, is probably the most reliable source from which a child can derive a sense of belonging to a family circle held together by loyalty and love. To know who one is and to whom one belongs is to have a sturdy support against the despair and joylessness of those who cannot find their real selves amid the fantasies of their minds.

Second, it is only reasonable to suppose that loss of authority within the family will affect a child's ability to live with authority in society. Parents who give strong and purposeful leadership teach their children to live with and recognize true authority. If a child develops personally in an atmosphere where trust, loyalty, and honor are expected of him, he is well on his way toward responsible life in a society whose health depends on mutual trust, strong loyalties, and a critical caution with regard to all claims of authority. Permissive parents rob society of people who can distinguish genuine authority from its counterfeits. . . .

From Jesus we can draw a few tentative guidelines for thinking about the authority parents have to lead and teach and direct their children.

1. Authority is a union of legitimacy and power; the right to use power to influence people, even to prevail over them, gives a person what we call authority.

2. A person's authority must be believed by the people he hopes to lead; no one can function as an authority unless people are willing to trust him.

3. Persons have genuine authority only when they use power over people to nurture people into responsible freedom.

What we see, then, is that authority is a reality which exists only in a relationship where the authority-bearer and the authority-follower are active. People have no real authority unless they are trusted and believed; and no one deserves to be trusted unless he or she helps people be free.

Derived from the family

Why does an adult who happens to conceive and channel a human being into the world have the right to shape and form that child's life? Is it because the mother and father are smarter and wiser than a child? Hardly, since other adults are smarter and wiser than the parent and they could teach the child even more efficiently. Is it because the child owes parents obedience in return for the lavish sum they spend on his or her care? Hardly, the right to expect a return on your investment does not give you authority to influence another person at the core of his life. No, if parents have authority, it comes from their special roles within that troubled community of care we call a family. So we should ask what a family is.

A family is a group of people bound together in a covenant of care for one another. Though blood is a family's natural bond, it does not create a family. The sheer fact that people live together under one roof does not create a family, contrary to the U.S. Census Bureau's definition of a family as "two or more persons related by blood, adoption, or marriage and residing together." In a moral sense, what binds people together as family is the covenant of loyalty to one another from birth to death. . . .

The Judaeo-Christian perspective, however, sees the circle of covenanted care as the right setting for the nurture of children into commitment to what is right and true about life. Parents are parents mainly to take care of the child's initiation into faith and morals. And the two go together. Morality has to do with what is truly important and right about life, and what is important about life depends on what is true about God. So, the heart of family is the parents' calling to pass on the moral and spiritual reality of life to their children. The covenant of caretaking, then, creates the family. In this context alone we can understand how a parent has authority and why the child has an obligation to honor the parent.

A family is not a spillover from our romantic passions, nor a product of society's requirement that parents provide their offspring with bed and board, nor a little circle of people deriving emotional support from living together, nor a social contrivance for keeping our broods in control, one which could become obsolete if a social planner were to find a better one. In a Judaeo-Christian sense, family is rooted in the Creator's design for the ongoing nurture of children who bring faith and moral value into the next generation. To undermine, neglect, or replace it is to wreck the core community that makes all other community possible. . . .

There is a curious twist to the working of authority in a family. True authority, I have tried to say, is exercised—and in a way created—in dialogue. You cannot exercise authority unless the people you want to influence. believe in you. This is as true of parental authority as of any other. A parent needs to exercise authority in order to awaken the child's belief in it. Belief for a child takes the form of trust. Where the simplest, least educated, and least skilled parent believes in his own authority as a parent, the child learns to trust him. The courage to tell my daughter what I believe helps make me credible in her eyes. A child does not lose trust when a mother makes a mistake, or when a father exposes his ignorance on a point of theology or ethics. A child loses trust when he senses that his father and mother do not really believe what they say they believe.

Aimed at the child's freedom

The goal of parental authority is freedom. Parents' authority aims at releasing the child from their authority. This does not mean that parents lead their children toward freedom from authority, but that they use parental authority to help the child develop a responsible freedom that will enable him to live with—and be critical of—all other human authority.

The authority pattern of the family teaches a child how to live freely and critically within the authority structures of society. Living with parents who believe in their own authority and understand its purpose, children learn what authority is really for. Thus they learn how to size up anyone who claims to be an authority. Any society has powerful people who claim the right to influence and control others. Cultists, on the fringes of society, religious and secular alike, deploy mesmerizing gifts to seduce people who never have had a life experience with genuinely caring authority into giving up their freedom for the sake of security.

Every parent who claims the right to respect for his authority must keep this in mind; parental authority aims at critical freedom under all authority.

—*pp. 70-75, 79-83.*

....

From a Christian feminist perspective, Mary Stewart Van Leeuwen puts family in its place: a high but secondary place within the mission of Christians' "first family," the church.

From *Gender & Grace*, by Mary Stewart Van Leeuwen:

Marriage . . . is part of God's basic creation order. That God intended it to be a lifelong, "one flesh" monogamous union is both affirmed in the creation accounts and reaffirmed by Jesus (Mk 10; Mt 19: Lk 16). Certainly one does not have to marry in order to image God or carry out the cultural mandate in cooperation with others. But neither is marriage simply God's "second best" solution for those who cannot contain their lust well enough to serve him as celibate singles, as some medieval theologians taught. Marriage is part and parcel of what God has approved for human life on earth, reflecting the unity-in-diversity of Father, Son and Holy Spirit, as well as being the vehicle through which future imagers of God are procreated.

Now if we could merely stop with a creation theology of marriage, we might be able to justify (or at least excuse) the idealized descriptions of family life which, as we have seen, some Christians espouse. But, as we know only too well, the Fall has introduced distortions into all aspects of creation, including the relationship between women and men. And the Old Testament is quite unsparing in its documentation of the results. It presents us with accounts of rape, adultery, incest and polygamy gone wild. (King Solomon had seven hundred wives and three hundred concubines!) It adds accounts of further sins aimed at covering up sexual sins, such as King David's plot to murder the husband of the woman he impregnated. And it presents such events not primarily as the acts of pagans trying to undermine Israelite society, but as the acts of God's own people. Nor are these abuses of creational sexuality limited to men. We have accounts of women scheming to get their favorite sons into positions of primacy in the family (Rebekah) and to get heirs in the first place by means God has forbidden—through incest, as in the case of Lot's daughters or by mating a husband with a servant, as in the cases of Sarah, Rachel and Leah.

None of this, of course, is meant to portray God's intentions for marriage and family life. Rather, in Gretchen Gaebelein Hull's words, it is "the true record of a false idea"—an accurate portrayal of fallen men and women, "warts and all." Just as importantly, it is intended to show the Israelites that, despite their special status as the nation through which the Messiah comes, they cannot save themselves by trying to manipulate their bloodlines—let alone by departing from God's norms for faithful marriage. When the Messiah comes, he comes in God's time and by God's means—and although his coming and his message reaffirm the creational shape of family life, they also *relativize* it for the rest of human history, in the interests of bringing God's kingdom to completion. . . .

Moreover, Jesus' own life and teachings underscore the fact that marriage and family now take back seat to the universal proclamation of God's salvation and the formation of a new "first family"—a world-wide kingdom-building company, in which membership depends not at all on bloodlines, but on faith in the Messiah. Note that though he radically affirms women's worth, Jesus himself stays unmarried in order to better fulfill his mission. Although he confirms God's intention for monogamous marriage and performs his first miracle in the context of a marriage feast, he announces that the final, eternal state of humanity will *not* include the marriage bond (Mk 12:25). Moreover, he demands that his disciples place marriage and family loyalty second to their allegiance to him, "If anyone comes to me and does not hate his own father and mother and wife and children and brothers and sisters, yes, and even his own life, he cannot be my disciple" (Lk 14:26).

None of this is a license for Christians to treat the marriage bond casually. Although the disciples "leave all to follow him," nowhere is there evidence that this meant literally hating or abandoning their wives. In fact, just after Peter's call, Jesus goes to the latter's home and heals his mother-in-law. Later, after Jesus' resurrection and ascension, we learn that Peter and various other apostles took their wives on missionary journeys. What Jesus' teaching does mean, for both women and men, is that commitment to Christ and his kingdom comes before any other commitment. "The radical mistake of the human race," writes Bromiley, "is that of pushing God into second or third or last place . . . of giving a higher value to other goals than to the purpose of God." In doing so, ironically, humans lose the means by which those other goals, including marriage and family, can become most satisfying. For it is only by making God's kingdom their primary commitment that humans avoid worshiping "the created, rather than the creator," a sure recipe for disappointment in the end.

The problem, then, with Christian romanticization of the "traditional" family is not primarily that it tries to freeze a particular set of gender roles in time (although this is certainly a problem) nor even that it underestimates the sin and violence that can take place in the family (although this too is a problem). *The root problem is one of creeping idolatry—of putting first what should come, at best, second.* Look [at statements] from popular Christian literature on the family. Do we "achieve security, a sense of well-being and belonging *only* through the family"? The first question of the Heidelberg Catechism asks: "What is your only comfort in life and death?" Answer: "That I am not my own [nor, by implication, my family's] but belong—body and soul, in life and in death—to my faithful Savior Jesus Christ." Is the family our "last bastion against depersonalization and dehumanization?" If so, then the family of God—the church universal—is in bad shape, and is not fulfilling its radical, kingdom-building function. Is the family "the basic institution that undergirds all else"? No, not in any of the acts of the biblical drama. God's covenant with humanity, first in creation, then in salvation, is the basis on which Christians build everything else.

Role versus Priorities

None of this is meant to imply that the institutional church is potentially any freer than the family from corruption and self-worship. The New Testament does not identify the kingdom of God with the church per se, but with the restored rule of God over all things. Thus abusive, authoritarian families . . . often find their way into churches whose leadership style mimics and reinforces the least healthy aspects of their own family life. Nor am I trying to suggest that families per se are unimportant—either psychologically or in the economy of God's kingdom. I am so convinced of the family's importance for children's development that I have made as strong a case as I can for increased fatherly involvement in childrearing. . . . The point, in Rodney Clapp's words, is simply this: "For the Christian, church is First Family. The biological family, though still valuable and esteemed, is Second Family. Husbands, wives, sons, and daughters are brothers and sisters in the church first and most importantly—secondly they are spouses, parents, or siblings to one another."

And Clapp goes on to point out that "exactly as family is how the New Testament church behaves." It extends hospitality to a wide range of Christians and others. Its central sacrament draws on the analogy of a family meal. At their best, both "first" and "second" families are a magnet for unbelievers who are drawn to the love that is shared within and beyond their boundaries. . . .

We should also note that by restoring the family to its secondary, biblical place we can come a long way toward recovering a biblical respect for singleness. For despite the fact that Christians pay lip service to the equal value of married and single people, their near-idolatry of the family over the past century has made single Christians feel like second-class citizens at best and moral failures at worst. But when both states are evaluated in kingdom terms, their functions are clearly complementary: a stable Christian family may have a missionary advantage in providing hospitality. But the single person, unencumbered with family duties, often has the missionary advantage of mobility. And both are vital to the spread of the church.

So the root issue is not primarily one of "proper" gender roles for husbands and wives, if by "proper gender roles" we mean some historically fixed way of structuring family economic, domestic, and childrearing tasks. The root question is one of priorities. How can a given Christian family, with its particular constellation of talents, limitations and needs, so structure itself that it contributes to the advancement of God's kingdom on earth? As one woman put it in response to Clapp's article: "Perhaps the best environment for children is not one in which the mother stays home, but one in which the whole family, as part of the larger family of God, reaches out to meet the needs of others." Just *how* an individual family accomplishes this at various stages of family life is a matter of responsible Christian freedom. There is no one, "best" answer that fits every case.

—*pp. 172-77.*

....

Rod Jellema's poetry is saturated with family themes. The following two poems tie the generations from son to great-grandfather together in a skein of memory, loyalty, love, and—pointing to our next section—daily labor.

Heading In

Night breeze stirs the hair on my arm.
I hear trees moving along the shore.
The mast of my little boat
plots arcs and points in the dark,
uncertain. She bobs no light.

Son John and I all day have reaped the wind
and made the daggerboard tick
as we cut through sunlight and breakers.
His hands are quick to tiller and line.

White stars bloom soft down this desert of water.
Only my hands remember the day.
Each slow flap of sail is an ache in the arms.
I wish all boats had still a man's work,
could bring something back.

I am not quite lost in these reflections of stars.
Pakke's old cells call through my bones
to say, "you are losing your son,"
but a neighbor's light on the dune points home.

Some night as he sails here alone
my son will pick up and bring back
senses the mind can never know about wind,
his past, work, losses, his hands.

—*Rod Jellema. From* The Eighth Day,
p. 56.

The Work of Our Hands

He would come home tired at night from making things,
his hands still dreaming the prints of handles:
my *pakke*, great-grandfather, maker of windmills
            in Friesland.

Out of the wind, he would probably stare at his fire.
The work could go on alone, sails and beams
angled to translate every pull and push of wind
to the balance of brake-wheel.
While hand-cut spur gears rhyme the shaft,

his shapes could turn in drowsy in his head.
Only the hands remember a good day's work:
it's like falling asleep with your bride,
or fishing in the dark after the fish have stopped
but you think you feel them still through the hand.

I know that space. Though my *pakke* died before I was born,
carving ornate balustrades in Chicago mansions,
I finally fished and nailed and felt the wind and bought
a sail and now I know that throb in my hand.

The gift is tension, drag. I'll never wish again
to feel the sail rise up from the water and soar
toward the thrill and loop of a hollow scream:
even birds when they sing grip their hands down hard
into bark that is rooted and cuts the wind.

My hands hug shape. The prow leaps down for more.
Pakke, I write and sail as a displaced, unemployed millwright.
                —*Rod Jellema. From* The Eighth Day,
              p. 57.

12. How should we spend our work and leisure time?

In our work, even in dull routine,
we hear the call to serve our Lord.
We must work for more than wages,
and manage for more than profit,
so that mutual respect
and the just use of goods and skills
may shape the work place,
and so that, while we earn or profit,
useful products and services may result.
Rest and leisure are gifts of God
to relax us and to set us free
to discover and to explore.
Believing that he provides for us,
we can rest more trustingly
and entertain ourselves more simply.

—*Our World Belongs to God, st. 51.*

T he Reformation began with the insistence that we are saved by grace, not by works. Yet as we noted before, Calvinism became famous for its "work ethic." Reformed people thus seem tempted to repudiate their confession in practice: to talk about grace and to live by labor.

Paul A. Marshall recounts the biblical teachings which made the Reformers esteem daily labor, then notes both the degradation and overestimation to which work in our day is prone.

From "Calling, Work, and Rest," by Paul A. Marshall:

The importance of the cultural mandate [Gen. 1:28] shows the importance of the work to which humans are called as stewards of the earth. The Scriptures are full of praise for the work of human hands, hearts, and minds. Even God is described by analogy to human work, as the one who makes, forms, builds, and plants (Gen. 2:4, 7, 8, 19, 23). Work skills are described as gifts of God: "the Lord has called Bezalel . . . and he has filled him with the Spirit of God, with ability, with intelligence, with all knowledge and with all craftsmanship" (Exod. 35:30-32; see also Pss. 65:9-13; 104:22-24; Gen. 10:8-9).

Nor is this a theme that diminishes in the New Testament. Here we find Jesus immersed in the life and problems of working people. The apostles were mainly of humble background and sometimes returned to their work after being called by him. Jesus was a carpenter for all but the last few years of his life. His parables refer to sowers (Matt. 13:3), vineyard laborers (Matt. 13:30), harvesters (John 4:35), house building (Matt. 7:24), swine tending (Luke 15:11), and women sweeping houses (Luke 15:8).

Paul criticized idleness and exhorted Christians to work (2 Thess. 3:6). He made no distinction between physical and spiritual work and he used the same terms to refer to both the manual labor by which he earned a living and also his apostolic service (1 Cor. 4:12; 15:10; 16:16; Eph. 4:28; Rom. 10:12; Gal. 4:11; Phil. 2:16; Col. 1:29; 1 Thess. 5:12). Often it is quite difficult to know to which he was referring, or whether he himself was making such a distinction. For Paul, all types of work originate in faith and are service to God. When he outlines the "new nature . . . created after the likeness of God," he urges "doing honest work with his hands." The new creature, restored in Christ, in God's image, is to work in God's world to supply the needs of others and shape the development of human life (Eph. 4:17-32, esp. v. 28; 2 Cor. 11:9; 12:13; 1 Thess. 4:9-12; 2 Thess. 3:8; Acts 20:35).

Paul himself worked with his hands so as not to be a burden to the church; he worked to support others and he urged this practice on other Christians. His advice to slaves, that they should work willingly as slaves of Christ, illustrates the same theme. It shows that he regarded even slave labor as service to the Lord on a par with his own work. He summarized his position in the remarkable assertion that "there is neither . . . slave nor free . . . you are all one in Christ Jesus" (Eph. 6:6-7; Ga. 3:28). Similarly, his declaration "if anyone does not work, let him not eat" was not an expression of callousness toward those who could not support themselves—his program for deacons, collections on behalf of the poor, and sharing of goods show that this was not the case. Rather, Paul was concerned not with those who could not find work but with those who refused to share the burdens of their fellows. He was asserting that a life of leisure, religious contemplation, or eschatological abdication was a deficient life—that all members of the church should work (2 Thess. 3:10). Clearly this view was in radical opposition to the attitudes of Hellenistic culture. Paul did not regard religion as a "spiritual" activity separate from work. He regarded all aspects of life as equally religious, as equally noble, when done in loving service to God.

Even the New Heavens and the New Earth will include work. Isaiah prophesies that

> They shall build houses and inhabit them;
> they shall plant vineyards and eat their fruit.
> They shall not build and another inhabit;
> they shall not plant and another eat;
> for like the days of a tree shall the days of my people be,
> and my chosen shall long enjoy the work of their hands.
> —*Isa. 65:21-22*

When we read that "they will beat their swords into ploughshares and their spears into pruning hooks" (Mic. 4:35), we should remember not only the destruction of implements for war but also the (new) creation of implements for work.

In short, human beings are made, *inter alia,* as workers: this is part of what it means to be created in the image of God. We are called to work, and we are to find fulfillment in our working. Work has fallen under the curse of sin and so is torn with pain and suffering. But the curse is not the core of work: it is a cancer upon it. Work can be and will be fully redeemed as in the new creation it becomes an authentically free human action.

The Restoration of Work

The biblical teaching on work has three immediate implications. First it shows that all human activities are equally God-given, are equally religious. No one type of human activity can claim religious priority over another. Therefore we must echo Tyndale's declaration that "to wash dishes and to preach is all one, as touching the deed, to please God" and we must reject the semi-Gnosticism that has pervaded much of the Christian church, and especially its evangelical wing. Human beings are not apprentice angels better suited to and waiting for an existence on another spiritual plane. We are those whom God has made to tend the earth and serve one another through work. While sin has caused and will cause pain and frustration, work has not lost its character as service to Creator and creature.

Second, work must not be regarded as the antithesis of human fulfillment. We are not creatures destined for freedom who are now trapped in an alienated realm of necessity. We are called to manifest the image of God and, hence, to be free precisely *in and through* our work, in and through the necessities of life. This emphasis opposes the drift of our society where, while certain professions are thought to be fulfilling, work is generally treated as what economists call a "disutility," something to be minimized. . . .

Third, work is the act of a creature made in the image of God. Consequently work should be an action of responsibility carried out by a free image-bearer. This too can be contrasted with dominant social patterns, for an understanding of work as an activity reflecting the *imago dei* necessarily brings to the fore the theme of human responsibility as well as the theme of human freedom. We must concentrate not on wages as a "compensation" for work (though all people have a right to be sustained in and through their work) but on making work genuinely responsible. . . .

The development of such responsibility has a subjective side that requires a renewed sense of vocation and willingness to rejoice in servanthood. But we must beware of portraying the relationship of work and responsibility only as a question of personal renewal. Our work does not depend merely on our own motivations: it depends also on the attitudes, motivation, and actions of others, especially those who came before us and those who have power over us. Such attitudes have *already* been built into our property relations, into the factories and workplaces we have designed, the types of products we manufacture, the types of machines we work with, and the rhythm and pace of our work itself.

Individuals in an auto factory in Detroit conceivably can have a strong sense of their vocation to make good, relatively cheap cars that people will be happy to drive. But it is almost impossible to maintain such a sense if all you do is endlessly repeat the same mechanical action on an assembly line amid howling noise. In fact, in this type of situation a sense of vocation may be out of place because it is out of touch with reality. You are not being treated as a responsible person, an image-bearer of God. You are not being allowed to serve your neighbor. Work has ceased to be a calling and has become a pain, and money is the compensation for it.

We must restructure work so that it can honestly be a service and calling. We need to design workplaces and corporate structures so that we both exercise genuine responsibility and are treated as God's image-bearers. This means a concentration on good work and a rejection of the notion that "labor" and the worker are commodities to be bought and sold in a "labor" market. Those who work in an enterprise are to be responsible for it and need authority commensurate with that responsibility.

The Limits of Work

I have stressed the biblical teaching on the goodness and the redemption of work. But, given the modern secular stress on the salvific nature of work, we must also stress that work is not the means of salvation. Work is not the mediation between God and humankind, it cannot eradicate sin, it cannot produce a new creation. We cannot achieve happiness and security through the control of our human and nonhuman environments. . . .

Because we must worship God rather than idols, we must find our true end in what God has given, not in what we can achieve. Consequently we must continually be aware of the limits of human achievement. We remain creatures, and we cannot become gods either through our work or through anything else.

The limits on our work and on our achievement arise from two sources—the nature of created reality, and the consequences of sin. We must be aware of both of these. And we must also distinguish them carefully lest we identify creation and sin and, in consequence, either accept the triumph of sin by identifying our present broken situation with the will of God, or deny our status as creatures by attempting a Promethean struggle to escape our creaturehood.

Because of who we are in the creation, we will always need to work, our work will always present challenges, and it will always call us to responsibility. This necessity will remain a necessity; neither diligent labor, advanced technology, radical insight, fervent repentance, nor political revolution will overcome it. An attempt to do away with such limits is hubris, a replay of Babel.

But we must also emphasize that, because of sin, the good things that God has given in the creation have become distorted. Work has become toil, it is enmeshed in pain and suffering, it is long, and it can reduce us to automatons, or to scarecrows, or kill us. We are called to fight against these evil consequences, just as we, because of Christ's victory, are called to fight against all the effects of sin. Though pain in work will not finally disappear until the Lord's return we can never accept it passively: we are called continually to the struggle to transform the work of all human creatures into secure, free, and joyful service.

> —*Published in* Christian Faith and
> Practice in the Modern World,
> *pp. 208-14.*

....

Lee Hardy recalls the Reformers' concept of vocation as including but going well beyond our paid labor, and he draws out some of that concept's practical implications.

From *The Fabric of This World*, by Lee Hardy:

The Calvinists not only retained the Lutheran insistence on the dignity of labor, but they also elaborated the Reformed theology of work into a general understanding of the divinely intended order for human society. This understanding begins from the fact that God did not create us as individuals sufficient unto ourselves. We cannot by ourselves meet all of our needs, even our basic bodily needs, through our own efforts. Rather we depend upon others, as they depend upon us. This indicates God's intent that human beings should live in a society bound together by common needs and mutual service. Our lack of self-sufficiency necessarily draws us together into an interdependent society of persons. Furthermore, although we were created with the same basic needs, we were not created with the same talents and abilities. Each one of us cannot do all things equally well. Not all of us would make good neurosurgeons. That requires, among other things, a rare degree of manual dexterity. Not all of us would make good theoretical physicists. That requires a formidable amount of mathematical ability. Not all of us would make good finish carpenters. Some of us couldn't connect hammer to nail if our lives depended upon it. Possessing different gifts, each person is to occupy that particular station in life where those gifts can be exercised for the common good.

On the Reformed understanding then, human life is to be lived out in a society of mutual service and support, each member contributing according to his specific talents and receiving according to his need. The emphasis on the connection between work and social justice was clearly sounded by Calvin, and continued to reverberate in the subsequent works of English and American theologians in the Calvinist tradition. . . .

This understanding of human society serves in turn as a basis for apprehending our social obligations. Our talents and abilities were not given to us as tools to heap up fame and fortune for ourselves; rather they are to be exercised for the common good. In his *Institutes*, Calvin asserts that "all the gifts we possess have been bestowed by God and entrusted to us on condition that they be distributed for our neighbors' benefit." . . .

Work and vocation are not the same thing. Work may be a part of my vocation, but it is not the whole of my vocation; work may be one thing that I am called to do, but it is not the only thing I am called to do. As a husband I am called to love, honor, and encourage my wife; as a parent, to care and provide for my children; as a citizen, to be an informed participant in the political process; as a parishioner, to identify and make use of my spiritual gifts, edifying the community of faith; as a teacher, to instruct and advise my students. My vocation has many facets. If I am gainfully employed, my employment will count as only one of those facets.

This broad, rich, and variegated sense of vocation, encompassing all of life, goes back, as we saw, to Martin Luther's initial formulation of the concept of vocation in the sixteenth century. In Gustaf Wingren's study of Luther we read that "one's occupation and place of work are, according to Luther, contained in vocation, but it is also a vocation to be a father, mother, son, daughter, husband, wife, etc. Everything that brings me into relation with other people, everything that makes my actions events in other people's lives is contained in 'vocation.'"

In spite of its auspicious beginnings, however, the concept of vocation soon fell upon hard times. By the late seventeenth century the meaning of the word "vocation" had, in the vocabulary of the Puritans, been whittled down to the point where it meant little more than paid employment. One's particular calling was simply one's "special business." And one's special business was often thought a secular affair, alongside, or even in competition with, one's general calling to be a Christian.

This is an unfortunate development. But it leads directly to our present-day notion that a vocation is nothing more than a job. "Vocational training" means "job training." If we are asked what our vocation is, we are expected to say what we do for a living. It follows that finding one's "calling in life" is a matter of finding an occupation; that a person without a job is also without a vocation; and that the aspects of a person's life outside work do not have the dignity of being vocations—they are merely the insignificant details of personal life.

To gain a full-orbed, properly nuanced and balanced view of the place of work in human life, it is imperative to recover the broad sense of vocation. For an occupation is only one element in the total configuration of my vocation. After I've done my job as an employee, I still have other things to do as a spouse, a parent, a parishioner, a neighbor, and a citizen—not to mention the fact that I am also called to rest in leisurely contentment with God's goodness on the Sabbath. If I pour myself into my work, with nothing left over to give to my spouse, my children, church, community, or country, I have neither heard nor heeded the full scope of God's call in my life. For, as [Karl] Barth points out, human life "is not exhausted in the process of labor." Work, family, church, education, politics, and leisure must each of them find their place, shoulder to shoulder, under the concept of vocation.

The fact that our vocation has many dimensions brings with it the problem of "vocational integration." Luther once remarked that once we comprehend the full range of our duties to our neighbors we will quickly realize that we couldn't possibly fulfill them all, even if we each had four heads and ten hands. Over-responsible people tend to burn out quickly. The limitations of time and energy create dilemmas and call for trade-offs: do I go to my daughter's track meet or the church council meeting? Do I go out with my wife on Thursday night for coffee, or stay home and polish the Kant Lecture for Friday? Do I take advantage of an opportunity to hear my congressional representative speak . . . or do I spend more time with the Gospel of Mark? We are constantly making choices as to how we will spend our time. The question is: do our claims reflect the right priorities and proper balance?

Few of us can claim that our lives are well-balanced. And in our own culture, work is often the part of our vocation which claims disproportionately large amounts of our time and energy. Especially for those in the professions, the constant temptation is to make an idol of one's work. Other human relationships, even the relationship to God, must often make way for the high-speed pursuit of a successful career. . . .

Work is an important part of life, but it is not the whole of life. Moreover, the proper place of work in a person's life is an issue that must be posed anew from time to time, and may demand creative answers. Life is dynamic. It changes over time. The various facets of a person's vocation will interact with each other in different ways as that persons enters into new relations with other persons and as those persons change. The old answers to the question of work will not always be adequate to new situations. When a single person marries, the question of work must be posed anew, for married persons must learn how to adjust the pursuit of their vocations to each other: shall only the husband seek paid employment, or only the wife; or shall both seek full-time employment; if both seek full-time employment, should they do so at the same time, or should they "take turns"; or should both seek part-time employment? If children enter the picture, new considerations arise concerning their care and feeding as they grow up from being wholly dependent kids to surly teenagers to relatively independent adults with their own vocations to fulfill. Should the mother care for the children while the father goes to work, or should a more equitable distribution of parental responsibilities be sought?

Illness in the family, aging parents, unemployment, retirement, economic downturns, war, crucial moments in the life of the church or the nation that call for extraordinary involvement—all such eventualities can demand a reevaluation of the place of work in a person's life. There is nothing particularly sacred about being employed full time at the same job from age 21 to 65. A certain amount of flexibility is required in the organization of life; those who remain too rigid may miss their calling as it comes to them afresh.

—pp. 60-61, 111-14, 118.

....

In reaction against the work ethic, contemporary affluent societies have developed a cult, a virtual religion, of leisure and play. But this too has become a matter of strenuous activity, sacrifice, discipline—of hard work. Lewis B. Smedes proposes that a playful attitude should animate both our work and our leisure. His essay ends our tour at the place where it started: grace overcoming sin and issuing in a life of service on God's good earth.

From "Theology and the Playful Life," by Lewis B. Smedes:

Can life before the face of a holy God be an ultimately playful experience? Can a serious orthodox theology support a playful attitude in this worrisome world? Can play serve as a parable to tell us how to be co-laborers with God? This is my question. . . . [because Calvinists traditionally seem to view play as "a waste of time," as sin.]

Two things suggest another way of looking at sin and playfulness. One is that sin itself is a culprit for turning playful people into straightforwardly serious workers. Pride, the root sin, set the hod-carriers of Babel to work on their God-defying tower. The same sin set religious people under the law to try like grim graduate students to earn a favorable grade point average with God. The hard-working Pharisees, in their sin, were offended at Jesus for making burdens light and yokes easy. And it was the people who tried to turn the gospel back into a work ethic who aroused Paul's deepest anger. Sin creates the illusion that we must be workers or die forever. It is sinfulness, then, as much as our awareness of it, that prevents us from seeing the light from the parable of play.

The other, more crucial thing, is that grace relativizes the seriousness of sin. Grace prevents us from taking sin with undialectical seriousness. Since God took sin with undialectical seriousness, we may take it only with a trans-serious attitude; that is, we must be serious in dealing with it, but must not take sin itself as ultimately serious. Grace rescues us from sin's ultimate word, from the labor camp into which sin transformed life. It further liberates us from the depressing guilt of sin. Finally, grace creates the possibility that we can look sin in its grisly face and still say, "The living of life is a great good." Grace does not turn the world back into an Eden; it does not lead us into make-believe pleasure domes. But it does give the ultimate word that relativizes the nonplayful effects of sin.

184

The doctrine of vocation. The Reformers called the monks out of leisurely contemplation and led them back to work. Calvin in particular called them to accept their station as God-appointed and there do the job God appointed them to do. "Every man's mode of life, therefore, is a kind of station assigned him by the Lord; that he may not be driven about at random . . ." (*Inst.,* III.x.16) People are redeemed by Christ to fulfil their triadic office of prophet, priest, and king. Office means duty. Duty means work. And work means getting something done. Having an office is not the sad consequence of sin, or merely a survival requirement. It is the privilege given creatures of serving under their Great Taskmaster's eye.

There is, of course, a lot of work to be done. There are secrets of nature to be ferreted out, stupid ideas to be disputed, chaos to be ordered, mouths to be fed, roads to be built, souls to be saved—and a great deal more. This essay is not against work: my point is to ask whether we can have a playful attitude about our work.

The seriousness of our vocation is intensified by the limits of our time. We are only people. Each day is limited by the clock, each year by the calendar, and each life by the tolling of the bells. And within our small time frame, we are limited by a small amount of energy and talent to fill it creatively. Meanwhile, the summons from every direction to help produce more good in the world leaves us without respite. And our inner sense of obligation keeps telling us that we ought to do more than we have done. Every child of God is expected to repeat every night: "Forgive us the good we have left undone." It is very easy for the doctrine of vocation to keep us from being playful.

The answer to the work ethic is that grace has come in the form of the promise of the Kingdom of God. God's future has broken through the compulsions of the work ethic to tell us that God alone can *and will* bring in the Kingdom. The sign of the future does not tell us to stop working and start playing. It tells us that what we cannot do in our lifetimes, or a thousand lifetimes, will be done in God's good time. Furthermore, the promise of the Kingdom is that the life of the children of God is ultimately a life of restored playfulness. "Old men and old women shall again sit in the streets of Jerusalem, each with staff in hand for every age. And the streets of the city shall be full of boys and girls playing in its streets" (Zech. 8:4,5). What this comes to in terms of playfulness is that we are encouraged to take our most serious work with a trans-serious attitude. We ought to be serious in it, but ought not to see it as being an ultimately serious business.

The secret of our various vocations is that we must be dialectically serious about them. The person who views his work too seriously is likely either to turn off in despair or turn to it with a seriousness that prevents him from being playful about it. The promise of the Kingdom gives us a right to wink at it, take it all with less than final seriousness, and only then throw ourselves into it seriously—as we do in play. . . .

The Sabbath-keeper. The Sabbath is a sign that God has written over man: "Destined for Playfulness." It is God's own day, given to man in the midst of his work to remind him that festival and celebration, not sweat and toil, are the final truth about man. The Sabbath is the "Lord's Day," dedicated to the faith-fact that "death is swallowed up in victory" and work is swallowed up in play. The Sabbath, to be sure, is in counterpoint to labor. There *"remains* a rest for the people of God" (Heb. 4:1); the time of rest is not yet wholly come. But, in the Sabbath, in the festival of victory, we experience a taste of the banquet that is the end of man. Sabbath unties the knot that shackles us to production and goals and achievements, even though it does not relieve us of them entirely. Monday still follows Sunday, but Monday's seriousness is relativized by the memory of Sunday's playfulness. . . .

In the festival of worship, something goes on that is akin to child's play. Does it not follow that child's play tells us something about both the Sabbath and that "eternal rest" which it signifies?

The Sabbath exists in dialectic with a world of seriousness. The festival was open to the worst kind of distortion when it was removed from the dialectical tension with the effects of sin in the world. The festival was corrupted in Israel because the Sabbath players perverted the real work of the world on the other days. The poor were defrauded; the weak oppressed; and both were robbed of a truly playful existence. The Sabbath pointed to a new world "wherein justice dwells" along with banquets and festivals. But the overly serious Sabbath-keepers forgot that the symbol of the future was meant to stimulate men to bring something of the playful future into the working present. This is why the prophets said: "Close down the temples and cancel the festivities. Your Sabbaths are a bad smell in God's nostrils." They were an offense because, in a world of sin and imperfection, those who keep the Sabbath must keep it in dialectic with the real work given to God's children, and the real work included making life more playful for those whose poverty and weakness prevented them from playing. But even here, the real work could be done playfully in view of the Sabbath promise that it was God who would complete it.

Man in grace. Now we must try to get a lot of things together within the concept of grace. What it will come to is this: in order to see the meaning of life in playful terms we must see it in grace-given terms.

Without grace, everything becomes either despairingly serious or playfully illusionary. It is burdensome to be serious without grace, for then one has to be serious without relief. But then, too, without grace, playfulness becomes an escape from seriousness. This is why it is futile to make play a parable for a life mood unless it is a parable to illuminate the reality of a free grace that alone transforms a bitterly serious life into a life of playful hope. Play as the metaphor or myth that illumines life *on its own* is escape from reality. But within grace play can be a parable of life's trans-serious meaning. . . .

Since the resurrection, the cross invites us to a trans-serious attitude about life. We are serious players; but, since Calvary, we know the game we play no longer has ultimately serious consequences. . . . Our trans-serious attitude is what the Bible calls hope. But hope is not inside information that the game is predetermined. Therefore we can be playful only as we work. There are injustices to be undone. There are burdens to be lifted. There are stomachs to be filled. There are op-pressed persons to be liberated. There are souls to be saved. But even here, it must all be done in a properly playful mood. The revolutionary thinks the world must be transformed tomorrow—by him—and is doomed to despair because he is undialectically serious about his work. The playful cop-out thinks the world can be a Xanadu tomorrow; he is undialectically serious about play—and is doomed to a tranquilized existence. The captive of the work ethic uses play only as an intermezzo in his life of work. Under the cross and in hope of resurrection, the Christian has a hopeful invitation to be playful *in* his serious work.

Looking ahead to being a dancer in the joy of freedom, celebrating with applause the glory of God, he enters life now with the mood of a player. I am not talking about the right to celebrate now and then—though that, too, is a Sabbath gift. I am not talking about turning the Christian mood into triviality and serendipity. I am not talking about play as a metaphor for an ultimately meaningless life. I am saying that the theology of the grace-full God . . . opens a window to a world that transcends routine cause and effect, transcends the moral calculus of work and merit. Grace transforms the notion of a rationally rigged universe, with God as the winner of a fixed contest that was never really a contest, transforms it into an adventure of God that gives believers a *hope* that he will be the winner, and that we sinful losers will share his victory. Grace makes it possible to feel that struggle and pain, even in their most horrible forms, are part of a world that is good and pleasant to play and work in. Grace judges that the worth of life is not calculated by productivity, that it has a worth independent of how much we accomplish.

The playful mood is, like true leisure, a state of mind. It is not a justification of longer vacations and more golf games. It is an invitation to look hard at and throw ourselves seriously into what is, under grace, no longer an ultimately serious contest.

—*Published in* God and the Good;
pp. 46, 54-55, 59-62.

Contributors

David Beelen is a pastor at Madison Square Christian Reformed Church in Grand Rapids, Michigan, a multiracial inner-city congregation.

John Bolt has taught in the religion and theology department at Redeemer College, Ancaster, Ontario, and is currently an associate professor of systematic theology at Calvin Theological Seminary, Grand Rapids, Michigan.

James D. Bratt is a specialist in Dutch-American history and teaches in the history department at Calvin College, Grand Rapids, Michigan.

Sietze Buning was the folk-poet pen name of Stanley Wiersma, a professor of English at Calvin College, Grand Rapids, Michigan, from 1959 until his death in 1986.

Cynthia M. Campbell taught theology and ministry at Austin Presbyterian Theological Seminary, Austin, Texas, and is currently the pastor of First Presbyterian Church, Salinas, Kansas.

James A. De Jong is president at Calvin Theological Seminary, where he also teaches historical theology. He previously taught history at Dordt College, Sioux Center, Iowa, and has chaired the Liturgical Committee of the Christian Reformed Church.

Henry De Moor is an associate professor of church polity and church administration at Calvin Theological Seminary, Grand Rapids, Michigan.

Max De Pree is chairman of the board at Herman Miller, Inc., Zeeland, Michigan, where he held various management posts for forty years. He sits on the board of trustees of Hope College, Holland, Michigan, and of Fuller Theological Seminary, Pasadena, California.

Jonathan Edwards, one of America's greatest theologians and philosophers, pastored Congregational churches in Northampton and Stockbridge, Massachusetts, from 1726 through 1757. He died in 1758 while serving as president of the College of New Jersey in Princeton.

Howard G. Hageman was the pastor of North Reformed Church in Newark, New Jersey, for twenty-eight years, and from 1973 to 1985 he was president at New Brunswick Theological Seminary, New Brunswick, New Jersey, where he also taught liturgics and church order.

Lee Hardy is a professor of philosophy at Calvin College, Grand Rapids, Michigan, and has written extensively on issues of work and vocation.

Eugene P. Heideman has been secretary for program in the Reformed Church in America since 1982. He was previously a missionary in India; a chaplain and professor of religion at Central College, Pella, Iowa; and academic dean and professor of theology at Western Theological Seminary, Holland, Michigan.

I. John Hesselink served as a missionary in Japan for twenty years and is a past president of Western Theological Seminary, Holland, Michigan, where he currently teaches systematic theology.

Anthony A. Hoekema pastored three congregations in the Christian Reformed Church and taught systematic theology at Calvin Theological Seminary, Grand Rapids, Michigan, for twenty years until his emeritation in 1978.

George R. Hunsberger is an associate professor of missiology at Western Theological Seminary, Holland, Michigan. He previously taught at Belhaven College, Jackson, Mississippi, and pastored a Presbyterian congregation in that state.

Rod Jellema, a native of Holland, Michigan, and a graduate of Calvin College, Grand Rapids, Michigan, is director of the creative writing program at the University of Maryland, where he has taught literature since 1955.

John H. Kromminga was a professor of historical theology and president at Calvin Theological Seminary, Grand Rapids, Michigan, for more than thirty years until his emeritation in 1983.

John H. Leith served as a Presbyterian minister in Alabama and Tennessee and then taught theology for thirty years at Union Theological Seminary, Richmond, Virginia, until his emeritation in 1990.

George M. Marsden taught for twenty years in the history department at Calvin College, Grand Rapids, Michigan, and is currently a professor of American church history at Duke University Divinity School, Durham, North Carolina.

Paul A. Marshall, a native of the United Kingdom, is a senior member in political theory at the Institute for Christian Studies, Toronto, Ontario.

Richard J. Mouw, formerly of the philosophy department at Calvin College, Grand Rapids, Michigan, is provost and a professor of Christian philosophy and ethics at Fuller Theological Seminary, Pasadena, California.

Lesslie Newbigin is a minister in the United Reformed Church in the United Kingdom. He has served as a missionary in India, as bishop of the Church of South India, and as general secretary of the International Missionary Council.

James H. Olthuis is a senior member in philosophical theology at the Institute for Christian Studies, Toronto, Ontario.

Richard Robert Osmer has taught at Union Theological Seminary, Richmond, Virginia, and is currently an associate professor of Christian education at Princeton Theological Seminary, Princeton, New Jersey.

M. Eugene Osterhaven was a professor of systematic theology at Western Theological Seminary, Holland, Michigan, from 1952 until his emeritation in 1986.

Herman N. Ridderbos is a professor emeritus of New Testament at the Theological School of the Reformed Churches in the Netherlands

(GKN), Kampen. For many years he was the theological mentor of the GKN and is internationally known for his work in New Testament interpretation.

James Calvin Schaap writes fiction and is an associate professor of English at Dordt College, Sioux Center, Iowa.

James W. Skillen taught political science at Dordt College, Sioux Center, Iowa, and is the executive director of the Association for Public Justice, Washington, D.C.

Lewis B. Smedes, formerly a professor in the religion and theology department at Calvin College, Grand Rapids, Michigan, has taught theology and ethics for the past twenty years at Fuller Theological Seminary, Pasadena, California.

Mary Stewart Van Leeuwen holds a doctorate in psychology and is a professor of interdisciplinary studies at Calvin College, Grand Rapids, Michigan.

Johanna W. H. van Wijk-Bos, a native of the Netherlands, received her advanced degrees in the United States and since 1977 has been a professor of Old Testament at Louisville Presbyterian Theological Seminary, Louisville, Kentucky.

Loren Wilkinson, a professor of English at Seattle Pacific College, is the editor of *Earthkeeping: Christian Stewardship of Natural Resources*, produced by a team of scholars at the Calvin Center for Christian Scholarship, Calvin College, Grand Rapids, Michigan.

Albert M. Wolters taught philosophy at the Institute for Christian Studies, Toronto, Ontario, and is currently a professor of religion and theology at Redeemer College, Ancaster, Ontario.

Nicholas Wolterstorff taught philosophy at Calvin College, Grand Rapids, Michigan, for thirty years and since 1989 has been a professor of philosophical theology at Yale University, New Haven, Connecticut.

Henry Zylstra was a professor of English at Calvin College, Grand Rapids, Michigan, from 1941 until his death in 1956.

Bibliography

Acts of Synod 1975. Grand Rapids, Mich.: Christian Reformed Church; 596-97, 601.

Beelen, David. "A Thirst for Expressive Worship." *Reformed Worship 20.* Grand Rapids, Mich.: CRC Publications, June 1991.

Belgic Confession, tr. from the French text of 1619. Adopted by Synod 1985 of the Christian Reformed Church. Grand Rapids, Mich.: CRC Publications; Art. 3, 5, 15, 31, 36.

Belgic Confession, based on the translation adopted by Synod 1985 of the Christian Reformed Church and on the original French text. Adopted by the General Synod of 1991 of the Reformed Church in America. Published in *The Acts and Proceedings of the General Synod, Reformed Church in America: June 10-14, 1991.* Copyright © 1991, Reformed Church in America. Used by permission: Art. 36.

Bolt, John. *Christian and Reformed Today.* Jordan Station, Ont.: Paideia, 1984. Used by permission of Paideia Press Ltd., P.O. Box 1000, Jordan Station, Ont. Canada L0R 1S0.

Buning, Sietze. "Calvinist Farming" and "Obedience." *Purpaleanie and Other Permutations.* Orange City, Iowa: Middleburg, 1978. Copyright © 1978. Used by permission of Middleburg Press.

_____. "Holy Water" and "The Sea of Forgetfulness: Lake Michigan." *Style and Class.* Orange City, Iowa: Middleburg, 1982. Copyright © 1982. Used by permission of Middleburg Press.

Campbell, Cynthia M. "Foreword." *Presbyterian Policy for Church Officers.* Joan S. Gray and Joyce C. Tucker. Atlanta: John Knox, 1986. Copyright © 1986, John Knox Press; copyright © 1990 Joan S. Gray and Joyce C. Tucker. Used by permission of Westminster/John Knox Press.

Canons of Dort, tr. based on Latin manuscript signed at Synod of Dort, 1618-19. Adopted by Synod 1986 of the Christian Reformed Church. Grand Rapids, Mich.: CRC Publications; Points III/IV: Art. 3, 10, 16.

De Jong, James A. *Into His Presence.* Grand Rapids, Mich.: CRC Publications, 1985; 13-16, 119-20.

De Moor, Henry. "Equipping the Saints: A Church Political Study of the Controversies Surrounding Ecclesiastical Office in the Christian Reformed Church in North America, 1857-1982." Ph.D. dissertation, Kampen Theological Seminary, Kampen, the Netherlands, 1986. Used by permission of the author.

De Pree, Max. *Leadership Is an Art.* New York: Doubleday, 1989. Copyright © 1987 by Max De Pree. Used by permission of Doubleday, a division of Bantam Doubleday Dell Publishing Group, Inc.

Edwards, Jonathan. "God Glorified in Man's Dependence." *Jonathan Edwards: Representative Selections*, rev.; ed. Clarence H. Faust and Thomas H. Johnson. New York: Hill and Wang, 1962.

Hageman, Howard G. "The Need and Promise of Reformed Preaching." *Reformed Review*, 28/2. Holland, Mich.: Western Theological Seminary, Winter 1975; 75-78. Used by permission of *Reformed Review*.

_____. *Pulpit and Table: Some Chapters in the History of Worship in the Reformed Churches*. Richmond: John Knox, 1962. Copyright © Howard G. Hageman. To be reissued by Wm. B. Eerdmans Publishing Company in Spring 1993. Used by permission of Wm. B. Eerdmans Publishing Company.

Hardy, Lee. *The Fabric of This World: Inquiries into Calling, Career Choice, and the Design of Human Work*. Grand Rapids, Mich.: Eerdmans, 1990. Used by permission of Wm. B. Eerdmans Publishing Company.

Heidelberg Catechism, tr. from the first German edition approved by a synod in Heidelberg, Germany, in January 1563. Adopted by Synod 1975 of the Christian Reformed Church; revisions approved by Synod 1988. Grand Rapids, Mich.: CRC Publications; Q & A 1, 32, 54-55, 86, 103-104, 110-111.

Heideman, Eugene P. *Our Song of Hope: A Provisional Confession of Faith of the Reformed Church in America*, with Commentary and Appendixes. Grand Rapids, Mich.: Eerdmans, 1975. Used by permission of Wm. B. Eerdmans Publishing Company.

_____. "The Americanization of Reformed Confessions." *Perspectives*, 6/6. Grand Rapids, Mich.: Reformed Church Press, June 1991; 13-16. Copyright © 1991, *Perspectives*. Used by permission.

Hesselink, I. John. *On Being Reformed: Distinctive Characteristics and Common Misunderstandings*. 2nd ed. New York: Reformed Church Press, 1988. Used by permission of the author.

Hoekema, Anthony A. *The Christian Looks at Himself*. Grand Rapids, Mich.: Eerdmans, 1975. Used by permission of Wm. B. Eerdmans Publishing Company.

Hunsberger, George R. "The Changing Face of Ministry: Christian Leadership in the 21st Century." *Reformed Review*, 44/3. Holland, Mich.: Western Theological Seminary, Spring 1991; 225-27, 239-40, 242. Used by permission of *Reformed Review*.

Jellema, Rod. "Incarnation," "Heading In," and "The Work of Our Hands." *The Eighth Day: New & Selected Poems*. Washington D.C. and San Francisco: Dryad, 1984. Copyright © 1985, Rod Jellema. Used by permission.

Kromminga, John H. "General Overview of the Relationship of Covenant and Mission in the Reformed Tradition." Presented at the Eighth Reformed Missions Consultation, Farmington, Mich., Mar. 8-10, 1984. Used by permission of the author.

Leith, John H. *An Introduction to the Reformed Tradition: A Way of Being the Christian Community*. Atlanta: John Knox, 1977. Copyright ©

1977, John Knox Press. Used by permission of Westminster/John Knox Press.

_____. *From Generation to Generation: The Renewal of the Church According to Its Own Theology and Practice.* Louisville: Westminster/John Knox, 1990. Copyright © 1990, John H. Leith. Used by permission of Westminster/John Knox Press.

_____. *The Reformed Imperative: What the Church Has to Say That No One Else Can Say.* Philadelphia: Westminster, 1988. Copyright © 1988, John H. Leith. Used by permission of Westminster/John Knox Press.

_____, ed. *Creeds of the Churches: A Reader in Christian Doctrine from the Bible to the Present,* rev. Atlanta: John Knox, 1982. Copyright © 1963, 1978, 1982, John H. Leith. Used by permission of Westminster/John Knox Press.

Marsden, George M. "Reformed and American." *Reformed Theology in America,* ed. David F. Wells. Grand Rapids, Mich.: Eerdmans, 1985. Used by permission of Wm. B. Eerdmans Publishing Company.

Marshall, Paul A. "Calling, Work, and Rest." *Christian Faith and Practice in the Modern World: Theology from an Evangelical Point of View.* Mark Noll and David F. Wells. Grand Rapids, Mich.: Eerdmans, 1988. Used by permission of Wm. B. Eerdmans Publishing Company.

_____. *Thine Is the Kingdom: A Biblical Perspective on the Nature of Government and Politics Today.* Basingstoke, England: Marshall, Morgan, and Scott; 1984. Reprinted, Grand Rapids, Mich.: Eerdmans, 1978. Copyright © 1984, Paul A. Marshall. Used by permission.

Mouw, Richard J. *Called to Holy Worldliness.* Philadelphia: Fortress, 1980. Copyright © 1980, Fortress Press. Used by permission of Augsburg Fortress.

Newbigin, Lesslie. *Mission in Christ's Way: Bible Studies.* Geneva: WCC Publications, 1987. Copyright © WCC Publications, World Council of Churches, Box 2100, 1211 Geneva 2, Switzerland. Used by permission.

Olthuis, James H. *I Pledge You My Troth: A Christian View of Marriage, Family, Friendship.* New York: Harper & Row, 1975. Copyright © 1975, James H. Olthuis. Used by permission of HarperCollins Publishers.

Osmer, Richard Robert. *A Teachable Spirit: Recovering the Teaching Office in the Church.* Louisville: Westminster/John Knox, 1990. Copyright © 1990, Richard Robert Osmer. Used by permission of Westminster/John Knox Press.

Osterhaven, M. Eugene. *The Spirit of the Reformed Tradition.* Grand Rapids, Mich.: Eerdmans, 1971. Used by permission of Wm. B. Eerdmans Publishing Company.

Our Song of Hope. *Worship the Lord.* Our Song of Hope is "a contemporary statement of faith adopted by the Reformed Church in America in 1978 for use in the church's ministry of witness, teaching, and worship." Revised from the 1975 statement published in *Our Song of Hope: A Provisional Confession of Faith* (Grand Rapids, Mich.:

Eerdmans, 1975). Copyright © 1987, Reformed Church in America. Used by permission. St. 2, 14-15.

Our World Belongs to God: A Contemporary Testimony. Approved by Synod 1986 of the Christian Reformed Church as "a testimony of faith for our times, subordinate to our creeds and confessions." Grand Rapids, Mich.: CRC Publications; st. 47-51.

Ridderbos, Herman N. "The Inspiration and Authority of the Holy Scripture." *The Authoritative Word*, ed. Donald K. McKim. Grand Rapids, Mich.: Eerdmans, 1983. Used by permission of Wm. B. Eerdmans Publishing Company.

Schaap, James Calvin. "Lord, Have Mercy: Lakeside Church Wrestles with Raised Hands." *Reformed Worship* 19. Grand Rapids, Mich.: CRC Publications, March 1991.

Skillen, James W. "Christian Action and the Coming of God's Kingdom." *Confessing Christ and Doing Politics*, ed. James W. Skillen. Washington, D.C.: Association for Public Justice Education Fund, 1982. Used by permission of the Center for Public Justice, 321 Eighth St. N.E., Washington, D.C. 20002.

Smedes, Lewis B. *Mere Morality: What God Expects from Ordinary People.* Grand Rapids, Mich.: Eerdmans, 1983. Used by permission of Wm. B. Eerdmans Publishing Company.

_____. "Theology and the Playful Life." *God and the Good: Essays in Honor of Henry Stob*, ed. Clifton Orlebeke and Lewis B. Smedes. Grand Rapids, Mich.: Eerdmans, 1975. Used by permission of Wm. B. Eerdmans Publishing Company.

_____. *Union with Christ: A Biblical View of the New Life in Jesus Christ.* Grand Rapids, Mich.: Eerdmans, 1983. Used by permission of Wm. B. Eerdmans Publishing Company.

Van Leeuwen, Mary Stewart. *Gender & Grace: Love, Work & Parenting in a Changing World.* Downers Grove, Ill.: InterVarsity, 1990. Copyright © 1990 by Mary Stewart Van Leeuwen. Used by permission of InterVarsity Press, P.O. Box 1400, Downers Grove, IL 60515.

van Wijk-Bos, Johanna W. H. *Reformed and Feminist: A Challenge to the Church.* Louisville: Westminster/John Knox, 1991. Copyright © 1991, Johanna W. H. van Wijk-Bos. Used by permission of Westminster/John Knox Press.

Wilkinson, Loren, ed. *Earthkeeping: Christian Stewardship of Natural Resources.* Grand Rapids, Mich.: Eerdmans, 1980. Used by permission of Wm. B. Eerdmans Publishing Company.

Wolters, Albert M. *Creation Regained: Biblical Basics for a Reformed Worldview.* Grand Rapids, Mich.: Eerdmans, 1985. Used by permission of Wm. B. Eerdmans Publishing Company.

Wolterstorff, Nicholas. *Until Justice and Peace Embrace.* Grand Rapids, Mich.: Eerdmans, 1983. Used by permission of Wm. B. Eerdmans Publishing Company.

Zylstra, Henry. *Testament of Vision.* Grand Rapids, Mich.: Eerdmans, 1961. Used by permission of Wm. B. Eerdmans Publishing Company.